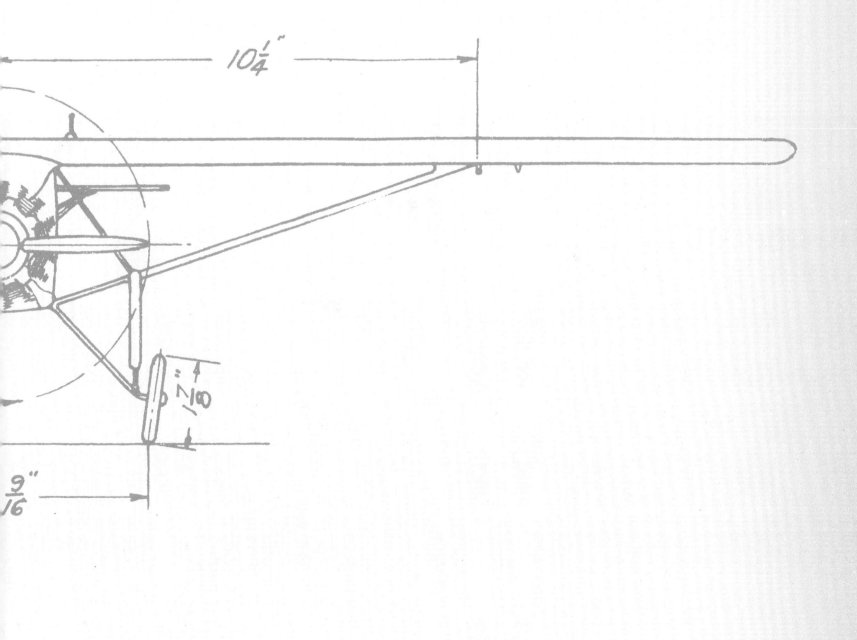

LINDBERGH

FLIGHT'S ENIGMATIC HERO

LINDBERGH

FLIGHT'S ENIGMATIC HERO

BY VON HARDESTY

CURATOR, SMITHSONIAN NATIONAL AIR AND SPACE MUSEUM

FOREWORD BY ERIK LINDBERGH

HARCOURT, INC.

NEW YORK   SAN DIEGO   LONDON

TEHABI BOOKS

TEHABI BOOKS conceived, designed, and produced *Lindbergh: Flight's Enigmatic Hero* and has developed and published many award-winning books that are recognized for their strong literary and visual content. Tehabi works with national and international publishers, corporations, institutions, and nonprofit groups to identify, develop, and implement comprehensive publishing programs. Tehabi Books is located in San Diego, California. www.Tehabi.com

President: Chris Capen
Senior Vice President: Tom Lewis
Editorial Director: Nancy Cash
Sales Director: Eric Pinkham
Director, Corporate Publishing: Tim Connolly
Director, Trade Relations: Marty Remmell
Editor: Garrett W. Brown
Art Director: Vicky Vaughn
Production Artists: Helga Benz, Mark Santos
Copy Editor: Lisa Wolff
Proofreader: Wendy M. Martin
Indexer: Ken DellaPenta

Image credits appear on pages 228–29.

cover image: *Standing next to the* Spirit of St. Louis, *Charles Lindbergh was the first to fly from New York to Paris in the "Transatlantic Derby." The man and his airplane became emblematic of aviation and its future.*
end-sheet image: *Oscar Schuwendt used the original Ryan Airlines drawings of the* Spirit of St. Louis *to produce outline sketches, including this front-view detail, two months after Lindbergh's historic flight. The outline claims that it may be relied upon as "an authentic model of the original."*
page 1: *Commemorative coin dedicated to "U.S. Air Hero" Charles Augustus Lindbergh, circa 1927.*
page 3: *A youthful Charles Lindbergh garbed in a flight suit, just before his transatlantic flight, May 1927.*
pages 4–5: *Roll-out of the* Spirit of St. Louis *at San Diego, California. The airplane had been designed and built at Ryan Airlines, Inc., in a mere sixty days, allowing Lindbergh to enter the competition for the Orteig Prize in May 1927.*
page 6: *Charles Lindbergh peers out the cockpit of his* Spirit of St. Louis *on the eve of his historic transatlantic flight, May 1927.*
pages 8–9: *A huge crowd, estimated at over 100,000 people, greeted Charles Lindbergh when he landed the* Spirit of St. Louis *at Le Bourget Airport on the night of May 21, 1927.*
page 10: *Charles Lindbergh lands the* Spirit of St. Louis *in England in June 1927.*

Requests for permission to make copies of any part of the work should be mailed to the following address: Permissions Department, Harcourt, Inc., 6277 Sea Harbor Drive, Orlando, Florida 32887-6777.

Excerpts from *Autobiography of Values* by Charles Lindbergh, copyright © 1978 by Harcourt, Inc., and Anne Morrow Lindbergh, reprinted by permission of the publisher.

Excerpts from *The Spirit of St. Louis* by Charles A. Lindbergh, reprinted with the permission of Scribner, an imprint of Simon & Schuster Adult Publishing Group. Copyright © 1953 by Charles Scribner's Sons; copyright renewed © 1981 by Anne Morrow Lindbergh.

www.HarcourtBooks.com

Harcourt Trade books may be purchased for educational use. For information, please write: Harcourt Trade Publishers, Attn: Director of Special Sales, 525 B Street, Suite 1900, San Diego, CA 92101. Specific, large-quantity needs can also be met with special editions, including personalized covers and corporate imprints. For information, please write: Tehabi Books, Attn.: Eric Pinkham, Sales Director, 4920 Carroll Canyon Road, Suite 200, San Diego, CA 92121.

Library of Congress Cataloging-in-Publication Data

Hardesty, Von, 1939–
    Lindbergh : flight's enigmatic hero / by Von Hardesty ; foreword by Erik Lindbergh.—1st ed.
        p. cm.
    Includes bibliographical references and index.
    ISBN 0-15-100973-2 (hardcover)
    1. Lindbergh, Charles A. (Charles Augustus), 1902–1974. 2. Air pilots—United States—Biography. I. Title.

    TL540.L5 H37 2002
    629.13'092—dc21
    [B]   2002027305

Printed by Dai Nippon Printing Co., Ltd., in Hong Kong

First edition
J I H G F E D C B A

Table of Contents

the spirit lives on

BY ERIK LINDBERGH

The rain is beating hard against *The New Spirit of St. Louis.* I call out, "Temperature, four degrees Celsius; altitude, 7,000 feet; airspeed, 174 knots." It's hard to believe that such heavy precipitation won't slow her down. One more check with my flashlight on the wing, "Negative icing." I remain vigilant, knowing that any accumulation of ice on the wings can keep me from reaching Paris—or worse. Later that night as I pass through the mid-Atlantic storm system, the stars come out. I start to relax in the clear, calm air. Polaris, the North Star, is holding steady off my left wing, the moon above my right. I was cradled in the same sky that had carried my grandfather across the ocean seventy-five years before.

Erik Lindbergh, grandson of Charles, waves from the cockpit of *The New Spirit of St. Louis,* the low-wing monoplane in which he recreated his grandfather's historic transatlantic flight from New York to Paris.

As a pilot and the grandson of Charles and Anne Morrow Lindbergh, I have often pondered my grandfather's flight across the Atlantic. The event hovered in my mind like a myth, somehow detached from reality. Perhaps it seemed that way because I needed to create my own identity apart from that of the world hero. Perhaps even my grandfather needed to move on from the legacy of the flight to contribute to society in other ways. I remember that, when somebody (even a family member) would ask him about the flight, he would say, "Read the book!" [*The Spirit of St. Louis*]. The resulting tendency within my family was a great resistance to revisiting almost anything related to the flight. For me to consider attempting a flight of my own was a definite taboo.

What I didn't count on was the seductive power that the plane itself held for me. While building a wooden sculpture of the *Spirit of St. Louis* in my shop, I became much more intrigued with its unique shape and symbolism. I started to fly it around in my hands and imagine *myself* in the cockpit. *I could fly across the Atlantic—couldn't I?* When I sanded and smoothed the waves of cedar grain undulating across the wing, I thought of flying alone above the ocean— *what would it be like?* I became so captivated by the *Spirit* that I felt compelled to explore the feasibility of doing the flight myself.

I couldn't have even contemplated the flight without recent advances in medicine. For over fifteen years, I'd contended with the often-debilitating effects of rheumatoid arthritis, an autoimmune disease that

causes inflammation in my joints. As a youth, I was a gung-ho skier and mountain climber and state-champion gymnast. But the constant pain of the disease took its toll, and by the age of thirty I was severely disabled. Thanks to some amazing "carpentry" on my knees and a breakthrough biotechnology drug called Enbrel, I've regained much of my mobility.

The breakdown and revival of my physical health allowed me to work through the "inherited taboo." My identity was now strong enough to follow my own path, even if it so closely mirrored the footsteps of my grandfather. Given a second chance in life, I wanted to do something special. I knew that grandfather's flight wasn't just about an adventure or a prize. More than that, it was about his vision for the future. My own vision of the future of flight and the quality of life on earth prompted my desire to raise awareness and money for the Arthritis Foundation, the X Prize Foundation, and also the Charles and Anne Morrow Lindbergh Foundation. The seventy-fifth anniversary also seemed an auspicious occasion to connect my own personal experience with my grandfather's appreciation for and contributions to modern medicine that you will read about in this book.

▲ *A woodworker by trade, Erik found the original inspiration for his flight in sculpting the shape of the* Spirit of St. Louis *out of red cedar. In July 2002, he completed another, more detailed model, shown above with a wingspan of forty-four inches.*

▼ *The New Spirit of St. Louis taxis on the runway at Republic Field on Long Island, New York, on May 1, 2002, in preparation for takeoff. A Lancair Columbia 300, the plane is capable of cruising at 220 mph, twice as fast as the original* Spirit of St. Louis.

I am fascinated and motivated by technological innovation. In fact, the quality of life that I enjoy right now is a direct result of medical innovation. Some technological advances find their inspiration from prizes. The $25,000 Orteig prize was the seed that prompted Grandfather to make his flight. Five major teams spent approximately $400,000 trying to win the prize. All of that research and development was dedicated to long-distance air travel, and Raymond Orteig only had to pay the winner!

Since 1996, I've been involved with the X Prize Foundation, an organization that has established a $10 million prize for the first privately funded team to send a three-person reusable launch vehicle into space. This prize does for space flight what the prizes of the 1920s and 30s did for aviation. Using my flight as a way to publicize the X Prize provided a way for me to link the history of flight with the future and to promote the next great step in space exploration, one that will open up space travel to the rest of us.

The Orteig prize prompted Grandfather to pull together the latest technology to overcome the oceanic barrier between Europe and the United States. That technology looks downright primitive today. Whereas he averaged 108 mph in the tube, wood, and fabric Ryan aircraft, I averaged 212 mph in a glass and carbon fiber Lancair. Grandfather couldn't talk to anybody once he was airborne and navigated by holding a compass heading and using checkpoints. I used a Global Positioning System for navigation and had

▲ *Upon landing at Le Bourget Airport in Paris at 11:23 A.M., Erik stands on the wing of his plane to wave to a crowd of his supporters and well-wishers. His total flying time is seventeen hours and seven minutes.*

▼ *Rare photograph of the Spirit of St. Louis taken in the first hour of Charles Lindbergh's 1927 flight.*

radio and satellite communications with mission control at the St. Louis Science Center that could provide me with up-to-date weather and technical assistance. Even with all these advantages, it was still a difficult flight for me—and I think that all goes to show the tremendous magnitude of difficulty that Grandfather faced.

If there's anything that makes one feel a part of something larger than oneself, it's the spectacular view from the cockpit. It gives you an "overview perspective"—insight into landforms, erosion, cities, roads, and farmland. It has made me appreciate what my grandparents noticed about changes in the environment as they flew all around the world from the 1920s to the 1970s. In this book you will read about the questions that arose from those experiences and led to a life of working toward a balance between technological advancement and the preservation of the environment. This work is carried on today by the Charles and Anne Morrow Lindbergh Foundation, which gives grants and annual awards to scientists and hosts educational programs, all working to promote their vision of balance.

As you read this book and follow along with the spectacular photographic timelines, I hope you are able to imagine *yourself* in the cockpit of the *Spirit of St. Louis.* More than that, I hope that you take heart in my grandfather's life and spirit and come away with questions of your own about the delicate balance between technology, nature, and our quality of life.

DEC. 17, 1903

Orville Wright guides the Wright Flyer across a 120-foot course above the windswept sands of Kitty Hawk, North Carolina—the first flight of a powered heavier-than-air flying machine. The Wrights inaugurate a new Air Age.

JUNE 23, 1905

The Wright brothers experiment with an advanced version of their flying machine, achieving a new benchmark in controlled flight.

OCT. 23, 1906

Alberto Santos Dumont wins the 3,000-franc Archdeacon prize for flying over 82 feet. Three weeks later, he wins a French Aero Club prize for a flight of 722 feet.

SEPT. 17, 1908

Orville Wright's passenger, Lt. Thomas Selfridge, is killed in a demonstration flight—the first fatality in an airplane crash.

JULY 25, 1909

Louis Bleriot wins the £1,000 prize offered by the *London Daily Mail* for being the first aviator to fly across the English Channel: 23 miles in 37 minutes.

MARCH 7, 1911

Eugene Renaux and Albert Senouque win the Michelin Grand Prize for the first passenger flight from Paris to Clermont-Ferrand.

1902   1905   1908   1911   19

SEPT. 20, 1904

Wilbur Wright completes a full circle in the Wright Flyer.

OCT. 5, 1905

Wilbur Wright, in Wright Flyer #3, flies 24.2 miles in 38 minutes and 3 seconds.

JAN. 13, 1908

Henri Farman wins the Deutsch-Archdeacon Prize for flying an aircraft over a kilometer.

DEC. 31, 1908

Setting the bar for future competitors, Wilbur Wright wins the first Michelin Cup with a flight of 78 miles.

WINTER 1910

William Randolph Hearst offers a $50,000 prize to the first aviator to complete a transcontinental trip within 30 days.

NOV. 5, 1911

In pursuit of the Hearst prize, Calbraith Rodgers completes the first transcontinental trip by airplane, enduring 75 crashes or mishaps, but exceeds the time limit by 19 days.

MAY 15, 1918

The U.S. Post Office establishes airmail service, with stops in Washington, D.C., Philadelphia, and New York City.

MAY 24, 1918

The U.S. Army formally establishes the U.S. Air Service, the forerunner of the modern-day U.S. Air Force.

JULY 1914

Igor Sikorsky flies the four-engine *Ilya Mourometz* on a roundtrip aerial journey from St. Petersburg to Kiev, setting a world's record for distance and duration.

MAY 31, 1919

The R-34 dirigible lands at Plymouth, England, after making the first round-trip flight from the British Isles to the United States in a lighter-than-air flying machine.

JUNE 4, 1920

The Army Reorganization Act, which establishes the basis for a modern air force, is signed into law by President Woodrow Wilson.

SEPT. 24, 1922

James Doolittle makes the first transcontinental trip within a single day: 22 hours and 30 minutes.

14   1917   1920   1923   1926

MARCH 3, 1915

The Advisory Committee for Aeronautics—later renamed the National Advisory Committee for Aeronautics, or NACA— is formed.

MAY 22, 1919

Raymond Orteig offers a $25,000 prize for the first aviator to cross the Atlantic from New York to Paris, or vice versa, nonstop in a heavier-than-air airplane.

JUNE 15, 1919

John Alcock and Arthur Whitten Brown win the £10,000 prize offered by Lord Northcliffe and the *London Daily Mail* for the first nonstop transatlantic flight between England and the United States.

Nov. 27, 1920

Newspaperman Ralph Pulitzer sponsors the first in a series of races to promote high-speed flight.

MAY 2–3, 1923

Oakley Kelly and John Macready make the first nonstop transcontinental flight from New York to San Diego: 26 hours and 50 minutes.

the prize

Raymond Orteig was an air enthusiast. He had observed the whole saga of early flight with keen interest, from the Wrights at Kitty Hawk and Louis Bleriot flying across the English Channel to the exploits of aces in World War I. With time, Orteig began to explore the idea of how he might promote the advance of aviation, not as an aviator but as a financial patron. After all, the *London Daily Mail* had offered a prize for the first aviator to fly across the English Channel, and this cash incentive played a key role in prompting Louis Bleriot to make his epic flight in 1909. He reasoned, why not create a cash award for the first person to make a transatlantic crossing between New York and France? Such a nonstop flight would be a remarkable aviation milestone, one that would connect the Old and New Worlds.

Raymond Orteig, a French-born entrepreneur and hotel magnate, offered a $25,000 prize to the first person(s) to make a transatlantic flight in an airplane between New York and France. Orteig made his offer in 1919, but only in 1926–27 did an international group of competitors emerge to attempt a transoceanic crossing to win the prize money.

Orteig had accumulated considerable personal wealth, so his dream was not an idle one. Born in France, Orteig had immigrated to New York City in the late nineteenth century and become a prominent businessman. He owned two hotels: the Lafayette and the legendary Brevoort. Orteig had renovated the old Brevoort in 1902, transforming it into an upscale hotel appealing to titled Europeans and America's own nouveau riche. For Orteig, these entrepreneurial activities were a prelude to his role as an international patron of aviation progress. He confidently believed his personal fortune could be the stimulus for some new aerial spectacular.

So in 1919 Raymond Orteig set aside $25,000 (roughly a quarter million dollars today) for his transatlantic prize. The conditions were simple and straightforward: The award would be granted to "the first aviator who shall cross the Atlantic in a land or water craft (heavier than air) from Paris or the shores of France to New York, or New York to Paris or the shores of France, without a stop."[1] To assure legitimacy for his initiative, Orteig later placed the administration of the prize under the control of the U.S. National Aeronautics Association.

Seven years passed, and no one stepped forward to claim Orteig's award. But then, in 1926, aviators began to make plans to fly the Atlantic. There was one reason for this sudden clamor to win the Orteig prize:

▲ The Wright Whirlwind radial engine, which helped revolutionize aviation in the 1920s.

▼ Richard Byrd (left) and Floyd Bennett, whose historic 1926 flight to the North Pole was in a Fokker plane powered by three Wright Whirlwinds.

the development of the Wright Whirlwind radial engine. Charles Lawrance designed the engine in the mid-1920s, and it made a revolutionary impact on aviation. For the first time, an airplane could be fitted with a powerful and reliable power plant, one that would allow long-duration flights. The Wright Whirlwind compared with the older OX-5s, Hispano-Suizas, and Liberties much like a modern race car compares with a Ford Model T. When Richard Byrd and Floyd Bennett made a round-trip flight to the North Pole on May 9, 1926, in a Fokker aircraft powered by three Wright Whirlwinds, aviation—in particular long-distance flying—entered a new era.

The celebrated French ace René Fonck stepped forward in 1926 to make the first attempt to win the Orteig prize. Fonck came to America to seek out a syndicate to support his project and then began his search for an airplane. He eventually sought out famed aircraft designer Igor Sikorsky, who was operating a small aircraft-manufacturing facility at Roosevelt Field, on Long Island, New York. Sikorsky, a Russian émigré, had received a medal from Tsar Nicholas II for his remarkable four-engine airplane, *Ilya Mourometz*, a giant of the air that once made a round-trip journey from St. Petersburg to Kiev. With the advent of the Russian Revolution, Sikorsky fled to the United States to escape a Bolshevik firing squad. Once in America he endeavored with a small group of

Russian émigrés to launch a second career, this time as an American aircraft designer.

Fonck had been impressed with Sikorsky's huge S-29 aircraft, which flew successfully in 1924, impressing all with its ability to transport two grand pianos from Roosevelt Field to Washington, D.C. While Sikorsky had earned a reputation for high-performance aircraft, his "factory" at Roosevelt Field was modest in the extreme. He and his workers occupied two old wooden hangars at the edge of the field. The hangars were spacious but lacked doors. Sikorsky's dedicated workers labored in these primitive conditions, braving leaky roofs and the extremes of

weather. René Fonck ignored the grim working conditions, seeing in Sikorsky's facility a diamond in the rough. Fonck proposed and Sikorsky agreed to manufacture a special multi-engine airplane, one that would carry Fonck and a crew of three to France.

Even as Fonck and Sikorsky began work in the summer of 1926 on their new plane, now dubbed the S-35, there was concern that it would not be ready in September, the last month available for safe flying in the North Atlantic. Sikorsky decided not to build the S-35 from scratch, proposing to Fonck that the fuselage of a partially completed twin-engine aircraft be transformed into a trimotor, the preferred design for a

▼ Igor I. Sikorsky, famed Russian-American aircraft designer, built the trimotor S-35 for René Fonck, the celebrated French ace, who made the first serious attempt to win the Orteig prize. The S-35 was a long-range aircraft built to accommodate a crew of four. The plane crashed and burned on takeoff at Roosevelt Field in September 1926, ending Fonck's campaign.

transoceanic flight. Both the wings and the forward section of the fuselage had to be redesigned, the latter to accommodate a third engine. Fitting fuel tanks posed another difficult challenge, but Sikorsky devised an ingenious method to allow the S-35 to carry a huge amount of fuel for any long-duration flight. To save weight, they decided not to equip the airplane with brakes. By August, to the delight of Fonck and his backers, Sikorsky completed the S-35, in his words, a "huge, elegant, efficient, modern looking airplane."[2]

Would it fly? More important, would it fly safely? Sikorsky first ran a series of taxiing tests, which were followed by short flights out of Roosevelt Field with only two engines running. Fonck joined Sikorsky for this critical round of test flights. On one such flight, Fonck and Sikorsky flew the S-35 over New York City. Now confident that the S-35 flew well, Sikorsky ordered the installation of an extra tank, special equipment, and newly designed

▲ *Igor Sikorsky (left) and Captain René Fonck in the cockpit of the Sikorsky-designed S-35 aircraft. Fonck's hastening of the plane's testing procedures to keep his flight on schedule may have precipitated its tragic demise.*

landing gear. The S-35 was flown from Long Island to Washington, D.C., where it was inspected by government officials. Their reaction was positive, giving the projected Fonck flight across the Atlantic wide publicity. Press coverage at Roosevelt Field intensified. As August gave way to September, Fonck increased his pressure on Sikorsky to complete the pre-flight tests. Calendar concerns—the frenzied effort to be ready for the flight in mid-September—ran counter to Sikorsky's deliberate style and desire to test the S-35 in a systematic fashion, but Fonck rejected the idea of delaying until spring 1927.

News reached Roosevelt Field that weather conditions would be ideal on or around September 20. Fonck did not hesitate. He instructed Sikorsky to have the S-35 ready for departure on that date, pending any shift in the weather. At midnight, Sikorsky taxied the S-35 to the runway, where the ground crew pumped 2,500 gallons of gasoline from barrels into the S-35's cavernous tanks. Electric lights cast a bright, silvery glow over the S-35 during the long fueling process, which lasted into the early morning hours of September 20. Alerted to the departure of the S-35, a huge crowd gathered on the edge of the field, intent on getting a good vantage point from which to observe the historic flight.

The *New York Times*, August 29, 1926

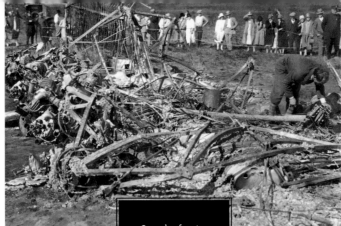

Just before dawn Sikorsky communicated to Fonck that the S-35 was ready. At around five o'clock Fonck and his three crewmen boarded the airplane, fired up the engines, and made their last-minute checks. On signal the fuel-laden S-35 began its long-anticipated takeoff run at Roosevelt Field, moving forward along a passageway between long lines of spectators. The S-35 gained speed slowly. Halfway down the runway, one of the auxiliary landing gears (added to accommodate the airplane's extra fuel tanks) broke away. The landing gear, now awkwardly hanging from the plane, began to plow a rut in the runway. The increased drag further slowed the overladen airplane. A huge cloud of dust arose, prompting gasps from the crowd of onlookers. As the S-35 reached the end of the runway, that critical point of no return, it failed to rotate upward for the climb out. It seemed as if the S-35, sliding forward with no way to stop, was held to the ground by some powerful force. Unable to stop or ascend, René Fonck labored to keep his airplane in the center of the runway. Finally the plane, with the landing gear in tow, hobbled awkwardly to the end of the field, careened down a steep incline, and disappeared from sight. A startled crowd looked on in silent apprehension. Seconds passed, and then

▲ Crowds of curious onlookers gather around the wreck of René Fonck's S-35, at Roosevelt Field, Long Island, New York, September 1926.

▶ Pin with image of aviator Clarence Chamberlin, a competitor of Charles Lindbergh for the Orteig prize. Chamberlin piloted a Wright Bellanca monoplane, the Columbia.

suddenly a spiraling, red flame shot upward, followed by a tall, billowing column of black smoke.

By the time the fire truck and crowds reached the burning airplane, Fonck and his copilot had managed to exit through the cockpit. The other two crewmen, the radio operator and the mechanic, were trapped and died in the inferno. Fonck's dream of a New York–to–Paris flight ended in this crash. His one chance had come and gone.

Fonck's ill-fated S-35 demonstrated the dangers inherent in any transoceanic flight, where prevailing thought dictated that an airplane had to be fitted with extra engines and multiple fuel tanks to cross the Atlantic. But his crash did not dampen the growing competition for the Orteig prize. Public interest in the "Transatlantic Derby" shifted to the remaining competitors, and it intensified considerably over the winter of 1926–27.

The odds-on favorite, at least for Americans, was U.S. Navy Lieutenant Commander Richard Byrd, the famed Arctic explorer and pilot. Byrd, backed with the financial largesse of Rodman Wanamaker, used these months to outfit and test his Fokker three-engine *America*. Another American, Clarence D. Chamberlin, with the critical backing of entrepreneur Charles Levine, offered a serious challenge with the sleek Wright Bellanca monoplane, powered by the advanced Wright Whirlwind nine-cylinder, 200-horsepower

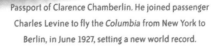

Passport of Clarence Chamberlin. He joined passenger Charles Levine to fly the *Columbia* from New York to Berlin, in June 1927, setting a new world record.

engine. The third major effort had been organized in Europe, where celebrated French ace Charles Nungesser and François Coli prepared for an east-west crossing of the Atlantic in *L'Oiseau blanc* ("the white bird"). All competitors awaited the arrival of favorable weather in the spring of 1927 to launch their flights. But who would be first? That question now preoccupied the public and the media.

By May, Richard Byrd remained the favorite, especially among gamblers who saw in Byrd's résumé the makings of a winner. Byrd had flown with Floyd Bennett from Spitzbergen to the North Pole on May 9, 1926, an extraordinary flight that many viewed as a dress rehearsal for the Orteig competition. In fact, Byrd's flight log was filled with remarkable aerial treks. And, as the *Aviation Yearbook* noted in 1927, his journey to the top of the world represented a "notable achievement from every standpoint."[3] That memorable year, Byrd emerged as the most likely candidate to win the Orteig prize.

For his transatlantic flight Byrd selected a Fokker trimotor, which was built in the winter of 1926. The *America* was an imposing flying machine with a wingspan of seventy-one feet. By design, the airplane could carry three thousand more pounds of fuel than Byrd had transported on his 1926 flight to the North Pole. Byrd added to the overall weight of the *America* by approving the installation of eight hundred pounds of "necessary" equipment, including a special radio set, two rubber boats for the crew of four, pistols for night signaling, a sextant and hand compasses, a wireless antenna, a special apparatus to make water, emergency

▲ Charles Nungesser and François Coli attempted an east-west crossing of the Atlantic in May 1927 in competition for the Orteig prize. After departing France, the pair disappeared.

▶ Richard Byrd (center), who in May 1926 completed the first round-trip flight to the North Pole, is greeted by South Pole explorer Roald Amundsen. Byrd was a favorite to win the Orteig prize.

• ◆ •

food for three weeks, and "equipment of all sorts."[4] The heavy-laden *America* would also carry the first bag of U.S. Air Mail for delivery to France. Byrd counted on his plane's three reliable Wright Whirlwind engines as the steady force to carry him and his crew across the Atlantic. He wrapped his endeavor in the language of scientific purpose: The collection of meteorological and navigational data would pave the way for future transatlantic commercial airline service.

Another competitor of humbler origins and with fewer pretensions had yet to make his appearance on the scene. Several days after the crash of Fonck's S-35, a twenty-four-year-old pilot from Little Falls, Minnesota, sat behind the controls of a war-surplus DH-4 biplane, flying the mail on a night run from St. Louis to Chicago. Charles A. Lindbergh had taken off with the confident expectation that his flight would be routine in all respects. That night flight to Chicago, viewed now in historical perspective, became a turning point in the course of the twentieth century. In his memoir *The Spirit of St. Louis*, Lindbergh tells the curious story of how this unremarkable flight became a personal epiphany, the moment when one unknown airmail pilot reordered his life. For those preparing to compete for the Orteig prize in the winter of 1926–27, this moment would produce a new, formidable, and unexpected challenger.

When Lindbergh began his descent into Chicago's airspace, just ten minutes from landing, he cast his eyes on the terrain below, seeing a bright moon casting its reflected light on the meandering rivers, woods, and fields along the flight path.

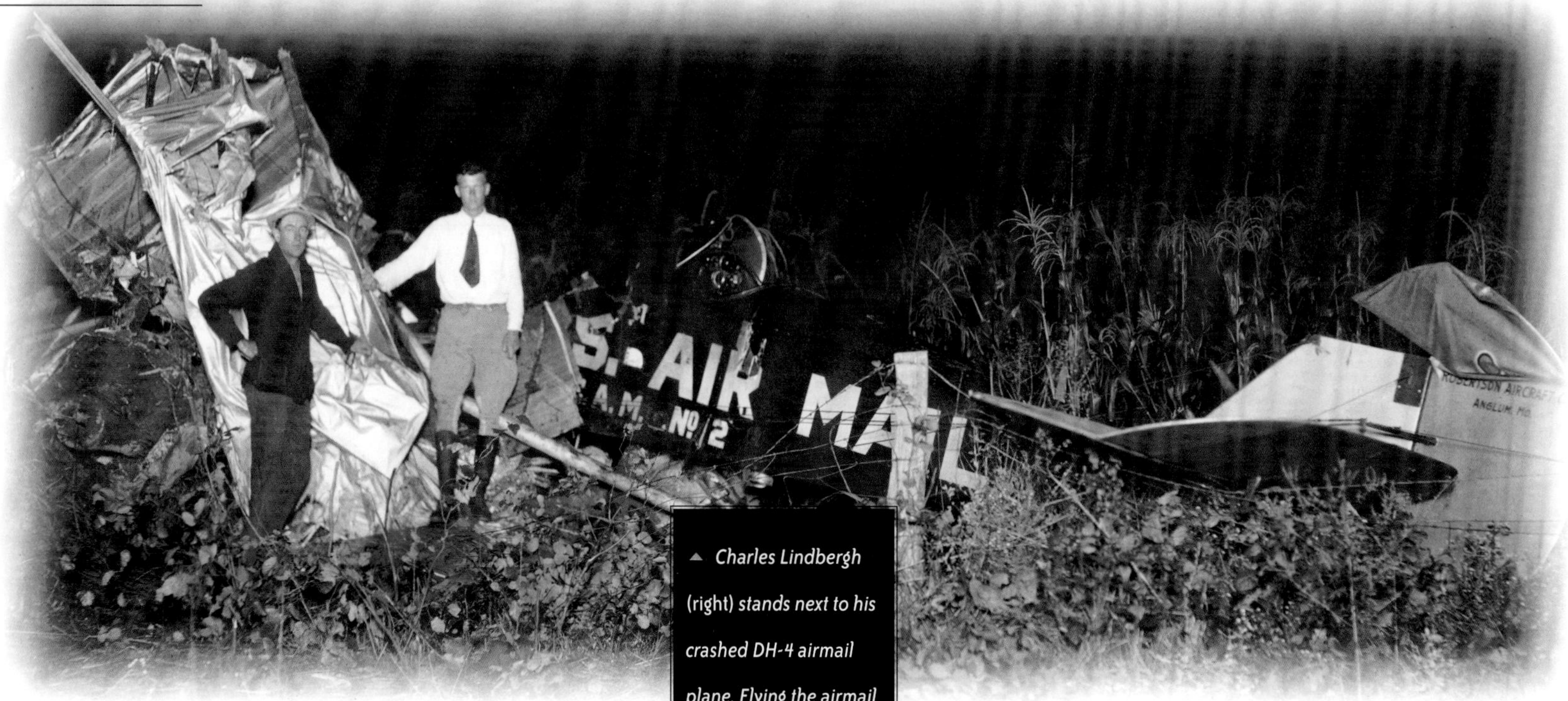

▲ *Charles Lindbergh (right) stands next to his crashed DH-4 airmail plane. Flying the airmail was a dangerous profession, requiring pilots to maintain precise flight schedules in all kinds of weather. Crashes were commonplace when airmail pilots attempted to fly through bad weather.*

Lindbergh picked up the navigation beacon out of Chicago. The lights of a small city came into view off the right wing. He made a mental note of his position, glanced quickly at his instruments, and then vectored his lumbering flying machine toward the distant airfield on the horizon.

At that instant, Lindbergh encountered an unanticipated rush of thoughts and emotions. In a moving passage in *The Spirit of St. Louis,* he records that he suddenly felt "aloof and unattached, in the solitude of space." This powerful sensation gave the young aviator a personal transcendence from the world below, from "the myriad lights, all the turmoil and works of men." He then thought about all those nameless people living around the points of light he saw along the flight path, as if they hung precariously on the earth, moving through the heavens as "a phosphorescent moss on its surface, vulnerable to the brush of a hand."[5]

Lindbergh then asked himself, "Why return to that moss; why submerge myself in the brick-walled human problems when all the crystal universe is mine?" Feeling a newfound kinship with the vast universe above, he added: "Like the moon, I can fly on forever through space, past the mail field at Chicago, beyond the state of Illinois, over mountains, over oceans, independent of the world below."[6]

Lindbergh's mood shifted as he became conscious of his airplane, basking in the greenish hue of the moonlight. Alone in the open

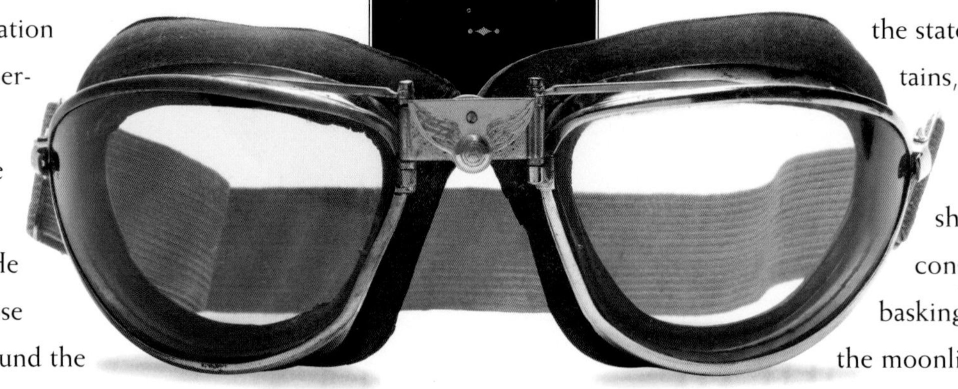

Type of flying goggles worn by Charles Lindbergh and other aviators in the 1920s

cockpit, surrounded by the noise of the slipstream and the growl of the DH-4's Liberty engine, he found himself restive at the controls of his old warbird, commenting, "I grow conscious of the limits of my biplane, of the inefficiency of its wings, struts, and wires."[7] He found himself annoyed at the thought of landing, realizing that his obsolete DH-4 was not a magic carpet capable of taking him effortlessly anywhere in the world. His airplane possessed a finite quantity of fuel and would soon have to land. Ahead there would be the mundane routine of unloading, sorting, and transferring the mail bags into a plane heading eastbound for the Alleghenies and New York.

Lindbergh questioned this roundabout method of flying the mail to Chicago to get it to New York: "Why shouldn't we carry it directly to New York from St. Louis?" He mused that a nonstop flight to New York could be made in one of the modern aircraft that were then flying American skies. Why not fly one of the new Lairds already in commercial service, or a fast and reliable Wright Bellanca? "With three planes like the Bellanca," he told himself, "we could easily carry the mail nonstop between St. Louis and New York, and on clear nights possibly two or three passengers besides."[8]

Chicago's airfield was nearing. But then Lindbergh reached a new insight: "If only I had the

▲ A young woman who had stumbled across Lindbergh took this rare photograph at Roosevelt Field after her vain quest to photograph Richard Byrd, then the odds-on favorite to win the Orteig prize. The fact that she could find Lindbergh alone and largely ignored by the crowds points to his underdog status in the "Transatlantic Derby."

Bellanca, I'd show St. Louis businessmen what modern aircraft could do; I'd take them to New York in eight or nine hours. They'd see how swiftly and safely passengers could fly. There are all kinds of records I could break for demonstration—distance, altitude with load, nonstop flights across the country. . . . Possibly—my mind is startled at its thought—I could fly nonstop between New York and Paris. . . . Why shouldn't I fly from New York to Paris? I'm almost twenty-five. I have more than four years of aviation behind me, and close to two thousand hours in the air. I've barnstormed over half of the forty-eight states. I've flown my mail through the worst of nights. I know the wind currents of the Rocky Mountains and the storms of the Mississippi Valley as few pilots know them. During my year at Brooks and Kelly [U.S. Army Air Corps bases] as a flying cadet, I learned the basic elements of navigation. I'm a Captain in the 110th Observation Squadron of Missouri's National Guard. Why am I not qualified for such a flight?"[9] Lindbergh's quick survey of his flight log becomes his apologia to join the race to be the first across the Atlantic.

Upon landing in Chicago, Charles Lindbergh emerged on the tarmac a new man, no longer content to be an airmail pilot. He now embraced a new and radical future, vowing, "I'll organize a flight to Paris!"[10]

FEB. 4, 1902

Charles Augustus
Lindbergh is born in
Detroit, Michigan, to
parents Charles August
and Evangeline Lodge
Land Lindbergh.

JUNE 22, 1906

Anne Morrow is born in
Englewood, New Jersey,
to parents Dwight
Whitney and Elizabeth
Cutter Morrow.

JUNE 1912

Lindbergh attends his
first air meet, the
Aeronautical Trials at
Fort Myer, Virginia.

1902   1905   1908   1911   19

MARCH 4, 1907

Lindbergh's father
begins his first of five
consecutive terms in the
U.S. House of
Representatives.

JUNE 28, 1914

Austrian archduke
Francis Ferdinand and
his wife are
assassinated by a
Serbian nationalist.
leading directly to
World War I, a conflict
that will rage for four
years and lead to ten
million casualties.

OCT. 1916

Lindbergh and his mother drive from Minnesota to California —a forty-day trip through bad weather and over poor roads.

JUNE 15, 1918

Lindbergh graduates from Little Falls High School in Minnesota.

FALL 1920

Lindbergh enrolls at the University of Wisconsin as a mechanical engineering student.

FEB. 1922

Lindbergh drops out of college and attends classes at the Nebraska Aircraft Corporation.

MARCH 1923

Lindbergh buys his first airplane, a war-surplus Curtiss "Jenny" with a ninety-horsepower engine.

MARCH 14, 1925

Lindbergh graduates first in his class from U.S. Army Air Service Advanced Flying School in San Antonio, Texas.

OCT. 1925

Lindbergh becomes the chief pilot for Robertson Aircraft Corporation in St. Louis, Missouri.

14 1917 1920 1923 1926

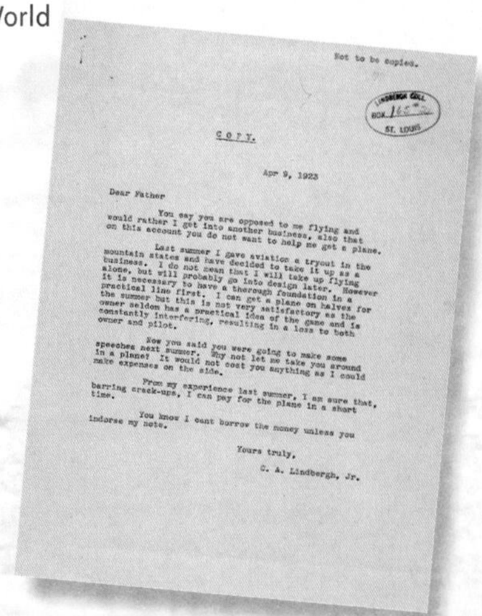

MARCH 1917

The Russian Revolution begins.

APRIL 1917

The United States enters World War I, providing the decisive measure of human and material resources to win the war for the Allies.

JUNE 28, 1919

Treaty of Versailles is signed, ending World War I.

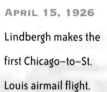

APRIL 1, 1922

Lindbergh makes his first flight as a passenger.

APRIL 9, 1922

Lindbergh makes his first solo flight—and nearly crashes.

MARCH 1924

Lindbergh enlists in flight training with the U.S. Army Air Service.

MAY 24, 1924

Lindbergh's father dies.

APRIL 15, 1926

Lindbergh makes the first Chicago–to–St. Louis airmail flight.

F ew people knew Charles Lindbergh when he decided to enter the "Transatlantic Derby" for the Orteig prize. The *Aircraft Yearbook,* an annual review published by the Aeronautical Chamber of Commerce, did not mention his name when highlighting the myriad events of

daredevil lindbergh

1926. He was known only to a small circle of aviators in the U.S. Army Air Service, the airmail business, and a few residents of the western states, where there were distant and fading memories of a "Daredevil Lindbergh" who flew as a stunt pilot in the barnstorming circuit in the early 1920s. When news began to circulate about Lindbergh's plan to win the Orteig prize, many aviation experts scoffed at his intention to fly the Atlantic alone. How could someone stay awake, for perhaps as long as forty hours, in a tortuous

Charles Lindbergh *(kneeling at center)* poses with fellow barnstormers, circa 1923.

aerial trek across a vast ocean? The *Chicago Evening Post* caught this mood of skepticism by labeling Lindbergh the "Flying Fool." All agreed that Lindbergh was an improbable candidate for the Orteig honors, the darkest of dark horses.

Yet a year later Charles Lindbergh would be the most celebrated aviator in the world. The *Aircraft Yearbook* would herald the former airmail pilot as the conqueror of the Atlantic, the symbol of aviation and its future, the exemplar of American values. It would also express wonderment at how Lindbergh catapulted himself to fame: "The whole Lindbergh performance was without publicity, like a job that was to be done, whether the world knew of it or not."[1]

Images of Charles Lindbergh began to appear in the press in the winter of 1926–27, when he made his eleventh-hour debut in the Orteig competition. Americans were slow to learn about Lindbergh and even slower to appreciate his high seriousness and potential to win the race. Byrd and Chamberlin, by contrast, were well known. The press followed their movements with intense interest, giving them most of the headlines. As the spring of 1927 neared, everyone expected one or more attempts to cross the Atlantic by plane, and in response to increasing demand, the press expanded their coverage to include Charles Lindbergh, but they didn't temper their skepticism regarding his chances.

Lindbergh possessed a certain charm that drew the press and the public to him. His quiet demeanor in the face of

▲ *Evangeline Land Lindbergh with her son, Charles. Evangeline took a keen interest in the affairs of her only child, and her family's interest in science and inventions had a profound impact on him.*

▼ *The home in Detroit, Michigan, where Charles was born.*

this growing scrutiny had an unintended consequence. In the absence of concrete knowledge, people began to project onto the Lindbergh persona all sorts of values. Tall, blue-eyed, and blond, he struck many as an "all-American boy." His personal style was controlled, understated, and purposeful, a contrast to the flamboyance of the typical barnstorming aviator of that era. Lindbergh appeared taciturn and shy, and behind his ready smile many perceived a boyish innocence. He exuded a certain naturalness, which also suggested self-confidence. In an age of gangsters, ethical lapses in government, and material excesses, the young flyer from the Midwest appeared to embody the best in the American character. And Lindbergh's background in flying the airmail circuit, arguably the most dangerous kind of flying at the time, evoked an image of personal heroism.

Less apparent to the growing circle of Lindbergh watchers in 1927 were other character traits, still largely hidden yet destined to shape the trajectory of his entire life: his innate intelligence; his futuristic vision of aviation as a tool to advance civilization; his instinct for privacy, always in conflict with his need to promote his projects; his strong prejudices and ethnocentrism; his immense capacity for disciplined work; his stoicism, often mislabeled as modesty; his infatuation with the idea of progress, in particular the power of science and technology to mold civilization (a set of values to be revised

"I was attracted to aviation by its adventure, not its safety, by the love of wind and height and wings."—Charles A. Lindbergh

in his mature years); and his stubbornness, just under the surface, always evident when he was challenged on matters of principle or personal integrity.

Even in his days of obscurity as an airmail pilot, Lindbergh had a strong drive to excel in his chosen profession. With time he articulated his own ideas about the future of aviation, particularly his dream of continents being linked together by commercial air service. Winning the New York–to–Paris race meant more than prize money or even setting a new air record. As Lindbergh noted in his *Autobiography of Values,* "the *Spirit of St. Louis* was a lens focused on the future, a forerunner of mechanisms that would conquer time and space."[2]

Lindbergh's family background and early years in Little Falls, Minnesota, helped to shape his approach to life. Born on February 4, 1902, he grew up in a dysfunctional family. His parents separated when he was five, setting into motion a life of constant movement as he divided his time between his mother and father, both of whom took a keen interest in his upbringing. He attended eleven separate schools. As a teenager

▼ Charles Lindbergh in 1904. Although his parents lived apart, he enjoyed fishing and hunting trips with his father and visits to his mother's family home in Detroit, where he took great interest in the inventions of his uncle, Charles Land.

Lindbergh became a loner, slow to make friends and always uncomfortable in group activities. He displayed no interest in girls, although the opposite sex found his good looks alluring. Lindbergh always appeared boyish, but his passage to adulthood came early in life. His peers from those formative years remembered his self-reliance, his restless nature, and his bent for a solitary life.

His father, Charles August Lindbergh, had served as a Minnesota congressman from 1907 to 1917, earning a reputation for political independence, agrarian populism, and spirited opposition to America's entrance into World War I. The elder Lindbergh was denounced as a traitor for his outspoken views. When the young Charles accompanied his father on an election tour during those turbulent days, he watched with alarm the angry crowds throwing eggs and rocks at him. His father's stoic response left an indelible impression on the boy. These painful incidents also gave the young Lindbergh a keen dislike of crowds and an apprehensive attitude toward the darker side of human nature.

Despite their many periods of separation, the elder Lindbergh took time to introduce his son to the Minnesota backwoods, taking him on numerous hunting and fishing trips. Once the young Lindbergh found himself in deep water and in danger of drowning. His father refused to come to his aid, insisting that his son find his own way to safety. Such lessons honed the boy's survivor skills. Both father and son could be unemotional in the face of crisis, devoid of sentimentality and outward displays of affection. The father's independent manner, pride, and stoicism, as biographers have noted, no doubt played a key role in shaping the son's future character.

Lindbergh's mother, Evangeline Land Lindbergh, came from a Detroit family known for their independent ways. Charles was her only child, and she devoted no small amount of her energy to his welfare, a pattern that would persist throughout her life. She was at her son's side at many critical junctures, including his departure from New York for Paris in 1927. Charles delighted in the company of his maternal grandfather, Dr. Charles H. Land, a Detroit dentist. He marveled at his grandfather's great energy, outspoken devotion to science, and many inventions. The young Lindbergh spent countless hours in Land's laboratory in Detroit.

Both parents sanctioned Charles Lindbergh's independent ways. When the United States entered World War I in 1917, they gave their permission for him to farm in lieu of completing his senior year of high school. During the war farming was deemed a vital part of national defense,

▲ As a boy, Charles Lindbergh took great pleasure in his canine companions, in this case his beloved dog Dingo. At the time he was living in Little Falls, Minnesota.

◄ Charles Lindbergh with his trophies on a hunting trip with his father in 1910.

Commemorative toys honoring the *Spirit of St. Louis*

and students were allowed to count a year of farming toward their high-school graduation. Lindbergh disliked school and thrived in this work environment. He also adamantly refused to attend Sunday school or church, seeing formal religious instruction as an unnecessary imposition. Throughout his life he would be a nominal Christian but at odds with the organized church and largely unknowing when it came the intellectual taproots of the Christian faith. With this lack of a consistent and complete education, Lindbergh developed a highly idiosyncratic approach to learning, reading only what narrowly interested him. Consequently, he entered adulthood largely untutored, but he possessed a raw intelligence and an innate curiosity that often compensated for what he lacked in formal learning.

When Lindbergh entered the University of Wisconsin in 1920 as an engineering student, he displayed little interest in a conventional academic course of study, and he eventually flunked out in his sophomore year. While at Wisconsin, however, he did excel as a member of the Reserve Officers' Training Corps (ROTC) rifle and pistol team, earning a reputation for marksmanship. Typically, such activity attracted him because it allowed him to compete as an individual.

Despite the shortcomings of Lindbergh's formal education, he demonstrated impressive mechanical skills and an insatiable urge to travel. He was at home repairing automobiles and motorcycles.

charles august lindbergh

Charles Lindbergh was the son of Charles August Lindbergh (often called "C.A."). Born in Sweden in 1859, C.A. was brought by his parents, Ola Månsson and Lovisa Callén (who renamed themselves August and Louisa Carline Lindbergh when they left Sweden), to Minnesota as an infant. His parents were pioneers in this newly settled territory and no strangers to adversity. From an early age, C.A. was driven to succeed. He studied law at the University of Michigan, and after graduating in 1883 set up a practice in Little Falls, Minnesota. C.A. married Mary LaFond in April 1887, and she bore him three daughters (one of whom died as an infant). In April 1898, she died suddenly from stomach cancer.

With the passing of time, the widower C.A. caught the eye of Evangeline Lodge Land, a chemistry teacher. Their whirlwind courtship led to marriage, despite the fact that C.A. was twenty years her senior. When she became pregnant Evangeline decided to return to her hometown of Detroit for the birth of their child, where her uncle, a physician, could handle the delivery. Charles Augustus Lindbergh was born on February 4, 1902. Shortly thereafter, C.A. and Evangeline moved back to Little Falls, where he had built a new home near the Mississippi River. There he took pains to introduce his son to the rugged Minnesota outdoors. The young Charles quickly adapted to this primitive environment, taking great delight in hunting and fishing, collecting arrowheads, and building rafts

A formal photograph of the young Lindbergh with his father, circa 1909

to navigate the Mississippi River. C.A.'s lifelong love of the Minnesota outdoors made an indelible imprint on his son.

The marriage of C.A. and Evangeline proved to be a troubled one, leading eventually to a separation, with the young Charles dividing his time between his estranged parents. However, both parents remained strongly involved in his upbringing. C.A. bequeathed to Charles a spirit of rugged individualism, personal discipline, and stoicism in the face of adversity.

From 1907 to 1917, C.A. served as a Republican congressman in the U.S. House of

The senior Lindbergh was an energetic and outspoken politician, shown here campaigning in rural Minnesota in 1909.

Representatives. Later he made unsuccessful campaigns for the U.S. Senate and the Minnesota governorship. At heart a reformer, the elder Lindbergh ardently campaigned for the agrarian West against moneyed interests, industrial trusts, and monopolies. His opposition to America's entrance into World War I, culminating in the publication of his outspoken book *Why Is Your Country at War?* (1917), led to his isolation and the end of his political career. Nonetheless, C.A.'s long tenure as a congressman allowed his son to live in Washington, D.C., and even afforded him the opportunity to meet two presidents, William Howard Taft and Woodrow Wilson. Always an attentive father, C.A. Lindbergh remained a powerful influence on his son's life until his death in 1924.

Like Henry Ford, he enjoyed tearing down mechanical devices to see how they worked. At the age of fourteen Lindbergh drove his mother to California and back, an arduous month-long trek each way across primitive roads. The following year he rode his motorcycle across much of the West and South. Although such activities further disrupted his formal education, Lindbergh's journeys gave full expression to his independent spirit and love of the outdoors. They also were training for long, solitary trips.

Flying captured Lindbergh's imagination at an early age. "When I was a child on our Minnesota farm," he remembered, "I spent hours lying on my back in a high timothy and redtop, watching white cumulus clouds drift overhead, staring into the sky. . . . How wonderful it would be, I'd thought, if I had an airplane. . . . Then, I would ride on the wind and be part of the sky."[3] Following his brief stint at the University of Wisconsin, in March 1922 Lindbergh headed for the Nebraska Aircraft Corporation in Lincoln for flying lessons. This personal

◄ *Charles Lindbergh at the University of Wisconsin in 1921. At Wisconsin he studied engineering, which seemed to fit his natural aptitude, but performed poorly in this highly structured academic environment and eventually left college. However, he displayed a keen interest in the Wisconsin rifle team and ROTC, where he excelled.*

▶ *Lindbergh purchased his own war surplus Curtiss Jenny biplane in 1923, which he used in his new career as a barnstormer pilot.*

decision, one that would require him to pay a fee of five hundred dollars, opened a whole new area of activity for him. While Lindbergh found the flying school lacking in many respects, he felt he had discovered a career path in harmony with his nature and skills.

Before 1922 ended, Lindbergh had made his debut in the world of barnstorming. The term "barnstorming" originated in the world of the theater, where it referred to touring actors who often performed in barns. The co-opted term suited the stunt pilots of the 1920s, who flew from town to town performing their death-defying aerobatics and offering plane rides to the brave in the crowd. Lindbergh began as a barnstormer's assistant but soon moved up in the ranks. He toured several western states, performing aerial stunts, parachuting, and wingwalking. In 1923 he purchased a war-surplus Curtiss Jenny biplane to perfect his skills and to earn money as a barnstormer. He flew the typical routine before rural crowds, flying figure eights, tailspins, and barrel rolls. Lindbergh was constantly on the move, often sleeping on a canvas hammock under the wing of his plane. Pay was minimal but enough to keep him alive in his new career in aviation.

The more Lindbergh flew as a barnstormer, the more restless he became. He yearned to enter a more legitimate and demanding arena of flight. Here his natural restlessness blended with his

Commemorative *Spirit of St. Louis* pencil-box set for children

growing ambition to make his mark in aviation. There was no real commercial aviation in those days, but the military did offer flight training. Accordingly, in 1924 Lindbergh joined a class of 104 cadets at the U.S. Army Air Service training program at Brooks Field near San Antonio, Texas, where for the first time in his life he embraced a formal course of training on its own terms and endeavored to succeed. The training was rigorous, consisting of a demanding round of ground-school studies followed by intensive flight instruction. Lindbergh reached the top of his class and moved to Kelly Field for the advanced phase of his training. The washout rate was high, with only nineteen of Lindbergh's original class winning their wings. Graduation from army flight training brought a commission of second lieutenant for Lindbergh. He subsequently joined the 110th Observation Squadron of the Missouri National Guard at Lambert Field in St. Louis.

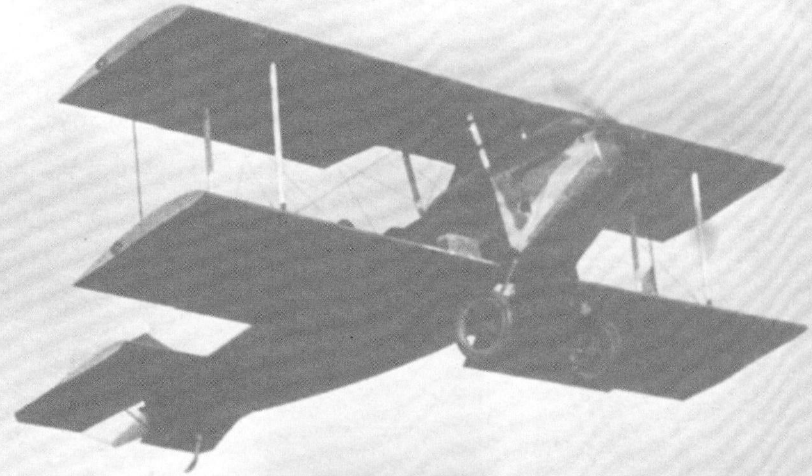

While in advanced training at Kelly Field, Lindbergh flew with a small cadre of highly skilled military pilots. Formation flying, gunnery practice, and cross-country navigation exercises filled his days at Kelly, but there were moments when the routine was broken. Once, in a nine-ship formation of SE-5 pursuit planes, Lindbergh participated in a practice attack maneuver on a DH-4 aircraft. Diving from an altitude of five thousand feet on the target, Lindbergh swept past the DH-4, only to find himself in a midair collision with another SE-5. The sudden crash fused the two airplanes together.

"The ships started to mill around and the wires began whistling," Lindbergh remembered. "The right wing commenced vibrating and striking my head at the bottom of each oscillation."[4] He acted quickly, releasing his safety belt and climbing out on the damaged wing. From this position, he leapt backward and into the void. "I had no difficulty in locating the pull-ring and experienced no sensation of falling," he recalled. "The wreckage was falling nearly straight down and for some time I fell in line with its path and only slightly to one side. Fearing the wreckage might fall on me, I did not pull the rip cord until I dropped several hundred feet and

▲ After his stint as a barnstormer, Lindbergh won his wings as a military pilot with the U.S. Army Air Service, training at Kelly Field in Texas. Upon graduation, on March 14, 1925, he entered the army reserves as a pilot with the 110th Observation Squadron of the Missouri National Guard.

UNITED STATES AIR SERVICE
This is to certify that
Chas. Augustus Lindbergh has been
appointed Second Lieutenant in the
AIR SERVICE
OFFICERS RESERVE CORPS
(INACTIVE STATUS)
of the
ARMY OF THE UNITED STATES
for period of five years commencing
March 14, 1925
He received the rating of Air. Plt.
per P.O. 73-7, OCAS, 3/28/25, 19
Ira F. Fravel, Lt. Col., A.S.
Chief, Personnel Division.

Age 23 Wt. 165
Hgt. 6 ft. 3 in.
Color Hair Light
Color Eyes Blue
Date of issue April 15, 1925.
(Card not official without Air Service Seal.)
Signature
Name Typed Chas. Augustus Lindbergh
Rank Second Lieutenant
Organization Air Service Officers Reserve Corps
Rating Airplane Pilot

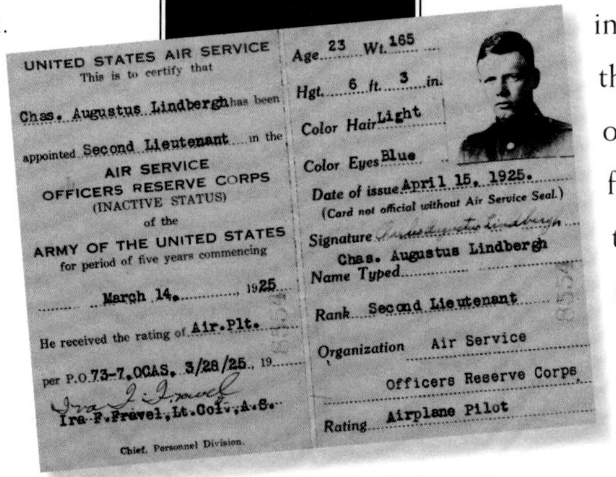

Lindbergh's military identification card

into the clouds. During this time I had turned one-half revolution and was falling flat and face downward."[5]

Lindbergh's parachute opened. As he descended, Lindbergh saw the other pilot's parachute open. Both made it to the ground safely, but not without danger en route. The wreckage fell around both men during their descent, missing them narrowly, and then bursting into flames upon impact. A DH-4 airplane picked up both downed pilots. Within an hour Lindbergh was flying again in a fresh SE-5, perfecting his skills at formation flying and mock air battles. This incident demonstrated his ease in the air and his coolness in the face of danger. His remarkable flying and personal bravery earned him the respect and acceptance of his peers in the U.S. Army Air Service.

In 1926 Lindbergh once again shifted careers, moving on to the demanding life of an airmail pilot. At this juncture, Lindbergh appreciated the regular income of his new job. His employer, the Robertson Aircraft Corporation, had won the competition for "Contract Air Mail Route No. 2," which covered the Chicago–St. Louis region. William B. Robertson, the owner of the airmail franchise, valued Lindbergh's talents and professionalism and designated him "chief pilot" for the St. Louis–to–Chicago route.

Flying the airmail offered unusual risks, and Lindbergh soon

▲ In the 1920s, Charles Lindbergh flew in the barnstorming circuit and in the more disciplined ranks of the U.S. Army Air Service. He often faced flight emergencies, displaying considerable coolness in the face of danger.

▼ Air races also drew large crowds in the decades of the 1920s and 1930s.

found himself in life-threatening situations. The tradition of the Pony Express seemed to be reincarnated in these intrepid aviators, who took great pride in getting the mail through on time, regardless of bad weather. Flying through storms, landing at night, and making forced landings because of engine failure were commonplace.

One of the great difficulties of night flying, as Lindbergh once observed, was finding a way to light the landing field. Navigation was done by "pilotage"—following highways and railroad arteries to a given designation. There were some primitive navigation aids such as lights and radio beacons, but there was no sure way to guide an airmail plane—typically a war-surplus DH-4—to a safe landing. Sometimes several cars were lined up with their headlights turned on. The beams of light were dim at best, but in those days they were a welcome alternative to complete darkness. Lindbergh remembered one dark night with minimal illumination: "I took off and landed by the light of a pocket flashlight which one of the men flashed constantly while I was in the air, to enable me to keep track of the landing field."[6] Some nights Lindbergh used the city lights to guide him to the landing field. The key element was to know the proper sequence of towns en route.

Emergency jumps were also commonplace on airmail routes. One of the more spectacular occurred on the night of September 16, 1926.

barnstorming

One of Charles Lindbergh's first jobs in aviation was as a barnstormer. The 1920s had become the heyday for barnstorming, a time when intrepid aviators toured the United States performing high-risk aerial stunts, offering plane rides, and popularizing the airplane as the new mode of transportation. In those days airplanes were a novelty, and

Lindbergh *(center)* poses with Lieutenant William C. Cornelius *(left)* and Lieutenant Irwin A. Wookring at Miles Field, California.

crowds predictably responded with enthusiasm to the staged, "death-defying" performances. Few towns or even cities had airports, so

barnstormers had to select a spacious open field to set up their operations. They frequently flew war-surplus Curtiss Jenny biplanes, slow and maneuverable flying machines that were ideal for the air-show circuit. Barnstormers operated alone, in small groups, or in "flying circuses." The Gates Flying Circus, the Flying Aces, and Jimmy Angel's Flying Circus, the most organized and financially viable of the touring air shows, deployed numerous planes and a large cast of performers. One of the most prominent barnstormers of the era was Clyde "Upside Down" Pangborn, who flew with the Gates Flying Circus.

When Lindbergh worked as a barnstormer, the crowds were often small, typical of an impromptu air show offered in a little town in the Midwest. However, there were occasions when a traveling troupe of stunt pilots drew large audiences. Publicity for such events mimicked the carnivals and circuses. Often the arrival of a barnstorming troupe was heralded by a plane pulling a banner or dropping flyers onto a town square. Well-organized air shows by the major barnstorm-

ing companies drew huge crowds in such cities as Chicago, numbering in the tens of thousands. For elite troupes, these shows offered considerable financial reward.

For an admission price of fifty cents or less, amazed onlookers watched barnstormers fly loops and spins. The aviators frequently flew their planes down to ground level to pick up riders from a speeding race car, using a ladder or rope. Wing-walkers, often women, performed spine-tingling aerial stunts: moving in a carefree manner across and over the wings, standing erect on the top of the wing as the plane made a complete loop, or dangling precariously from the lower fuselage as the plane sped through the sky. One of the most spectacular stunts called for the transfer of a wing-walker from one plane to another in midair, often without a parachute. A number of intrepid women such as Gladys Ingle and Georgia "Tina" Broderick gained considerable fame in this risky profession. Broderick entered the record books in 1913 as the first woman to parachute from a plane.

Even in an era of widespread racial discrimination, a small coterie of black aviators managed to break into the barnstorming circuit, if on a segregated basis. Bessie Coleman won fame as a barnstormer and is remembered as one of the first licensed black pilots in the country. To earn her license, Coleman traveled to France for flight training. She managed to sustain herself financially as a stunt pilot at a time when most blacks, men and women, were routinely barred from American flight schools. The Blackbirds flew out of Los Angeles and performed before thousands at an all-black air show in 1931, but this celebrated team of stunt pilots failed to launch a "100 City Tour" for lack of funding. However, the organization of viable black flying clubs in Los Angeles and Chicago set the stage for black pilots and aerial performers to organize their own air shows and to join the craze for barnstorming.

Barnstorming posed many dangers. Air mishaps and even death became part of the barnstorming script. Lincoln Beachey performed as a stunt pilot at the very dawn of aviation, becoming an inspiration for the

Anne and Charles Lindbergh sit with Cliff Henderson, managing director of air races, at the National Air Races in Los Angeles, 1930.

barnstormers of the 1920s. Among Beachey's many exploits, he is best remembered for flying through the gorge at Niagara Falls. He died when his plane crashed into the harbor at San Francisco Bay. Beachey's fate was shared by many barnstormers in the 1920s; Bessie Coleman died in 1926 while performing an aerial stunt in Florida.

By the end of the 1920s, barnstorming had lost its general appeal. The older Jennys had become difficult to maintain in flying condition. Barnstormers found the newer aircraft faster, but expensive to maintain and not cost-effective for the barnstorming circuit. And, as many barnstormers had entered their profession as young pilots, the allure of the barnstorming life waned with the passing of time. Like Lindbergh, many viewed their lives as stunt pilots as temporary, a way to get into aviation and set the stage for more serious endeavors. Talented pilots were often lured away to participate in air races or record-breaking flights. The military and commercial airlines also drew some away from the high-risk, low-paying lifestyle of the barnstormer. No less important, increased federal regulation of all aspects of aviation during the 1920s—and, later, the onset of the Great Depression—forced an end to the carefree atmosphere that had allowed barnstorming to thrive.

◆ Barnstorming reached
its peak of popularity in
the 1920s, as daredevil
aviators, such as the
Black Cats, drew avid
crowds to their shows.
Pilots flew loops and
spins, often with wing-
walkers performing
stunts on their planes.
This exciting new form
of entertainment was
accessible to the
masses, with many
tickets costing less than
fifty cents.

That night Lindbergh departed from Lambert Field in St. Louis for Maywood Field in Chicago, with scheduled stops in Springfield and Peoria, Illinois. He left from Peoria around dusk. The weather was fine, with a clear night sky and only a light ground haze to challenge the navigational skills of the pilot. However, shortly after Lindbergh's departure he encountered fog, which soon thickened. He dropped a flare and planned to land. In those days, it was routine in bad weather for the airmail pilot to land and transfer his mail bags to the nearest train for delivery. The flare, however, did not ignite. Lindbergh decided to continue on, hoping the enveloping fog would eventually dissipate. As he approached Maywood Field, the fog grew worse still—only a dull glow at the top of it indicated a town below. On the airfield, ground crews turned on searchlights and started to burn gasoline in drums in the hope that Lindbergh would spot the field.

At 8:20 P.M. his engine stopped, having consumed the last drop of fuel. At that point Lindbergh pointed his airplane toward the open countryside, nosed up, and parachuted out of the right side of the cockpit. He estimated that he was at around five thousand feet when he abandoned the fuel-starved flying machine. As Lindbergh began his long descent, he heard the distinct roar of an airplane engine! His plane's engine had re-ignited and resumed flying on its own. (Apparently, when the airplane nosed down, residual fuel drained into the carburetor and restarted the engine.) Once the engine restarted, the plane fell into a series of powered spirals. Emerging from the fog-shrouded sky it made several close passes to Lindbergh, one coming as close

◆ Barnstormer Lindbergh dislocated his shoulder testing an airplane at Lambert Field, St. Louis, on June 2, 1925. Later, as an airmail pilot, he flew through severe weather on mail routes. Lindbergh displayed great coolness in flight emergencies, on one occasion parachuting to safety when his plane ran out of fuel.

as three hundred yards. Remarkably, he managed to touch down safely. By 3:30 A.M. he had retrieved his mail bags from the crash site and was on board a train to Chicago with the bags in hand.

It was on an airmail flight that Lindbergh would decide to seek the Orteig prize. His own accounts of how and why he made this decision vary and, to some degree, are contradictory. When he wrote his first account of the New York–to–Paris flight in his July 1927 book, "We," he merely observed that he had made up his mind to pursue the Orteig prize in September 1926 on a flight from St. Louis to Chicago. In 1953, when he published The Spirit of St. Louis, he provided a dramatic and lyrical account of his own Damascus Road experience, a moment when the whole course of his life had been transformed. Still, his motives were complex, from boredom with flying the airmail to the alluring temptation of taking on the high-risk transoceanic flight to Europe.[7]

Whatever the circumstances, Lindbergh began his quest for the Orteig prize in the fall of 1926. His first obvious task was to secure financial backing, since his personal savings of $2,000 fell short. This small fund would be his seed money. Lindbergh felt he needed a minimum of $15,000 to purchase or build an aircraft. Such a budget, he knew, was modest. Richard Byrd had solicited about $100,000 for his project, and it was rumored that the American Legion had budgeted a similar amount for Noel Davis and Stanton

▲ When Lindbergh completed his historic transatlantic flight, there was a huge demand for a book on his extraordinary achievement. His memoir "We" became a bestseller in 1927; in 1953 Lindbergh published a more detailed account in his book The Spirit of St. Louis.

Wooster's multi-engine Keystone Pathfinder and their projected flight to Europe. Lindbergh needed backers, and he needed them as soon as possible.

Solicitation of the St. Louis business community became Lindbergh's priority. For example, he spoke with Major Albert Bond Lambert about his vision of a transatlantic flight. Lambert offered a donation of $1,000 and indicated that his brother, J. D. Wooster Lambert, would match that amount. Lindbergh's airmail boss, William B. Robertson, endorsed the idea and offered to lend his name to the project, but he lacked the funds himself to be a financial patron. Later, Lindbergh recruited Harold Bixby, head of the St. Louis Chamber of Commerce, and Harry F. Knight, a prominent banker, to lead the effort to complete his solicitation of $15,000. Two other men, Earl Thompson and E. Lansing Ray, joined the group of St. Louis businessmen and civic leaders. With the active involvement of these men, Harry Knight cut a check for Lindbergh in February 1927.

His St. Louis backers did not offer their support without asking some tough questions. They reacted with surprise, as most people did, to Lindbergh's plan to fly the Atlantic alone. Was such a venture plausible? They realized that if Lindbergh actually made the first transatlantic flight, his success would cast reflected glory on St. Louis. But, if he failed, there would be a

Commemorative shadow box of Charles Lindbergh and the Spirit of St. Louis

public outcry about the misdirected largesse of the sponsors.

Lindbergh's scheme was controversial, to say the least, even among some aviation experts. He called for a single-engine airplane to make the long flight, not the multi-engine machine favored by most contenders, including the experienced Richard Byrd. In Lindbergh's mind, they were expensive and unnecessarily dangerous, especially when overloaded at takeoff, as in the case of René Fonck. Moreover, their safety features were illusory: With three engines, he argued, you tripled your chances of engine failure. From the start, Lindbergh believed the single-engine Wright Bellanca WB-2 was the optimal machine. It was single-wing, streamlined, and a recordholder on duration flying. (A world endurance record of fifty hours and thirty-three minutes without refueling was set in 1926.)

The key technological breakthrough, Lindbergh noted, was the durable Wright Whirlwind engine. The existence of such a modern engine made the success of his plan to fly the Atlantic possible. Throughout the 1920s the demand grew for a reliable air-cooled aircraft engine, one that would be simultaneously lightweight and powerful. Water-cooled engines were heavy and, in those days, typically underpowered and highly unreliable. The Wright Whirlwind was not

▲ Charles Lindbergh recruited a group of St. Louis businessmen to provide financial backing for his campaign to win the Orteig prize. Clockwise from left: Harold M. Bixby, Harry Knight, Harry F. Knight, Major A. B. Lambert, Earl Thompson, E. Lansing Ray, William B. Robertson, and J. D. Wooster Lambert.

only reliable, it also incorporated several innovative design features such as sodium-cooled valves and self-lubricating rocker arms, making it relatively maintenance free. These modern features allowed the new engine to perform flawlessly for hundreds of hours, and the time between engine overhauls was greatly extended. For Lindbergh and his rivals, the advent of the Wright Whirlwind made nonstop long-distance flying, even across oceans, feasible for the first time.

Lindbergh also argued for severe austerity in the aircraft's design. His airplane would be minimalist in every respect—no radios, no special instrumentation, no creature comforts. Consistent with his single-pilot concept, he preferred an extra fuel tank to a copilot. There was an elegant and persuasive simplicity to Lindbergh's approach that did not escape the attention of his financial backers.

In late November 1926, Lindbergh traveled east to meet with officials of the Wright Aeronautical Corporation. On this journey he met the Italian-born aircraft designer Giuseppe Bellanca himself. This was an exploratory trip, to see if he could arrange the purchase of a Wright Bellanca WB-2. On a second trip, two months later, he met businessman Charles Levine, who at the time owned the fabled Wright Bellanca.

Lindbergh's trip to New York City to negotiate this purchase turned out to be a fiasco. The chance that Levine would sell the aircraft outright was minimal, since he jealously guarded the option of determining how his aircraft would be used for any transatlantic flight. Levine might have been interested in allowing Lindbergh and his backers to invest, but he was determined to retain control. When Levine made his position clear, especially his right to have the final word on the crew, Lindbergh was angered and abruptly ended the negotiations. For Lindbergh, Levine's posture was at odds with his own approach to the entire flight and his desire to be in the cockpit. He left New York disappointed but determined now to build his own airplane—one that would mirror the sleek silhouette of the WB-2 and, of course, be powered by a reliable Wright Whirlwind engine.

Hurriedly, he pursued his last option, Ryan Airlines, Inc., in San Diego, California. This small and financially pressed firm had built some modern airmail planes for

▼ While the Spirit of St. Louis was under construction, Lindbergh test-flew the Ryan M-1 to gain experience with the high-wing Ryan designs. On one occasion he flew the M-1 to Los Angeles to obtain Atlantic sailing charts for navigation planning. Lindbergh made his inaugural test flight of the completed Spirit on April 28, 1927.

service along the West coast. The company had been founded by aviation pioneer T. Claude Ryan, but was now under the effective control of Frank Mahoney. The Ryan staff analyzed Lindbergh's specifications for his new plane, to be called the *Spirit of St. Louis,* and offered to build it within budget. Lindbergh traveled to San Diego to see the plant for himself and, satisfied, finalized the agreement on February 23, 1927. The new airplane was to be designed and built in a mere sixty days.

At the Ryan factory, Lindbergh would depend on the dedicated work of three men: Frank Mahoney, the man in charge who approved the deal and at the start oversaw the operation; Donald Hall, Ryan's talented aeronautical engineer; and Hawley Bowlus, the factory manager. Extra workers were hired to assure compliance with the short deadline to complete the project. Lindbergh himself took up residence in the Grant Hotel for $2.50 a night to be close to the factory. There was no part of the process that Lindbergh did not oversee, and he could be a demanding boss.

Hall and Lindbergh worked on the detailed design of the aircraft. Hall decided that a new design development was required since the two current Ryan models could not support 750% more fuel. To compensate for the added weight planned for the aircraft, the wingspan was extended to forty-six feet. The new plane would be equipped with a Wright Whirlwind radial engine, for certain. But Hall and Lindbergh chose the latest model, a special series J-5C with 223 horsepower. Upon hearing that Lindbergh planned to fly alone, Hall was shocked, but soon he accepted this idea because it allowed certain favorable compromises in the new design, in particular the placement of the fuel tanks and the savings in overall weight. The *Spirit of St. Louis* carried 450 gallons of fuel in its fuselage and forward tanks (all controlled manually by an elaborate set of petcocks). The construction of the plane consisted of wood and metal components, steel-tube framing, and cotton fabric skin treated with cellulose and painted aluminum.

Lindbergh's exacting standards led to some peculiar design features in the *Spirit of St. Louis,* which, in retrospect, enhanced the performance and ultimate success of the new airplane. To make room for the large forward fuselage tank, the windscreen had to be eliminated; the pilot could see forward only through a periscope or out the side windows by

▲ 1927 telegram from Ryan Airlines to Robertson Aircraft.
▼ The construction of the *Spirit of St. Louis* called for the extensive use of lightweight materials, as evident here in the thin plywood instrument panel and wicker seat for the pilot. The entire cockpit area was specially designed to accommodate the reach of the lanky Lindbergh.

making shallow banks in flight. To save weight, Lindbergh decided on a simple wicker chair for the pilot, the built-in discomfort of the seat being viewed as a distinct asset—a way to prevent sleepiness on a long flight. The wicker seat was positioned more toward the aft, as a safety measure. Navigation would be a critical factor, and Lindbergh insisted on the best—an Earth Inductor Compass linked to a rotor and generator mounted on top of the fuselage. Space was also allotted for a magnetic compass. By modern standards, the instrumentation was minimal: an air speed indicator, an eight-day clock, an inclinometer (for the angle of attack of nose), an altimeter, two gauges for the measurement of oil pressure and oil temperature (key devices to monitor the condition of the engine while in flight), a turn-and-bank indicator, a fuel-pressure gauge, a magneto switch, and a mirror—all situated on a thin plywood dash of lightweight construction. A dunnage bag for maps, charts, and Lindbergh's minimal survival gear (a hunting knife and fishing tackle) was fitted behind the pilot's seat. Flares and water canteens, deemed essential, were given a place in the tightly designed cockpit area.

Lindbergh studies navigation charts in preparation for his transatlantic flight.

The *Spirit of St. Louis emerges from the Ryan factory in April 1927, equipped with a 223-horsepower Wright Whirlwind engine and boasting a range of over four thousand miles. Lindbergh oversaw every detail of the manufacturing process of his specially designed airplane.*

While in San Diego, as the *Spirit of St. Louis* grew in the cocoon of the Ryan factory, Lindbergh lived an ascetic life, spending long days at the factory overseeing the manufacturing process, working on his numerous checklists, gathering charts and maps, and studying the many details associated with the weather and navigation over the North Atlantic. Occasionally, he took long hikes alone to prepare himself physically for the flight ahead. Rumors circulated that he even stayed awake for over forty straight hours to test his capacity to control his normal urge to sleep. Even at this early point in his career, Lindbergh displayed a keen dislike for the local press, finding their questions silly and their reporting often inaccurate. His resentment of the Fourth Estate led to personal isolation, except from the Ryan workers—a pattern that became more severe and unyielding as the day approached for the *Spirit of St. Louis* to take to the air.

The Ryan crew completed their work on April 28. Their dedication, hard work, and long hours had allowed Ryan Airlines to meet the sixty-day deadline to manufacture the airplane. That same day Lindbergh took the *Spirit of St. Louis* on its first test flight and was pleased with the speed and agility of his aircraft. He then flew to nearby Camp Kearney, where he conducted a series of additional tests. One critical sequence was to load the airplane with graduated amounts of fuel. Once he reached the 300-gallon level, there was some minor damage to landing gear because of the enormous weight. The problem was quickly fixed, but Lindbergh decided not to fly the plane with

Drafting instruments lent to Lindbergh for use in preparing his flight maps

"He Built the Ryan New York to Paris Plane"

◆ Building the Spirit of St. Louis *required the labors of a talented team of specialists. Lindbergh worked closely with Donald Hall and the Ryan Airlines staff to design a sturdy, reliable plane for a nonstop flight from New York to Paris. Throughout the manufacturing process no small detail escaped his attention.*

◆ ◆ ◆

RED CROWN
THE GASOLINE OF QUALITY

the tanks topped off; he would wait until the day of the flight to make that last test.

On April 14, just as work on the *Spirit of St. Louis* entered its final stages, the press reported that Clarence Chamberlin and Bert Acosta had flown the Wright Bellanca on a fifty-one-hour nonstop flight. Such a demonstration indicated that Chamberlin was ready for a transatlantic flight. With great fanfare, Chamberlin announced that he would make the flight to Paris from Roosevelt Field in May, as soon as the weather was favorable. Two days later news reached Lindbergh that Richard Byrd had crashed his Fokker

America while landing, but the damage had been minor. Byrd indicated that his plane would be repaired in short order, and he, too, would be ready for a May departure across the North Atlantic. While Lindbergh's major rivals at Roosevelt Field were preparing for their flights, there was an unexpected turn of events: Noel Davis and Stanton Wooster had died in a crash of their Keystone Pathfinder near Hampton, Virginia. Their deaths came during the final test flight of their trimotor. Lindbergh learned of this grim news at about the same time as the Ryan workers rolled out the *Spirit of St. Louis* for flight testing.

On May 8, on the eve of Lindbergh's long-awaited departure for the east, there was more

▲ *Charles Lindbergh at Rockwell Field before his departure for St. Louis, en route to New York. He would reach St. Louis in record-breaking time.*

◄ *Lindbergh peers into the cockpit of the Spirit of St. Louis.*

dramatic news, which at the time cast a dark shadow over the entire Lindbergh team in both San Diego and St. Louis. Newspaper headlines reported that Charles Nungesser and François Coli had departed from France and were making their way toward New York over the North Atlantic. Nungesser and Coli had emerged as strong candidates to win the Orteig prize, and now it was only a matter of hours before they reached their destination. Lindbergh began to prepare himself for the huge disappointment of losing the race even before he had reached Roosevelt Field. He began to consider alternatives: Should he now make a flight across the Pacific?

Hours passed with no word from Nungesser and Coli. Lindbergh continued with his plans for a transcontinental flight, with its first leg to St. Louis and second to New York. On May 10 he departed San Diego, flying to St. Louis in a record-breaking four-teen hours and twenty-five minutes. He landed at Lambert Field at 8:20 A.M. on May 11.

▲ *Lindbergh greets the camera with a smile after the successful flight tests of his* Spirit of St. Louis.

◀ *The* Spirit of St. Louis's *motor is started by a Ryan worker, as Lindbergh inspects the cockpit.*

Shortly after landing, Lindbergh consulted with his backers. What should he do next? Nungesser and Coli had disappeared somewhere over the Atlantic. No one had heard from them for three days, suggesting that they had perished at sea. Reports were circulating that they had crashed in Maine or Newfoundland, but these theories appeared fanciful. Weather reports were now projecting good flying conditions over the North Atlantic in the week ahead. Byrd and Chamberlin were already at Roosevelt Field, like coiled springs, ready to go as soon as the weather cleared. There had been plans for Lindbergh to meet with his supporters in St. Louis. Should he stay? He decided that the window of opportunity was narrow and closing. There was no choice: He had to press on.

Lindbergh quickly refueled the *Spirit of St. Louis* for another nonstop flight to New York, and he departed on May 12 at 8:13 A.M. "The wind was west and the weather clear for the greater part of the distance," Lindbergh observed. "Over the Alleghenies, however, the sky was overcast and some of the mountain tops were in low hanging clouds and I followed the passes. At 5:33 P.M. New York Daylight Saving Time, I landed at Curtiss Field, Long Island."[8]

Charles Lindbergh now awaited his fate.

▼ Publicity photo of the Spirit of St. Louis, in association with Red Crown Aviation Gasoline and Gargoyle Mobil Oil. The two firms had donated fuel and oil, respectively, for the newly built Ryan airplane. Charles Lindbergh is pictured third from right, and Donald Hall, the Ryan chief engineer, second from right.

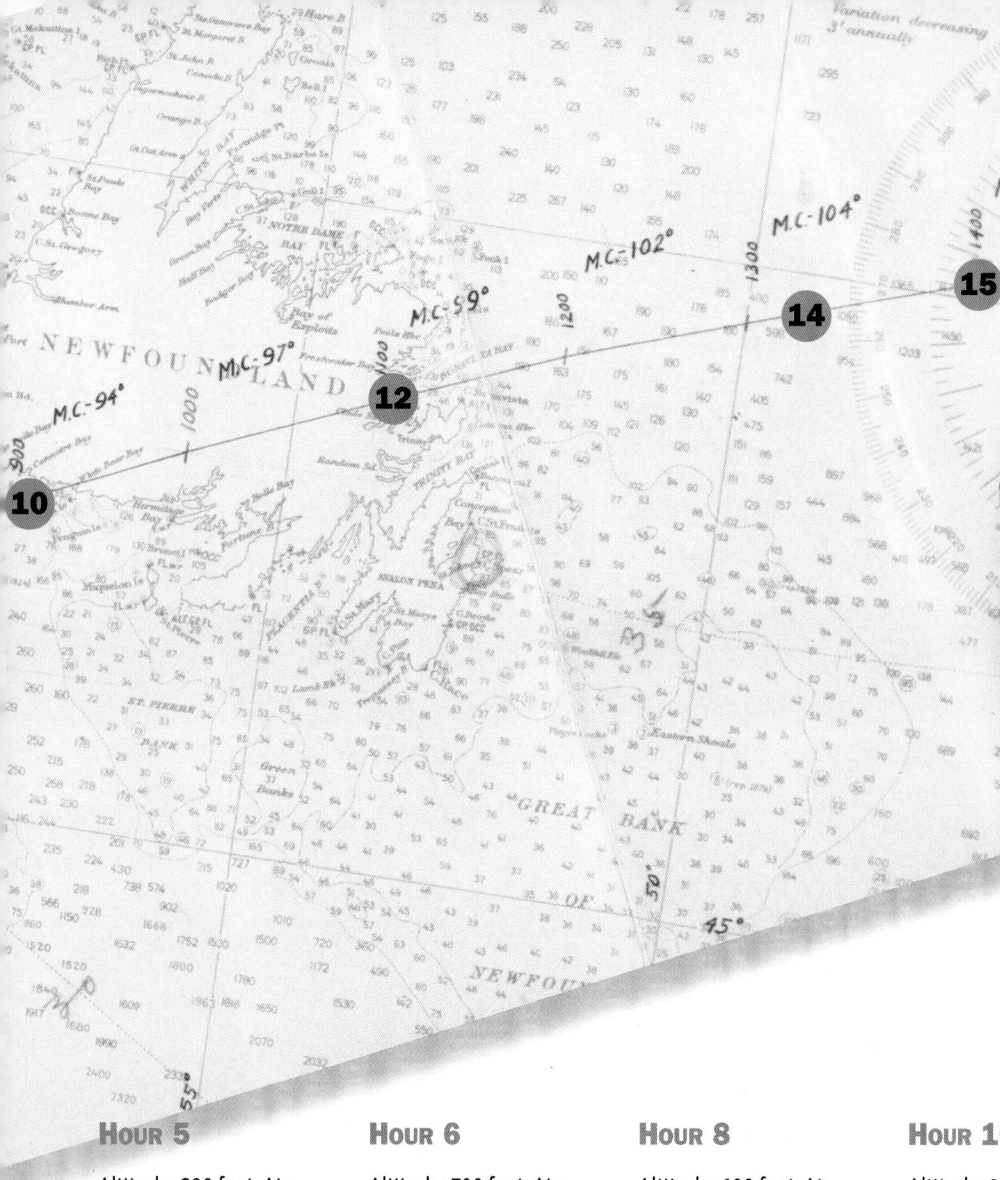

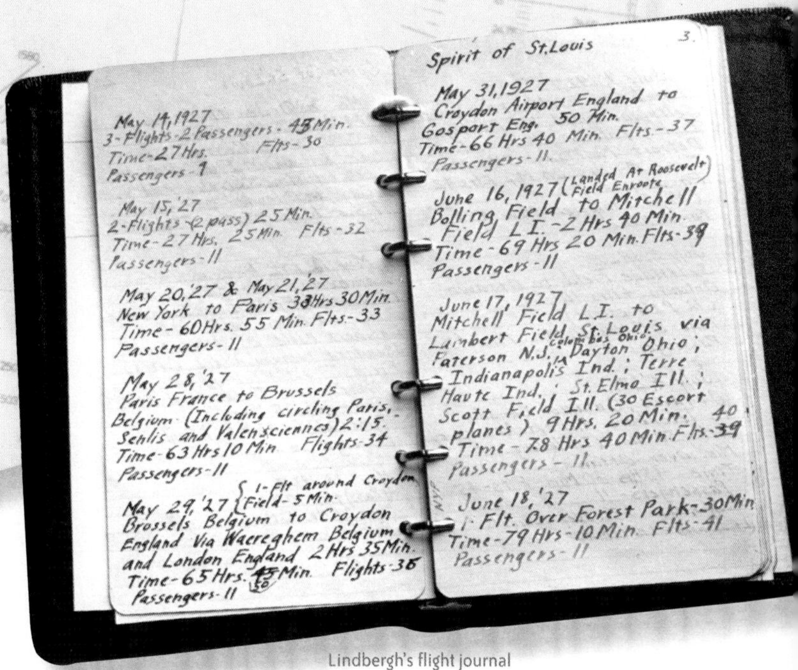

M.C.-110° M.C.-110°

M.C.-108°

M.C.-107°

M.C.-104°

M.C.-104°

M.C.-102°

M.C.-99°

M.C.-97°

M.C.-94°

NEWFOUNDLAND

GREAT BANK OF NEWFOU...

Lindbergh's flight journal

Spirit of St. Louis

HOUR 5

Altitude: 200 feet. Air speed: 103 mph. Nova Scotia appears ahead, Lindbergh's first turn-back marker. After flying over 400 miles, the *Spirit of St. Louis* is only six miles, or two degrees, off course. Lindbergh continues confidently.

HOUR 6

Altitude: 700 feet. Air speed: 101 mph. Wind velocity has increased from 0 to 30 mph. Rain clouds fill the north sky, and the *Spirit of St. Louis* encounters heavy turbulence as it approaches the storm.

HOUR 8

Altitude: 600 feet. Air speed: 96 mph. The storm changes direction and Lindbergh flies through clear skies once more. Only hours into his flight, the already exhausted pilot struggles to stay awake.

HOUR 10

Altitude: 150 feet. Air speed: 95 mph. Lindbergh flies over ice sheets in the Atlantic on his way to Newfoundland.

HOUR 12

Altitude: 700 feet. Air speed: 98 mph. In order to notify his supporters of his progress, Lindbergh makes a detour to fly over St. John's, Newfoundland. This is his last contact with North America.

HOUR 14

Altitude: 9,300 feet. Air speed: 85 mph. Nightfall brings a dense and dangerous fog. To avoid a rapidly gathering storm, the *Spirit of St. Louis* climbs to almost 10,000 feet. Lindbergh must also fly off course in order to escape from the hazardous ice that accumulates on his plane.

33½ hours

THE GREAT CIRCLE ROUTE

Much of Lindbergh's triumph lay in his planning and ingenuity. Previous flights to Paris had crossed the Atlantic by way of the Azores, but Lindbergh took advantage of the curvature of the earth by following the Great Circle route, the shortest distance between two points on a sphere. He plotted his course by first drawing a straight line between New York and Paris on a gnomonic projection chart. He then carefully transferred that path to the Mercator chart shown here, which he carried with him on his epic flight. The resulting arc curved gracefully over Nova Scotia and Newfoundland; Dingle Bay in Ireland; Cornwall at the southwest tip of England; and Cherbourg, France. Following this route shortened the flight by about 490 miles, bringing the total distance to about 3,610 miles. Lindbergh noted benchmarks at hundred-mile intervals, roughly the distance covered in one hour of flying.

Lindbergh departs from New York for Paris.

HOUR 1

Charles Lindbergh takes off from Roosevelt Field, Long Island, New York. In order to see through the hazy weather, Lindbergh flies just high enough to clear treetops and buildings.

HOUR 2

Altitude: 500 feet. Air speed: 102 mph. The sky clears and Lindbergh sees his first glimpse of the Atlantic Ocean.

MAY 9, 1926

Richard E. Byrd announces that he and copilot Floyd Bennett are the first to fly an airplane over the North Pole.

JULY 2, 1926

Army air service is restructured as the U.S. Army Air Corps.

OCT. 1926

Byrd announces that he intends to fly from New York to Paris the following summer.

1926

MAY 20, 1926

President Calvin Coolidge signs the first federal legislation regulating civil aeronautics and mandating the registration and licensing of pilots and planes.

SEPT. 15, 1926

In an overloaded plane, World War I fighter pilot René Fonck crashes at takeoff, ending his quest to be the first to fly the Atlantic.

SEPT. 1926

Bored with flying the airmail, Lindbergh decides to enter the race for the Orteig prize.

NOV. 29, 1926

Lindbergh meets with an executive at the Wright Aeronautical Corporation about the possibility of buying a Wright Bellanca airplane.

19

FEB. 19, 1927

Negotiations with Charles Levine to purchase the Wright Bellanca fall through.

FEB. 25, 1927

Lindbergh meets with Donald Hall and Franklin Mahoney at Ryan Airlines and, pleased with their figures, signs the order to have them build the *Spirit of St. Louis*.

APRIL 8, 1927

The Wright Whirlwind radial engine arrives at the Ryan plant.

APRIL 20, 1927

Orteig prize competitor Byrd crash-lands on his first test flight, injuring three crewmen and damaging the plane.

APRIL 28, 1927

Lindbergh makes the first test flight of the *Spirit of St. Louis* from Dutch Flats in San Diego and remains aloft for 20 minutes.

MAY 8, 1927

Frenchmen Charles Nungesser and François Coli depart France for New York. Although a radio report claims that their plane had been spotted over the Atlantic, the two men are never seen again.

MAY 20–21, 1927

Lindbergh flies the *Spirit of St. Louis* from New York to Paris, becoming the first pilot to cross the Atlantic alone.

27   1928

MARCH 7, 1927

Lindbergh flies to Los Angeles from San Diego in search of charts for his transatlantic journey.

APRIL 26, 1927

Noel Davis and Stanton Wooster are killed in a crash while testing their aircraft, The Keystone Pathfinder, for a transatlantic flight to win the Orteig prize.

MAY 3–4, 1927

Lindbergh completes additional flights of his *Spirit of St. Louis* to test various fuel loads from 38 to 300 gallons of gasoline.

MAY 10–12, 1927

Lindbergh flies the *Spirit of St. Louis* from San Diego to St. Louis and from St. Louis to Long Island, setting a transcontinental record.

MAY 13–15, 1927

Lindbergh conducts test flights from Curtiss Field. The total flying time of the *Spirit* stands at 27 hours and 25 minutes.

MID-MAY 1927

Orteig prize competitor Clarence Chamberlin is temporarily stalled by a legal suit, clearing the way for Lindbergh.

HOUR 32

Lindbergh reaches the French city of Cherbourg. His destination is only 200 miles away.

HOUR 33

Lindbergh follows the navigation beacons down the Seine River on his night approach to Paris. The steady roar of the *Spirit of St. Louis*'s Wright Whirlwind engine assures a steady momentum toward Le Bourget Airport.

HOUR 34

After circling the Eiffel Tower, Lindbergh lands the *Spirit of St. Louis* at Le Bourget Airport, Paris, France. Local time: 10:22 P.M. Total flight time: 33 hours, 30 minutes, 29.8 seconds.

The *Spirit of St. Louis* is greeted by a throng at Le Bourget.

Sunglasses and case taken by Lindbergh on his transatlantic flight

Hour 15

Altitude: 10,500 feet. Air speed: 87 mph. Safely out of the storm, Lindbergh encounters other problems: Both his Earth Inductor Compass and his magnetic compass have suddenly stopped working. Lindbergh is forced to pilot the plane unaided in the dark for over an hour.

Hour 19

Altitude: 9,000 feet. Air speed: 87 mph. Reaching the halfway point in his trip, Lindbergh encounters fog, which hides the first signs of daybreak. The drowsy pilot struggles to remain awake and stops recording flight information.

Hour 22

Not having slept in forty-three hours, Lindbergh repeatedly falls asleep. He imagines land in the horizon and sees phantoms in his cabin. The fog clears, but there is still no land in sight.

Hour 27

Lindbergh sees several fishing boats. While unable to get directions from the fishermen below, the first signs of civilization revitalize him.

Hour 28

Lindbergh observes a coastline in the distance, which he correctly identifies as the southern tip of Ireland. Despite detours and fatigue, Lindbergh had remained almost exactly on course.

Hour 31

Lindbergh reaches Cornwall at the southwest tip of England, his second land fall in Europe.

L anding his sleek *Spirit of St. Louis* at Curtiss Airfield on Thursday, May 12, 1927, Lindbergh sparked a new wave of public interest in the New York–to–Paris race. For the first time, the radio and press coverage began to

solitary passage

focus on Lindbergh as a serious contender for the Orteig prize, no longer a "Flying Fool" or merely a footnote in the news coverage of his more prominent rivals. By Friday, headlines appeared across the nation with breathless commentary on the unfolding drama on Long Island. Two days later, on Sunday, some thirty thousand people had gathered at Roosevelt Field, anticipating one or more of the Atlantic racers to take off. The recent disappearance of Nungesser and Coli, along with the unexpected deaths of Davis and Wooster on the final test flight of their Keystone Pathfinder, lingered in the public's

A reenactment of Charles Lindbergh at the controls of the *Spirit of St. Louis,* as seen from the overhead window, clearly showing the instrument panel. While the photograph contains some inaccuracies, it gives dramatic sense of the cockpit area that was Lindbergh's "cabin in the sky," as he described it, on his thirty-three-hour transatlantic flight.

consciousness—a reminder that already six men had died in the race to win the Orteig prize. Such a grim tally of deaths further heightened public interest, which now reached a fever pitch.

None of the contenders for the prize had made any concrete moves to fly out of Long Island for France. Bad weather over the North Atlantic negated any such plan. With everything on hold, Lindbergh accepted an invitation from Colonel Theodore Roosevelt Jr. for lunch at the family estate on Oyster Bay. This timely and welcome luncheon allowed Lindbergh to escape the rush of radio and newspaper reporters seeking interviews and photographs. That same week Lindbergh's mother, Evangeline, arrived from Detroit to see her son on the eve of his historic flight. The press hounded her without mercy, asking probing questions about her state of mind, her awareness of the dangers facing her son on a transatlantic flight, and her reaction to the fact that no less than six deaths littered the competition for the Orteig prize. Lindbergh

▲ Charles Lindbergh's application for the $25,000 Raymond Orteig prize for the first aviator to make a nonstop crossing of the Atlantic.

▼ Lindbergh with his mother, Evangeline Land Lindbergh, on the eve of his historic flight.

responded angrily and made the decision never to write about his flight for the tabloid press, "no matter what they'd pay me."[1]

The week of May 16 became the time frame for some unforeseen events. Lindbergh entered the week still the underdog; he would emerge the first to get airborne. His contenders, heralded by the media as the best prepared for a transoceanic flight, seemed to be gripped by inertia, even as the weather began to change along the two-thousand-mile stretch of ocean between Newfoundland and Ireland. A high-pressure system slowly moved into this area as the week progressed, clearing the skies of storms and fog. Lindbergh properly interpreted this change in weather as the long-awaited moment to fly, while his rivals, Byrd and Chamberlin, could not or would not make the preparations for departure.

The hidden vanities and personality quirks of Lindbergh's rivals came to the fore in this narrowest of time frames. Byrd had styled his project as part of the "science of transoceanic flying," not just another aviation stunt, suggesting that he was more of an explorer than an adventurer. He seemed wedded to the cultivation of his reputation and the maintenance of proper test procedures. Seemingly indifferent to the calendar, he ordered additional tests of his Fokker aircraft just as the weather began to break. His pride in the "scientific" purpose of his flight in the *America* was echoed by his main backer, Rodman Wanamaker, who endorsed the additional round of tests. Wanamaker, with his casual attitude toward the calendar and shifting weather fronts, actually ordered a gala christening of the *America* for May 21, ironically the date the world would celebrate Lindbergh's landing at Le Bourget. Consequently, Byrd and his team were busy installing instruments and testing various systems of the *America* as Lindbergh monitored the daily weather reports. In his book *Skyward* (1928), Byrd took pains to answer his many critics, some who accused him of cowardice in not acting decisively that week: "To hasten . . . for the sake of notoriety," he wrote, "was to undermine the scientific character of our expedition."[2]

While Byrd adorned himself in the cloak of science, Clarence Chamberlin, keen on flying first to Paris, found himself caught up in an eleventh-hour lawsuit—one that proved to be more frustrating than any imaginable technical problem. Pugnacious Charles Levine, the owner of the Wright Bellanca (newly christened the *Columbia*), displayed an uncertainty over the crew makeup that history would record as an unfortunate exercise in egotism. Chamberlin had been scheduled to fly with Lloyd Bertaud, but once Bertaud got into an argument with Levine, purportedly over the distribution of the prize money, the whole *Columbia* project fell into a legal fog. Levine lost his confidence in Bertaud, and the whole matter led to a suit that grounded the *Columbia*. This legal hassle meant simply that Chamberlin would not fly that week.

In contrast, Lindbergh enjoyed enormous freedom. He could decide his own destiny, weather permitting. From the very beginning, from his initial

▲ *Two French pilots made a highly publicized effort to win the Orteig prize: François Coli (foreground) and Charles Nungesser (in cockpit). On May 8, 1927, they took off from France for New York in their airplane,* L'Oiseau blanc, *only to disappear without a trace.*

▶ *Clarence Chamberlin (left) stands with his supporters next to his Wright Bellanca monoplane, the* Columbia. *Chamberlin was a strong contender for the Orteig prize, but a legal suit grounded him the week Charles Lindbergh flew to Paris.*

thoughts about competition for the Orteig prize in September 1926, Lindbergh had exercised sovereignty over the design and use of the *Spirit of St. Louis*. He alone would decide when to fly. In retrospect, one could argue that he had mastered the "science of transoceanic flight" before he actually landed on Long Island. His theory that the Orteig prize could be won by one pilot flying a single-engine aircraft now seemed prescient. He was no "flying fool." The press would be slow to realize Lindbergh's unanticipated advantage after his arrival on Long Island. His flight, by definition, would be risky, and his fate would ride on the constant roar of the nine-cylinder Wright Whirlwind engine. But there he was on Long Island— confident, purposeful, free to act.

On the morning of May 19, light rain and cloudy skies cast a pall over Long Island. However, that same day reports reached Lindbergh that the long-awaited clearing over the North Atlantic was underway, offering a window of time to attempt a crossing. Lindbergh ordered his *Spirit of St. Louis*, still parked at nearby Curtiss Field, to be removed to the more spacious Roosevelt Field. With the engine covered in a tarpaulin, workers attached the rear skid of the aircraft to a truck for the transfer across a soggy road. No one has described this dramatic moment better than Charles Lindbergh himself: "My plane lurches backward through a depression in the ground. It looks awkward and clumsy. It appears incapable of flight—shrouded, lashed, and dripping. Escorted by motorcycle police, pressmen, aviators, and a handful of onlookers, the slow, wet trip begins. It's more like a funeral procession than the beginning of a flight to Paris."[3]

▲ *Ryan plant manager Hawley Bowlus (in white shirt and tie) appears with the* Spirit of St. Louis *at San Diego. Note the airplane is without its propeller, spinner, or wheel fairings.*

▼ *The* Spirit of St. Louis *is fueled on the morning of May 20, 1927.*

▶ *Lindbergh suits up for his flight.*

Lindbergh left the care of the *Spirit of St. Louis* in the hands of his ground crew, who attended to the final phase of fueling and the myriad last-minute preparations. Lindbergh returned to his hotel room, in hopes of getting some rest. He had decided to fly the next morning, May 20. As fate would have it, the young pilot managed to get less than three hours of sleep that night. When Lindbergh returned to Roosevelt Field at dawn, he was surprised to learn that he was the only aviator preparing for a departure. While his chances of completing the flight appeared plausible, he remained haunted by the old question: Could one man, flying alone, endure the physical challenge of flying 3,600 miles from New York to Paris?

With the yank on the ropes holding the chocks in place, Lindbergh began his takeoff run. He gave the *Spirit of St. Louis* full throttle. The time was 7:52 A.M. The overladen airplane moved slowly at first, and then

gathered momentum. For Lindbergh, as he later reported, the *Spirit of St. Louis* felt like an "overloaded truck." On board there was enough fuel to fly over four thousand miles. But the first hurdle was to get airborne. To add drama for Lindbergh's ground crew, this was the first time the tanks in the *Spirit of St. Louis* had been topped off. The Ryan aircraft now struggled with a payload of five thousand pounds. Everyone remembered the fate of René Fonck. Takeoff was the most dangerous moment in the "Transatlantic Derby." Men rushed forward to push on the struts of the airplane, hoping to add to its forward thrust across the wet runway.

At the one-hundred-yard mark the last person pushing on the struts dropped away, even as the Wright Whirlwind engine gave full power, and the airplane gained speed. Lindbergh remembered: "Pace quickens—turf becomes a blur—the tail skid lifts off ground—I feel the load shifting from wheels to the wings."[4] As Lindbergh held the course, the plane's wheels splashed repeatedly in puddles of water, giving a reassuring sense of speed. He pulled the stick back at the optimal moment, and the *Spirit of St. Louis* left the ground for the first time, only to bounce back and then leap skyward. Over two thousand feet of runway were left. Lindbergh climbed out with the "controls taut, alive, straining."[5] Ahead were telephone lines, and the onlookers watched in apprehension as

▲ The *Spirit of St. Louis attracted crowds wherever it appeared. A sleek silver monoplane with distinctive machine-tooled cowling, it possessed a range of four thousand miles. Lindbergh ardently believed that a single pilot in a single-engine aircraft could make it across the Atlantic.*

Lindbergh approached this man-made peril. "Now, I have to make it—there is no alternative," Lindbergh thought at that historic moment. "It'll be close, but the margin has shifted to my side. I keep the nose down, climbing slowly, each second gaining speed. If the engine can hold out for one more minute—five feet—twenty—forty—wires flash by underneath—*twenty feet to spare!*"[6]

Having escaped his first dangerous obstacle, Lindbergh banked the *Spirit of St. Louis* and headed out over Long Island Sound, passing by the grand estates and homes, hugging the beach. A Curtiss Oriole chase plane with a photographer suddenly appeared off his wing. The uninvited guest kept abreast for awhile, taking photographs. Then the escort turned back. Now Lindbergh found himself at the controls of his silver monoplane, alone in the sky, cruising at about one hundred miles

"What kind of man would live where there is no danger? I don't believe in taking foolish chances. But nothing can be accomplished by not taking a chance at all." —Charles A. Lindbergh

per hour. His heading was now roughly northeastern, with Rhode Island and Cape Cod as the initial milestones on the long passage to Paris.

Being alone, he thought of his father, who had died in 1924, a self-reliant man who had warned his son about depending too much on the aid of others. Lindbergh reflected on a truism uttered by the settlers of Minnesota and repeated often by his father: "One boy's a boy. Two boys are half a boy. Three boys are no boy at all."[7] Now he was alone, a solitary figure following a trajectory over a vast ocean. He had no one to depend on but himself.

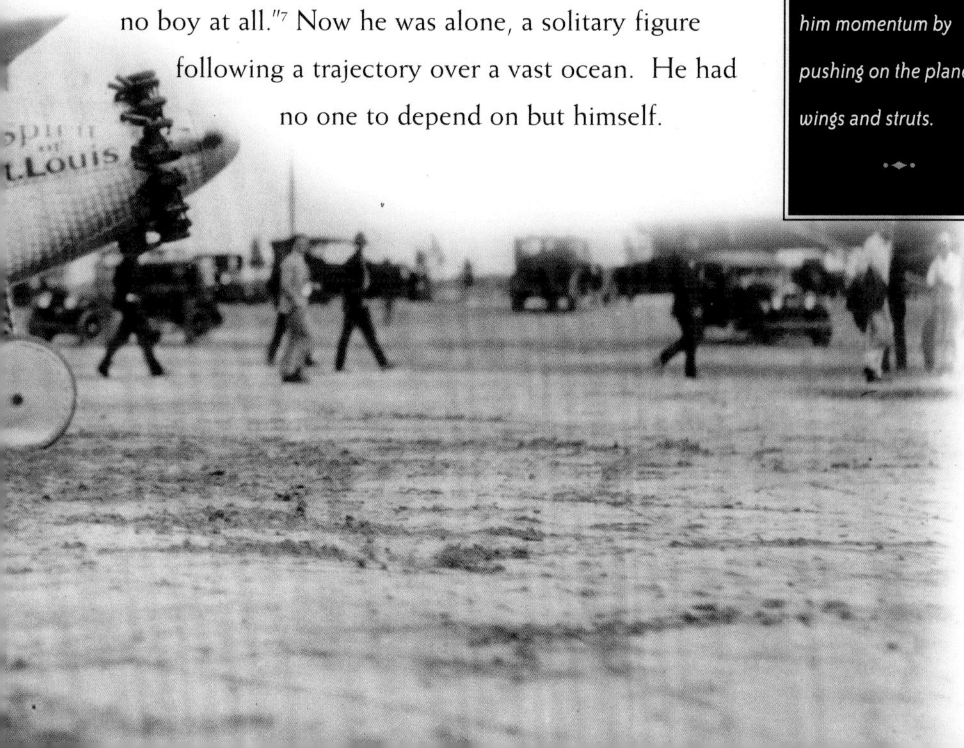

▼ *The takeoff sequence was the most dangerous moment in flying the* Spirit of St. Louis. *Lindbergh required a long runway to get airborne. Ground crewmen routinely gave him momentum by pushing on the plane's wings and struts.*

• ◆ •

Navigation now dominated his thoughts. He had chosen to fly the "Great Circle" route across the North Atlantic, which represented the shortest surface distance between two points on a sphere. The route called for Lindbergh to follow an initial heading of about sixty-five degrees over New England to Nova Scotia to Newfoundland. The curving route then dictated that he break out into the open Atlantic and fly a two-thousand-mile leg to landfall in Ireland. The final curving leg would take him over England to Cherbourg, where he planned to follow the Seine River to Paris. Lindbergh divided the route into one-hundred-mile segments with his Earth Inductor Compass as the trusted guide for navigational adjustments along the way, although he would use the stars and landmarks to define his course. He flew with no radio or even a sextant; his cockpit contained only charts and maps for reference.

The middle passage across the ocean from Newfoundland to Ireland constituted the greatest challenge. Much of the flying would be at night. Lindbergh had no experience in night-flying over

▼ The Spirit of St. Louis *lifts off at San Diego during a test flight. Charles Lindbergh conducted a series of flight tests on the new airplane in April 1927. Note the fairings (to reduce drag) on the landing gear have not yet been installed.*

oceans; there would be no convenient farmer's field to land on in case of an emergency. The North Atlantic, even in the most congenial moods, is a difficult space to master. For centuries, mariners had endured the ocean's shifting weather and rogue storms; by the mid-1920s only a few aviators had braved the open Atlantic (most notably, John Alcock and Arthur Whitten Brown in 1919). None had ever attempted the nonstop route of Lindbergh. At such a northerly latitude there are icebergs and freezing water in the spring; winds, fog, and rain define the harsh climate. Lindbergh had been told to brace himself for strong head winds, fog, and possible icing. Although weather reports projected clearing weather along the Great Circle route, there was no guarantee that he would encounter fair weather and excellent visibility while "crossing the pond."

Other challenges were psychological. Writing nearly a half century after his 1927 flight, Lindbergh mused about the phenomenon of fear. "Fear," he wrote in his *Autobiography of Values*, "is conditional. For me, there is a kind of fear related to responsibility, and another kind related to inevitability. In the one case, I am apprehensive of disaster. In the other, I am just plain scared."[8] His approach to fear was to dampen its impact by exercising control over his airplane whenever possible. As an airmail pilot, he had displayed

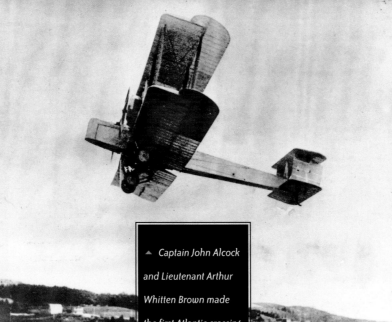

▲ Captain John Alcock and Lieutenant Arthur Whitten Brown made the first Atlantic crossing in their Vickers Vimy on June 14, 1919, flying from St. John's, Newfoundland, to Ireland. Their nonstop flight took nearly sixteen hours and covered a distance of 1,936 miles. For their precedent-setting flight, Alcock and Brown won a prize offered by the Daily Mail newspaper.

᠆●᠆

considerable coolness in handling storms and the dangers of night flying. Now, heading for the open Atlantic, Lindbergh remained serene, ready to embrace his fate. Along the way there would be benchmarks to gauge progress and also to mark places where, if the weather turned really harsh, he could turn back. He reminded himself: This was not a suicide mission, as some might say, but a bold adventure, even a calculated one, in perfect harmony with his character and background.

The hours slipped by effortlessly for Lindbergh on this first leg. By the third hour, he found himself over Cape Cod. Departing Massachusetts, his faithful airplane hugged the coast, but then for the first time Lindbergh found himself over a large stretch of water as he headed for Nova Scotia. He observed later that, between Massachusetts and Nova Scotia, "there's nothing but the black line on my chart and the waves of ocean beneath my plane."[9] The haze cleared and the clouds lifted, prompting Lindbergh to fly on the deck, near the surface of the ocean, where aviators believed a cushion of air adds lift. With no radio he could not signal his position or describe to his countrymen the progress he was making, now about 250 miles out.[10]

Noon found the silver monoplane from San Diego over Nova Scotia—"What an out-of-the-way place," Lindbergh observed, "hanging there precariously on the eastern edge of Canada, green and cold against the pink tint of New Brunswick."[11] The sixth and seventh hours also passed uneventfully as Lindbergh marveled at the vast emptiness of the province, the rugged interior covered with spruce and pine, seeing only a few farms dotting the land along his flight path. At 2:52 P.M., he saw Cape Breton Island in the distance. Pressing on, he managed to complete the pivotal two-hundred-mile leg to Newfoundland on time.

My cockpit," Lindbergh described, "is small, and its walls are thin; but inside this cocoon I feel secure,

◆ Rare photographs of the Spirit of St. Louis in flight shortly after its takeoff from Roosevelt Field on May 20, 1927. Powered by its highly reliable 223-horsepower Wright Whirlwind engine, the plane flew without mishap or mechanical failure from New York to Paris.

• ◆ •

despite the speculations of my mind. It makes an efficient, tidy home, one so easy to keep in order that its very simplicity creates a sense of satisfaction and relief. It's a personal home, too—nobody has ever piloted the *Spirit of St. Louis*, but me."[12] Flying the plane, he admitted, was like living in a "hermit's mountain cabin."[13] Here, too, Lindbergh was alert to weather, his navigation tasks, and the routine of shifting and recording the transfer of fuel from one tank to another. The airplane, by design, required constant attention. It did not fly itself. Still, he observed, "A cabin that flies through the air, that's what I live in; a cabin higher than the mountains, a cabin in the clouds and sky."[14]

the spirit of st. louis

The design of the *Spirit of St. Louis* tells us a great deal about Charles Lindbergh's thoughts on the best way to conquer the Atlantic. Unlike Richard Byrd and other competitors for the Orteig prize, Lindbergh did not believe a large, multi-engine aircraft was the ideal design for a long-distance ocean crossing. He opted to fly a single-engine airplane alone to reach France. A single-engine plane, in his mind, possessed greater range and was arguably safer: Trimotor designs were less streamlined and presented multiple chances for a fatal engine failure en route. This innovative concept, backed by state-of-the-art technology, gave Lindbergh the advantage he needed over his competitors.

During his days as a barnstormer and in the army air service, Lindbergh had flown a series of slow-moving biplanes of an older design. These aircraft, with their open cockpits, exposed struts and engines, and multiple wings, lacked streamlining. In contrast, the *Spirit of St. Louis* possessed a silhouette that anticipated the future—a monoplane with modern streamlining evident in the design of its cowling, wings, and landing gear. Lindbergh's simple idea for a long-distance plane marked a revolution in aircraft construction and was destined to radically alter the design and performance of future flying machines. By the next decade, these trends would shape a whole new generation of sleek, all-metal, stream-lined aircraft.

In pursuit of his novel concept, Lindbergh contracted with Ryan Airlines to build a single-engine monoplane with a fuselage constructed of tubular steel, with wings and ribs fashioned of wood and with a fabric-covered skin (a light-

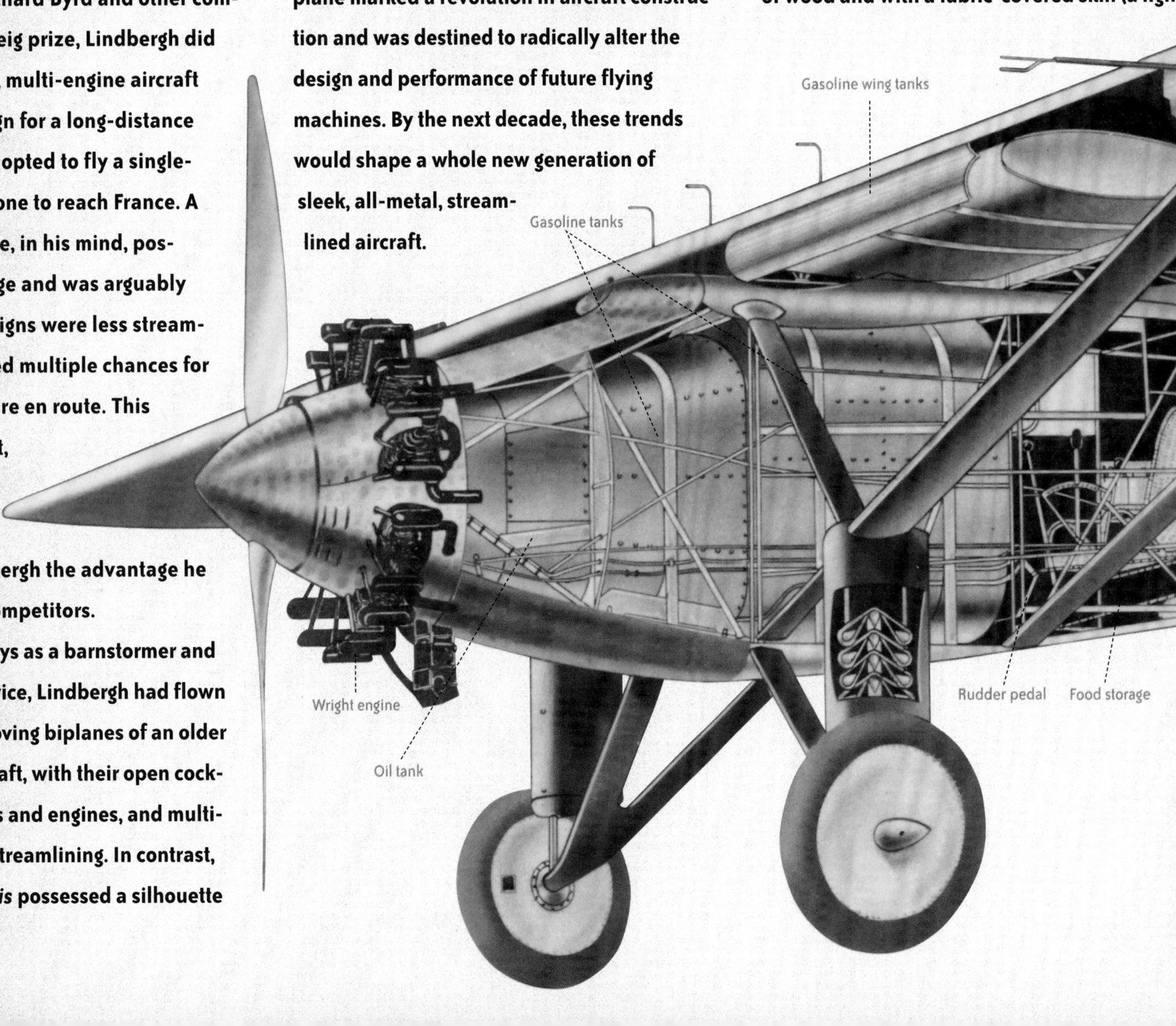

Gasoline wing tanks

Gasoline tanks

Wright engine

Oil tank

Rudder pedal   Food storage

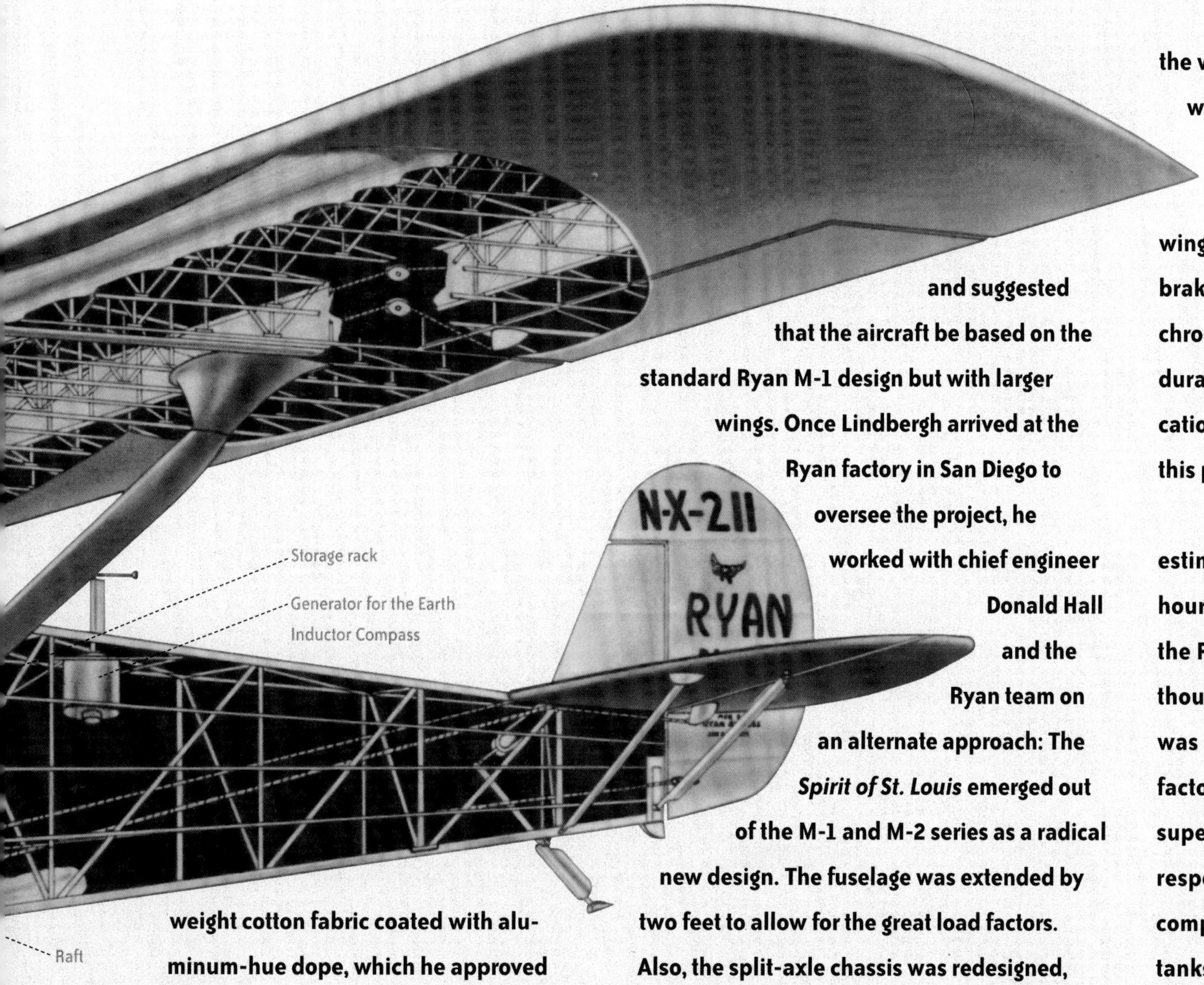

Storage rack

Generator for the Earth
Inductor Compass

Raft

and suggested that the aircraft be based on the standard Ryan M-1 design but with larger wings. Once Lindbergh arrived at the Ryan factory in San Diego to oversee the project, he worked with chief engineer Donald Hall and the Ryan team on an alternate approach: The *Spirit of St. Louis* emerged out of the M-1 and M-2 series as a radical new design. The fuselage was extended by two feet to allow for the great load factors. Also, the split-axle chassis was redesigned, again to accommodate the huge fuel capacity necessary to make a transatlantic crossing.

While the *Spirit of St. Louis* shared the sleek contours of the Ryan M-2, it possessed a longer wingspan of forty-six feet. Care was taken to redesign the wing for optimal lift, with the wing ribs spaced close together and plywood sections fitted on the leading edge.

The best spruce and mahogany wood components were incorporated into the wing structure. A tail skid (there were no brakes) was fashioned from heat-treated chrome molybdenum steel tubing, the same durable tubing used in the axles. Other modifications of the standard M-2 design added to this profile of strength and durability.

Hall, who kept a personal work log, estimated later that he had devoted over 775 hours to the engineering of the design, with the Ryan workers contributing over three thousand hours to build the airplane. Hall was ably assisted by Hawley Bowlus, the factory manager, and Bert Tindale, the shop superintendent. Various technicians took responsibility for purchasing materials and components, for the construction of the fuel tanks, and for cowling, fitting, and final assembly. Because of the tight schedule, extra workers were hired to assist in the project. Remarkably, the aircraft was built in sixty days, giving Lindbergh just enough time to compete in the race for the Orteig prize in the spring of 1927.

weight cotton fabric coated with aluminum-hue dope, which he approved later). Frank Mahoney, then in charge of the company, first wired Charles Lindbergh on his proposed design in early February 1927

The internal truss frame for the fuselage of the *Spirit of St. Louis*

The most critical component of Lindbergh's concept was to fit his sleek airplane with a durable Wright Whirlwind engine. Charles Lawrance had designed a series of

Spirit wing being moved from the Ryan building

Whirlwind radial engines of five, seven, and nine cylinders. Lindbergh selected the nine-cylinder J-5C model for its 223-horsepower rating at 1,800 revolutions per minute. For its time, the Wright Whirlwind was the most advanced aero propulsion system in the world—the same engine that had transported Richard Byrd to the North Pole and allowed the Wright Bellanca to set new records for endurance flying. The J-5C was made of light-weight aluminum and steel, totaling a dry weight of 508 pounds. The engine boasted a compression ratio of 5.2 to 1 and possessed optimal fuel and oil consumption rates.

Lindbergh's particular engine incorporated the latest modifications of the Lawrance design. It was fitted with a self-lubricating valve system, which at the time represented a quantum leap in engine design, allowing for greater reliability and easier maintenance. The engine's new "sodium cooled valves," where the valve stems were hollowed out and filled with sodium, allowed for an effi-cient means of heat transfer. This innovation improved engine compression and ensured longer interludes between engine overhauls. Few engines at the time could match the Wright Whirlwind's power-to-weight ratio, which guaranteed maximum lift for the *Spirit of St. Louis* when its fuel tanks were topped off for the transatlantic flight. The powerful Wright J-5C was fitted with a two-blade Duralumin propeller, manufactured by the Standard Steel Propeller Company of Pittsburgh, Pennsylvania.

Fuel for the Wright Whirlwind came from an elaborate cluster of tanks, controlled by petcocks in the cockpit. An engine-driven fuel pump carried the fuel to the carburetor. Because of the placement of the fuel tanks in the forward fuselage, there was no forward-looking windscreen. Three wing tanks possessed a capacity of 152 gallons, with the center fuselage and forward fuselage tanks carrying 310 and 68 gallons, respectively (a total of 450 gallons, weighing 2,750 pounds). The fuel tanks were linked together by a Lunkenheimer distributor, which allowed Lindbergh to tap and move fuel freely from tank to tank. A thirty-five-gallon oil tank was fitted between the pilot and the engine.

When Lindbergh wrote his Pulitzer Prize–winning book *The Spirit of St. Louis*, he gave considerable coverage to the faithful Wright Whirlwind engine that propelled him across the Atlantic. Following the epic Lindbergh flight, Charles Lawrance received the Collier Trophy for his remarkable engine. Lawrance ruefully observed that receiving this recognition was not unlike giving

The *Spirit of St. Louis* at Dutch Flats

an award to Paul Revere's horse. His comparison made light of the fact that the Wright Whirlwind had provided the motive force for one of history's most memorable flights.

The *Spirit of St. Louis*, at Lindbergh's insistence, was austerely equipped in cockpit design and instrumentation. The entrance to the cockpit was through a single door on the starboard side, fitted with a removable window, not unlike a side curtain on a

The *Spirit of St. Louis* nearing completion

Six men, including Lindbergh *(bottom center)* and Donald Hall *(bottom left),* atop *Spirit* barrels at Camp Kearney on May 4, 1927

phaeton-style automobile of the era. A skylight allowed for additional natural illumination of the interior. Rather than equip the cockpit with a standard seat of wood or metal, Lindbergh chose a wicker chair with a leather pad, which was attached to the frame. Lightweight plywood was employed to fashion both the floorboard and the instrument panel. Given the fact there would be only one pilot of the aircraft, the placement of the

wicker seat and control stick were customized to match the physical height and reach of the lanky Lindbergh.

For purposes of reducing weight, Lindbergh allowed for only the bare essentials when it came to flight instruments. However, the instruments he selected for the *Spirit of St. Louis* had to be of the latest design and proven reliability. For navigation, he selected an Earth Inductor Compass and a standard magnetic compass. The Earth Inductor Compass, which was highly accurate and allowed Lindbergh to correct for the magnetic deviation of the earth, was powered by a wind-driven generator mounted on the top of the fuselage. Other standard instruments assured proper flight management: an

Receipt for the lettering of the wing of the *Spirit of St. Louis.*

inclinometer to discern the angle of attack of the nose, an altimeter, a tachometer, gauges for oil pressure and oil temperature, an eight-day clock, a turn-and-bank indicator, and an airspeed indicator. Ryan worker Claude Randolph built a special periscope that could be extended out the side of the fuselage to give Lindbergh forward visibility. All the instruments were mounted on a black plywood panel.

Lindbergh was a minimalist in packing equipment and emergency gear. He rejected the idea of taking a parachute, because such an item added unnecessary weight, though he approved of the installation of a rubber raft in case of a water landing. He also carried an emergency water ration, an Armburst cup (to gather water from his breath), a hunting knife, a hacksaw blade, some fishing tackle, matches, flares, and a flashlight. For warmth, Lindbergh chose to wear a simple wool flying suit. He kept a dunnage bag for his survival gear under his wicker seat. This same bag contained his

carefully selected, cropped, and marked-up maps and charts for navigating the route from New York to Paris.

In 1928, Charles Lindbergh donated the *Spirit of St. Louis* to the Smithsonian Institution to become part of its national aeronautical collection. Today the famous airplane is suspended in the "Milestones of Flight" gallery in the National Air and Space Museum. Exhibited in simulated flight, the silver monoplane is positioned above and near the central artifact of the gallery, the Wright Brothers' Kitty Hawk Flyer. Lindbergh's fabled aircraft shares this remarkable gallery with other artifacts of the Air Age: the Bell X-1, the X-15, the Apollo 11 command module, a Goddard rocket, a model of *Sputnik,* and other aerospace milestones. For visitors to the museum, the *Spirit of St. Louis* remains an enduring symbol of aviation and a witness to an extraordinary flight that altered history.

The *Spirit of St. Louis* flies over San Diego.

While flying over Newfoundland, Lindbergh decided to divert slightly off course so he could fly over St. John's. The time for this maneuver was approximately 6:50 P.M., with night fast approaching. Behind Lindbergh were some 1,100 miles. Newfoundland represented an important milestone in the journey and was the last rugged edge of land jutting into the Atlantic before Lindbergh crossed over the open ocean. Flying over St. John's offered a chance to alert the world he had made the fateful decision to brave the North Atlantic. He thought of his backers in St. Louis, his mother in Detroit, and the workers at the Ryan factory in San Diego; they would all want to know of his progress. He guided the *Spirit of St. Louis*, now lightened by eight hundred pounds after nearly nine hours of flying, into a slow glide over St. John's: "I come upon it suddenly—the little city of St. John's, after skimming over the top of a creviced granite summit—flat-roofed houses and stores, nestled at the edge of a deep harbor. . . . There's no time to circle, no fuel to waste. It takes only a moment, stick forward, engine throttled, to dive down over the wharves (men stop their after-supper chores to look upward), over the ships in the harbor (a rowboat's oars lose their rhythm as I pass), and out through the gap, that doorway to the Atlantic."[15]

A vast, empty Atlantic now loomed ahead of the *Spirit of St. Louis*. Lindbergh adjusted carefully to his eastward heading. He could see behind him the black silhouette of the mountains, which slipped over the horizon in the twilight. He

▲ *Lindbergh departed the rocky New England coast for Nova Scotia on his first flight across open ocean. Hours later he departed from Newfoundland across the North Atlantic.*

Lindbergh's transport pilot's license, which he carried with him on his flight to Paris

calculated that he was now some ninety miles south of the Great Circle. He then adjusted his compass heading to resume his course along the black line on his chart. He noted that at this juncture he had consumed one third of his fuel. What if in another hour the engine began to miss, or the oil pressure suddenly dropped? He could turn back, for certain. "I look back again at the lowering silhouette of the mountains, still sharp against the western sky," he recorded later. "That is America. What a strange feeling—America at a distance! It's as though I were saying: 'That's the Earth'— far away, like a planet. There are no more reassuring islands ahead . . . I've given up a continent and taken on an ocean in its place—irrevocably."[16]

As darkness enveloped Lindbergh and his plane at about 8:15 P.M. New York time, he immediately noticed a thin line of fog. Also, he spotted icebergs, not the first he had seen along the way, but these stood out as ghostly islets in the gathering shadows on the horizon. As the fog thickened, Lindbergh flew to an altitude of ten thousand feet to avoid being engulfed. Nearly at the top of his ceiling, he could see the stars overhead—a welcome celestial marker, since there was no moon. In the enveloping darkness, Lindbergh flew on: "As I fly through the body of night, haze lessens, and I discover that I'm among the cloud mountains themselves—great shadowy forms on every side, dwarfing my plane, dwarfing earthly mountains with their magnitude, awesome in their weird, fantastic shapes. Huge pillars push upward thousands of feet above the common mass. Black valleys and chasms open below me to unfathomed depth."[17]

Flying at over ten thousand feet through the night sky ushered in a new danger—icing. Tired and preoccupied with the cockpit routine, Lindbergh admitted later that he had been slow to notice the danger. He reasoned that the problem arose after flying through a thunderhead for ten minutes. To determine how much ice had accumulated on the plane, he moved the beam of his flashlight from one spot to the next. There was no ice on the bottom of the wing, but it was evident on the strut, which meant that there was ice on the leading edge of the wing. He detected a drop of five miles per hour with the increased drag. Darkness made maneuvering difficult, but Lindbergh boldly directed his plane around pillars of clouds, in which he sought breaks. He considered diving to a lower altitude, perhaps skimming the waves for a period of time, but rejected this idea because the icing conditions no doubt extended down to the ocean surface. "The pillars of cloud multiply and thicken," Lindbergh remembered. "I followed narrow canyons between them, weaving in and out around thunderheads, taking always the southward choice for a course, edging toward the ship lanes and what I hope is clearer weather. Dark forms blot out the sky on every side, but stars drop down to guide me through the passes."[18]

Pressing on, Lindbergh marked his fifteenth hour in flight. The time was 9:53 P.M. To his delight the icing began to dissipate slowly, ending what could have been a fatal encounter with the

▲ The passport Lindbergh carried on his historic flight. He later expressed concern about arriving in Paris without a visa or proper diplomatic clearance.

Lindbergh's flight suit from the transatlantic trip

weather—a silent disaster at sea, beyond the sight of the growing global audience listening to the radio reports on the fate of the young Minnesotan pilot. As the ice thinned, the haze began to lift slightly, then more dramatically. Lindbergh had endured another tense gauntlet over the stormy North Atlantic.

Sleep, or the compelling urge to close his eyes and rest, oppressed Lindbergh throughout the flight. No challenge was more pressing and filled with danger than this one. "There comes a point," he wrote later on this matter, "when the body's demand for sleep is harder to endure than any pain I have encountered, when it results in a state of semi-consciousness . . . The rational mind I had previously known and relied upon had less and less effect on my body's responses."[19] He fell in and out of an alert state of mind, seemingly both asleep and awake. During the second day, on the night passage across the ocean, the perils of sleeplessness became acute and threatening. Lindbergh described his condition as one where his eyes, "under their weighted lids," seemed "completely disconnected from my body."[20]

The *Spirit of St. Louis* had been designed to be an unstable airplane—on Lindbergh's insistence. This fact, in the end, came to his aid, a situation where the pilot and flying machine assisted each other in a weird ballet of survival: "The slightest relaxation of pressure on either stick or rudder," he remembered, "starts a climbing or a diving turn, hauling me back from the borderland of sleep. Then, I fix my eyes on the compass and determine again to hold it where it belongs."[21]

Such moments of control and alertness would give way to semiconsciousness, forcing a repeat of the routine. Lindbergh's discipline—mental and physical—became the key to his survival.

His extreme physical fatigue set the stage for one of the most peculiar episodes in the flight—his encounter with "phantoms." When Lindbergh wrote his book *"We"* in the summer of 1927, he did not mention this most unusual and inexplicable event. Later, in *The Spirit of St. Louis* and his *Autobiography of Values,* he gave the topic proper reflection. Lindbergh told of phantoms appearing in the rear of the fuselage while he was flying through the fog. These "transparent" and "mistlike" creatures were visible although his eyes were focused straight ahead. Humanlike, they appeared to move effortlessly through the cabin, passing in and out of the fabric walls of the fuselage. More remarkable, one or more would actually linger to talk to the fatigued pilot and then rejoin the group of phantoms hovering in the rear of the fuselage. He confessed that

A silver model of the *Spirit of St. Louis,* set with rhinestones

even in advanced age he could still remember clearly these phantomlike creatures, but once he landed at Paris he could not recall any details of the conversations. Like a dream, the phantoms had generated vivid memories, only to slip away.[22]

Lindbergh acknowledged that this experience could be easily dismissed as the hallucinations of a tired pilot, "the ravings of a sleepless brain," as he

▲ *These minimal items are associated with Lindbergh's flight: a canteen, pilot's license, passport, leather notebook, flashlight, and oil bottle.*

▶ *Zula Kenyon, a noted artist from Wisconsin, painted this dramatic depiction of Lindbergh's flight across the Atlantic Ocean.*

THE SPIRIT OF AMERICA
THE VIKING OF THE AIR

noted in his *Autobiography of Values*.[23] For Lindbergh, the keen believer in rationality and science, such an experience was as confusing as it was embarrassing, given his worldview. In time he would be more open to the idea that a nonrational world existed. The "phantoms" would linger in his mind as a stimulus to think about earthly reality in an altered way. As he recorded in his autobiography, "the longer I live, the more limited I believe rationality to be. I have found that the irrational gives man insight he cannot otherwise attain."[24]

At dawn, Lindbergh finally escaped the grip of foul weather, drowsiness, and phantoms. He recorded this welcome epiphany in vivid images: "Mist lightens—the *Spirit of St. Louis* burst into brilliant sunlight, dazzling to fog-accustomed eyes—a blue sky—sparkling whitecaps. The ocean is not so wild and spray-lashed. It's less ragged with streaks of foam. The wind's strength has decreased, and it has shifted to my tail."[25] Once he reached the twenty-third hour, he estimated that he was ten hours out of Newfoundland, with an estimated eight hours to reach the Irish coast. Reaching Ireland, he reminded himself, would take the same amount of time he had logged on his flight from San Diego to St. Louis, or the equivalent of a full working day for all the folks at the Ryan factory. He had moved across a vast stretch of ocean, but there was still a substantial amount of flying ahead: "I'm in mid-Atlantic, nearly a thousand miles from land!"[26]

Hours passed as Lindbergh continued his relentless passage across the vast ocean, changing his

▶ *View of the Atlantic Ocean at sunrise. This scene greeted Charles Lindbergh after his long and exhausting interlude of ocean flying on the night of May 20–21, 1927. With the welcome arrival of sunrise on the second day, he was still roughly halfway to Paris, with a long stretch of sea to cross before reaching Ireland, his first landfall. Fighting the impulse to sleep, he pressed on and reached Paris for a night landing that same day.*

A carved pipe commemorating the flight of the *Spirit of St. Louis*

altitude whenever he deemed it necessary to exploit the most favorable flying conditions. So far he had seen a number of porpoises and birds, but no ships or fishing vessels. Then he saw a small fishing boat a few miles ahead and several miles south of his route. He banked toward the boat, seeing for the first time that there were several fishing boats grouped together. His pass over the first boat revealed no human presence on deck. He then circled over the second boat, and the roar of the engine prompted a man to appear and wave. This first human contact on the

Lindbergh reasoned correctly that he was approaching the southwestern sector of Ireland. But where, precisely, was he? He then altered his heading to pass over the Irish coast at the nearest point. Once he flew over the coastline and checked his maps, he determined that he had reached Cape Valentia and Dingle Bay. It was afternoon, with the evening approaching. Lindbergh estimated at this point that he had to fly six one-hundred-mile segments still marked on his chart, some six hundred miles to Paris.

"Time is no longer endless, or the horizon destitute of hope," he wrote in *The Spirit of St. Louis*. "The strain of take-off, storm, and ocean, lies behind. There'll be no second night above the clouds, no more grappling with the misty walls of ice. There's only one more island to cross—only a narrow tip of an island. I look at England's outline on my map. And then, within an hour, I'll see the coast of France; and beyond that, Paris and Le Bourget."[27]

Now the pace quickened. At the thirtieth hour, Lindbergh passed over St. George's Channel. It was 12:52 P.M. New York time, about 5:30 P.M. local time. The next hour he was above England, passing over Cornwall and Plymouth, not far from where the Pilgrims sailed to the New World three centuries before. He then crossed the English Channel at an altitude of 1,500 feet. Haze slowly closed in behind Lindbergh as he pushed on toward Cherbourg and the French coast. The sun was now behind him and low on the horizon. He reached Cherbourg just as the sun began to set.

▲ *Lindbergh strictly limited the survival gear he allowed on board the Spirit of St. Louis. This passion to reduce weight meant he took only the most essential items with him, including his Ever-Ready and Yale flashlights. The flashlights proved useful at one point in the flight, allowing Lindbergh to confirm icing on wings and struts of the plane.*

approach to Europe was exciting. Lindbergh made a futile effort to get the man to point in the direction of Ireland, shouting at him in a level pass with the engine throttled down. When the gesture elicited no response, he resumed his flight eastward.

Less than an hour lapsed before Lindbergh sighted land for the first time, catching an opaque view of the Irish coastline on the northeastern horizon. At the time, he was flying at an altitude of merely two hundred feet off the ocean. The coastline in the distance, perhaps some ten or fifteen miles away, came down from the north and curved toward the east.

mahoney & hall

Mahoney Airport, San Diego, in the late 1920s and the deposit and bill of sale for the *Spirit of St. Louis*

In February 1927, Charles Lindbergh signed a contract with Ryan Airlines, Inc., in San Diego, California, to build a single-engine monoplane capable of a New York–to–Paris flight. Two men, Benjamin Franklin Mahoney and Donald Hall, played pivotal roles in transforming Lindbergh's vision into reality, mobilizing the necessary human and material resources to build the *Spirit of St. Louis* in just sixty days.

In 1919, Mahoney moved from Pennsylvania to San Diego, where he became a bond salesman. In time the young and enthusiastic Mahoney met up with T. Claude Ryan, a former U.S. Army Air Service pilot, who taught him how to fly. Ryan owned a flight school and operated sightseeing and charter flights. Recognizing the commercial opportunities in Ryan's business, Mahoney proposed the idea of a commercial airline service between San Diego and Los Angeles and offered to put up his own money for a share of the profits. The two became

business partners and on March 1, 1925, established what would become the first regular passenger service between Los Angeles and San Diego—the first service of its kind in the United States. Ryan Airlines began manufacturing their own airplanes in the fall of 1925. When their commercial airline service began to falter in the fall of 1926, the two men, unable to reconcile their differing ideas about the direction of their company, agreed to end their partnership. Mahoney bought out Ryan for $25,000, but continued to use Ryan's name. In February 1927, Mahoney met with Lindbergh for the first time and worked out the necessary business arrangements for

Ryan Airlines to accept the job. Mahoney proved to be instrumental in his support for Lindbergh's vision and in assuring Lindbergh that Ryan Airlines could deliver the completed plane within two months.

Donald Hall, the chief engineer at Ryan Airlines, worked directly with Lindbergh on the design of the *Spirit of St. Louis*. A native of Brooklyn and a graduate of the Pratt Institute School of Engineering, Hall started his career at the Curtiss Aeroplane and Motor Company. He had migrated to California to advance his career in aircraft design with an eye toward starting his own design company. Just prior to his work on the Lindbergh project at Ryan, Hall had been associated with another important aviation pioneer, Donald Douglas. To fashion for

Lindbergh *(right)* with Frank Mahoney, president of Ryan Airlines

Charles Lindbergh at San Diego, after the final assembly of the *Spirit of St. Louis*

Lindbergh an airplane with a 450-gallon fuel capacity was no easy task, but Hall accepted the challenge with relish.

For Hall, there was the challenge of meeting Lindbergh's precise technical and design standards. This meant a new design for a single flight and purpose. Lindbergh preferred this approach because he wanted a monoplane type, to be powered by a single engine, in this case a Wright J-5C. Hall worked with this essential formula to design an airplane with the capacity to take off with a fuel load of 450 gallons.

Joined by the talented Ryan factory staff, Hall worked under a very tight schedule to complete the aircraft on time. In one marathon session, Hall spent thirty-six straight hours at the Ryan factory

working on the Lindbergh monoplane. One of his major concerns with the design of the *Spirit of St. Louis* was the problem of weight. The new Lindbergh airplane called for an optimal amount of fuel to reach the goal of four-thousand-mile range. To achieve this end Hall was attentive to the smallest detail, even

The *Spirit of St. Louis* on the eve of the historic flight

setting precise limits on the amount of solder to be used in the construction process.

Hall's artistry in the design of the *Spirit of St. Louis* required taking the M-2 template and fashioning what, in effect, became a new design. Hall's elaborate blueprint called for new wings and chassis, an elaborate cluster of wing and fuselage fuel tanks, the optimal use of lightweight materials, and a customized cockpit. While the *Spirit of St. Louis* possessed the genetic code of M-2, it emerged from the Ryan cocoon as a radical new airplane, one capable of flying 4,000 miles nonstop. Lindbergh credited Hall's expertise as a key

factor in his winning the Orteig prize. Lindbergh's affection for Hall was reflected in 1953, when he invited his old friend to write the technical appendix for his Pulitzer Prize–winning book, *The Spirit of St. Louis.*

In the aftermath of the flight of the *Spirit of St. Louis* from New York to Paris, Mahoney and Hall continued to advance in their careers in aviation. For Mahoney there was a welcome rush of business after the Lindbergh flight, and as a shrewd businessman he recapitalized his company to exploit fully the legendary Ryan name in aviation. Hall chose to stay in San Diego and, for a brief time, owned his own firm, the Hall Aeronautical Development Company. Eventually, he accepted an executive position at Convair, where he worked from 1936 to 1949. He finished his career in aviation at the North Island Naval Air Station, where he worked as supervisor in the helicopter engineering branch. Both Hall and Mahoney contributed in important ways to a pivotal moment in aviation history.

Lindbergh with Frank Mahoney

Lindbergh quickly sought out the Seine River, his key terrestrial marker for the flight to Paris and Le Bourget. While he adjusted his heading, he noted the beacons along the Seine, used to direct airplanes flying the Paris-to-London route. His thoughts turned now to his faithful airplane, the Ryan-built *Spirit of St. Louis:* "It's like a living creature, gliding along smoothly, happily, as though a successful flight means as much to it as to me, as though we shared our experiences together . . . *We* have made this flight across the ocean, not *I* or *it*. . . . I throw my flashlight on the engine instruments. Every needle is in place. For almost thirty-three hours, not one of them has varied from its normal reading . . . For every minute I've flown there have been more than seven thousand explosions in the cylinders, yet not a single one has missed."[28]

Lindbergh's passage down the Seine River corridor went smoothly, and he naively anticipated a quiet landing at Le Bourget, to be followed by a long stint of sleep. Although he knew that the successful flight would spark celebrations in France and America and that he would be required to attend to the ceremonial part of his achievement, he looked forward to a leisurely tour of European cities in the *Spirit of St. Louis* before returning to the United States. Little did Lindbergh realize that his landing at Le Bourget—in his own words later—would be a "match lighting a bonfire."[29]

Paris aglow appeared on the horizon at about 10:00 P.M. local time. A few minutes later Lindbergh made a dramatic sweep around the Eiffel Tower, as he looked to the northeast for Le Bourget Airport. Flying

▲ *A Celtic cross at Cornwall from 900 A.D. Lindbergh reached the southwest coast of England shortly after his flight over Dingle Bay.*

◄ *The longest and most dangerous segment of Lindbergh's flight was the two thousand miles of open ocean between Newfoundland and Dingle Bay, Ireland. He reached the southwest coast of Ireland after twenty-eight hours of flying, only three miles off course.*

on for five miles or so, he reached the airport, which was clearly visible below with its partially lighted runway and hangars. And Lindbergh noticed something else, which he found inexplicable. The roads to the field appeared to be backed up with long lines of automobiles. He made one pass over the runway to confirm that it was indeed Le Bourget and then turned for a final approach.

Charles Lindbergh is unsurpassed in his vivid description of this landing: "I've never landed the *Spirit of St. Louis* at night before. It would be better to come in straight. But if I don't sideslip, I'll be too high over the boundary to touch my wheels in the area of light. That would mean circling again—Still too high. I push the stick over to a steeper slip, leaving the nose well down—Below the hangar roofs now—straighten out—A short burst of the engine—Over the lighted area—Sod coming up to meet me—Deceptive high lights and shadows—Careful—easy to bounce when you are tired—Still too fast—Tail too high—The surface dims—Texture of sod is gone—Ahead, there's nothing but night—Give her the gun and climb for another try? The wheels touch gently—off again—No, I'll keep contact—Ease the stick forward—Back on the ground—Off—Back—the tail skid too—Not a bad landing, but I'm beyond the light—can't see anything ahead—Like flying in a fog—Ground loop?—No, still rolling too fast—might blow a tire—The field *must* be clear—Uncomfortable though, jolting into blackness—Wish I had a wing light—but too heavy on the take-off—Slower, now—slow enough to ground loop safely—left rudder—reverse it—stick over the other way—The *Spirit of St. Louis* swings around and stops rolling, resting on the solidness of earth, in the center of Le Bourget. I start to taxi back toward the floodlights and the hangars—But the entire field ahead is covered with running figures!"[30] So Lindbergh described his reentry into the terrestrial realm. The transoceanic odyssey ended precisely at 10:22 on the night of May 21, 1927, a lapsed time of thirty-three hours, thirty minutes, a nonstop flight of 3,610 miles.

Edwin L. James, reporter for the *New York Times,* was at Le Bourget that memorable night, and his reports to the folks back home dramatized the bonfire set by Charles Lindbergh: "There come moments in every newspaperman's life when he is all but overwhelmed by a feeling of insufficiency to tell what he has seen— when superlatives seem mere inadequacies."[31]

News of Lindbergh's approach to Paris had sparked a rush to Le Bourget by thousands of people, a migration that had begun in the early hours of the evening. Parisians rushed to the airport in hopes of seeing the extraordinary young pilot who had done the impossible—a nonstop flight from New York to Paris. James reported that the crowd pushed against a seven-foot-high fence circling the airport. At 8:30 P.M. the enthusiastic crowd of onlookers, ever growing in size, broke through the fence and ran onto the field. Soldiers worked

▼ *Over 100,000 people greeted Charles Lindbergh at Le Bourget Airport when he landed at 10:22 P.M. on May 21, 1927. News of the impending arrival of the Spirit of St. Louis reached Paris early in the evening, and soon the roads to Le Bourget were clogged with cars. When Lindbergh's plane was sighted, crowds broke through a fence and streamed onto the landing field. News of his extraordinary feat set off an unprecedented outpouring of popular interest.*

to keep the crowds behind a line. Off to one side there was a reception committee, and James estimated some fifty cameras in readiness. By 9:00 P.M. thecrowd was about 60,000 people, later to grow to 100,000. The roads out of Paris were jammed with cars; perhaps as many as nine thousand vehicles of various types endeavored to reach Le Bourget that night. Police and more soldiers arrived to reinforce the tenuous sense of order on the airfield.

James wrote about the landing from his perspective on the ground: "Ten o'clock struck. A sort of shiver went through the crowd and we were thinking of all the tears which were going to be shed, when all of a sudden the thousands were electrified by the sound of a motor. There was a plane above us somewhere. The landing lights went up. Everyone thought it was Colonel Lindbergh and a vast silence swept over and through as more than 100,000 pairs of eyes strained. And then the sound of the motor died out and the lights went down."[32]

Time passed and Lindbergh returned to land. "There, 500 meters above us," James continued his story, "a gray-white monoplane, right over our heads. Then it faded and the noise of the motor stopped. We thought it a hallucination, and a glance at the crowd showed that very few had seen it. Certainly the officer in charge had not, for the lights did not go on. Then in a moment, cold forgotten, the glares went on, and turning we saw, just as if thrown on a silver screen, a white-gray monoplane, twenty feet from the ground and softly settling."[33]

▲ Commemorative pillow honoring the historic flight of Charles Lindbergh.

▶ Soldiers of the French Thirty-Fourth Air Regiment set up a human cordon around the Spirit of St. Louis just moments after Lindbergh's night landing at Le Bourget Airport.

Lindbergh remembered that moment as one of chaos. The crowd broke for the plane. Lindbergh shut down his engine, for fear someone in the onrushing crowd would be killed by the propeller. Police failed to restore order.

The milling crowd pulled Lindbergh from the airplane as he attempted to exit. "For nearly half an hour I was unable to touch the ground," he wrote in the immediate aftermath of the historic flight.[34] Only with great effort did the police extricate Lindbergh and his airplane from the crowd. Military personnel at Le Bourget managed to rescue the Spirit of St.Louis from the encircling crowd, but not

before some souvenir seekers had torn away some of the fabric covering on the fuselage. In time, the new hero of the Atlantic found his way to the U.S. Embassy for a much-needed rest. James and the press throughout Europe and North America signaled the news flash: "He did it! Lindbergh lands in Paris!"[35]

Lindbergh himself saw the bonfire he had ignited: "I had entered a new environment of life and found myself surrounded by unforeseen opportunities, responsibilities, and problems."[36]

For America, the Lindbergh achievement was epic in its impact. Novelist F. Scott Fitzgerald expressed the moment well: "In the spring of 1927 something bright and alien flashed across the sky. A young Minnesotan who seemed to have nothing to do with his generation did a heroic thing, and for a moment people set down their glasses in country clubs and speakeasies and thought of their old best dreams."[37]

▲ On the morning of May 22, 1927, it was discovered that the Spirit of St. Louis had suffered minor damage during a crowd melee at Le Bourget Airport: Several strips of fabric had been torn from the airplane as souvenirs.

JUNE 11, 1927

Lindbergh and the *Spirit of St. Louis* return to the United States on board the USS *Memphis*.

JUNE 16, 1927

Raymond Orteig awards Lindbergh the $25,000 prize for his nonstop flight between New York and Paris.

DEC. 13, 1927

Lindbergh flies to Mexico City on the first leg of his Central and South American tour in the *Spirit of St. Louis*.

DEC. 21, 1927

Lindbergh meets Anne Morrow at the U.S. Embassy in Mexico City.

APRIL 30, 1928

Lindbergh makes the final flight of the *Spirit of St. Louis* to Bolling Field in Washington, D.C., where the plane is donated to the Smithsonian Institution. After 174 flights, the total flying time of the *Spirit* stands at 489 hours and 28 minutes.

JUNE 22, 1930

The Lindberghs' first child, Charles Augustus Jr., is born.

NOV. 28, 1930

Lindbergh and Alexis Carrel meet for the first time at the Rockefeller Institute of Medical Research.

1927

1930

JUNE 17, 1927

Lindbergh embarks on his tour of the United States in the *Spirit of St. Louis.*

SUMMER 1927

Lindbergh's book *"We"* is published.

FEB. 13, 1928

Lindbergh returns to the United States from his flights abroad.

MAY 27, 1929

Lindbergh marries Anne Morrow at the Morrow home in Englewood, New Jersey.

OCT. 1929

The stock market on Wall Street crashes, initiating a chain of events that would lead to the Great Depression.

JULY 27, 1931

Charles and Anne depart from New York on the first leg of their survey flight to the Orient by the Great Circle route.

SEPT. 19, 1931

The Lindberghs reach Nanjing, China, where they conduct a number of survey flights over flooded areas.

OCT. 5, 1931

Hugh Herndon and Clyde Pangborn successfully complete the first nonstop flight across the Pacific Ocean, winning them a 50,000-yen prize from Tokyo's *Asahi Shimbun* newspaper.

OCT. 5, 1931

Dwight Morrow dies in his sleep from a stroke.

MARCH 1, 1932

The Lindberghs' son is kidnapped from their Hopewell, New Jersey, home.

MAY 12, 1932

The Lindberghs' son is found dead some four miles from their home, after an exhausting seventy-two-day search.

JAN. 30, 1933

Adolf Hitler becomes chancellor of Germany.

JULY 9, 1933

Charles and Anne depart Long Island on the first leg of their Atlantic survey flight.

APRIL 5, 1935

Lindbergh and Alexis Carrel successfully perfuse the thyroid gland of a cat for the first time. They keep the tissue alive for a remarkable eighteen days.

SEPT. 15, 1935

The Nuremberg Laws are passed in Germany, depriving Jews of the rights of citizenship.

1933

1936

OCT. 23, 1931

The Lindberghs arrive home in New Jersey, having ended their survey flight prematurely.

MAY 20, 1932

Amelia Earhart becomes the first woman to fly across the Atlantic alone.

AUG. 16, 1932

The Lindberghs' second son, Jon, is born.

DEC. 19, 1933

The Lindberghs land at Flushing Bay, Long Island, ending their five-month survey flight.

JULY 1, 1935

Lindbergh and Carrel appear on the cover of *Time* magazine with their "mechanical heart."

FALL 1935

Anne Morrow Lindbergh's book *North to the Orient* is published.

DEC. 21, 1935

The Lindberghs set sail for England and, within a few weeks, take up residence in Kent.

Landing the *Spirit of St. Louis* at Le Bourget Airport at 10:22 P.M. on May 21, 1927, Charles Lindbergh found himself enveloped by thousands of frenzied devotees. His night passage out of the heavens to the earth, in the words of **triumph and tragedy** one biographer, evoked "demonstrations of emotion appropriate to the coming of some long-awaited god."[1] Alone and against improbable odds, he had traversed a vast ocean, earning mythic stature in the minds of his contemporaries. His silver monoplane, illuminated in the floodlights of Le Bourget, appeared as a ghostly harbinger of a new technological future.

An ecstatic Louis Bleriot, the famed French aviator who flew across the English Channel in 1909, greets Charles Lindbergh.

Later in life, Lindbergh wrote wistfully of the godlike transcendence he enjoyed at the start of his flight from New York to Paris: "No man before me had commanded such freedom of movement over the earth. I had enough gasoline to fly northward to the Pole, or southward to the Amazon . . . if I wish to change my course."[2] As we know, Lindbergh did not change his course; to do so would have been inconsistent with his nature and at odds with his highly scripted flight plan. His trajectory into history, mirrored in the steady compass heading for Paris, had been foreordained by his innate character, sense of purpose, and personal discipline.

Lindbergh's triumph in the "Transatlantic Derby" unleashed forces that fatefully transformed his life, catapulting him in an instant from obscurity to universal fame. And fame, in turn, entrapped him. Over the next eight years, from 1927 to 1935, he discovered that his heroic stature opened new doors to promote his personal vision of aviation. Yet there was a darker side to his celebrity. Lindbergh experienced a variety

Orteig medal

◀ Myron Herrick, the American ambassador to France (front, right), leads round of cheers for Charles Lindbergh (center) upon the completion of his transatlantic flight.

▼ Lindbergh's arrival in the United States is greeted by parades and public ceremonies.

▶ President Calvin Coolidge presides over a large and enthusiastic celebration in Washington, D.C., in which Lindbergh is awarded the Distinguished Flying Cross.

of intrusions into his life, from the flash of press cameras to the ultimate personal tragedy of the kidnapping and murder of his firstborn son. Throughout this turbulent period of time, Lindbergh mobilized all his energy and wits to wrestle with the hydra-headed monster of celebrity. In the end, he chose exile rather than to endure life in America.

Looking back on the events of May 1927, Lindbergh recalled that the pandemonium he encountered at Le Bourget came as a surprise: "I was astonished at the effect my successful landing in France had on the nations of the world."[3] Without false modesty, he viewed the successful flight of the *Spirit of St. Louis* as the handiwork of myriad people, a point the press failed to emphasize in the glare of hero worship. Press accounts of Lindbergh were extraordinary in terms of coverage and tone. For example, the *New York Times* devoted the first sixteen pages of one edition to cover the epic landing at Paris. Americans eagerly followed radio and newspaper coverage of the former

Minnesota farm boy, seeing in the transatlantic flight an epic episode in the human experience—one that mirrored individual courage and heralded a new phase of the Air Age.

Lindbergh's decorum in the immediate aftermath of his historic flight set the stage for his enduring role in American life. In Paris he welcomed the patronage of American ambassador Myron Herrick, who viewed the historic flight as a way to cement good relations with France. Lindbergh, in a borrowed suit, attended a frenetic round of dinners and parades, receiving the Legion of Honor and meeting Louis Bleriot, the famed French flyer who had crossed the English Channel in 1909. He then flew the *Spirit of St. Louis* to Brussels and London. At each stop, Lindbergh encountered huge crowds and festive public ceremonies. All were impressed, especially Americans, with his apparent humility, personal charm, and nobility. There was an intense interest in

▲ This Los Angeles Times *special section is typical of the coverage Lindbergh's flight received across the country. The* San Diego Independent *announces the awarding of the Orteig prize. Raymond Orteig (left) arrived in Paris on May 25, 1927.*

◄ *Lindbergh at city hall in Brussels.*

► *Lindbergh greets well-wishers.*

Lindbergh's return home. President Calvin Coolidge responded to this popular sentiment by sending the cruiser USS *Memphis* to England to retrieve Lindbergh and his plane. Huge parades and ceremonies then followed in Washington, D.C., and New York City.

Famed journalist Frederick Lewis Allen attempted to analyze the Lindbergh phenomenon in his best-seller *Only Yesterday* (1931). Looking back from the grim context of the Great Depression, Allen considered the 1920s the "Age of Ballyhoo," an era given over to materialistic excess and corruption, a nadir in American culture. "For years," he wrote, "the American people had been spiritually starved" and debased by the "corrosive influence of events and ideas."[4] Americans, in Allen's view, had lost their natural idealism.

Hollywood offered heroes on the silver screen and scoundrels in real life. And, in the world of business and politics, there were all sorts of bogus heroes. Among these cardboard celebrities, Lindbergh

The ticker-tape parade in New York City for Lindbergh, who rode with mayor "Jimmy" Walker, drew a huge crowd.

stood out as a towering personality. To be sure, the 1920s also had its sports heroes, such as Babe Ruth and Bobby Jones, who represented a real measure of achievement, but they seemed dwarfed by Lindbergh. In Allen's view, it was this cultural context, more so than Lindbergh's actual accomplishment, that explained the spontaneous outpouring of adulation for him.

Over time, Allen's bemused and disdainful chronicle of the 1920s became a sort of orthodoxy when people talked about the Lindbergh phenomenon. But what is overlooked in this oft-repeated critique is the fact that Lindbergh's aerial feat, in objective and historical terms, represented a genuine act of heroism. What Lindbergh accomplished on May 21, 1927, was worthy of the global enthusiasm it prompted. This reality stands apart from any real or imagined cultural void that Lindbergh may have filled in that extraordinary decade. Popular perceptions of the flight's technological significance developed slowly. The sense of time and distance for those living in the 1920s was radically different from our own today, when jets routinely cross oceans and link continents together. In the Coolidge years—and for several decades to follow—the Atlantic Ocean stood as an immense natural barrier separating America from Europe. Accordingly, that generation sensed in Lindbergh's accomplishment something epochal, and in the aviator a pathfinder who ushered in a new epoch, a man worthy of comparison with Columbus or Magellan. Their reaction to Lindbergh's aerial feat, if exaggerated at times, expressed an essential truth about the aviation milestone they had observed. The Lindbergh phenomenon was more than a frivolous display of popular hero worship.

Among aviators, Lindbergh's flight sparked a reckless drive to set new transoceanic records. In the spring and summer of 1927, forty pilots attempted high-risk ocean crossings, of whom twenty-one lost their lives. In a single competition to fly a vast stretch of the Pacific Ocean between San Francisco and Hawaii, seven people perished, including one woman.[5] The transpacific flights were high risk, but offered cash awards through the patronage of James D. Dole. Two Army Air Corps pilots, Lester J. Maitland and Albert F. Hegenberger, flew a Fokker trimotor with Wright Whirlwind engines across 2,400 miles of ocean from Oakland to Honolulu on June 28–29, 1927. However, the aerial feat of the two army pilots failed to generate much publicity, becoming a sort of footnote to the Lindbergh flight.

Raymond Orteig traveled to France in late May 1927, in anticipation of some aviator winning his award. This colorful check for $25,000 was awarded to Charles Lindbergh for his successful flight.

Transported by seaplane and yacht to New York Harbor after his return flight, Lindbergh was greeted by thousands of admirers.

Lindbergh's old rivals at Roosevelt Field, Richard Byrd and Clarence Chamberlin, also flew the Atlantic in the weeks that followed the successful landing of the *Spirit of St. Louis* at Le Bourget. Byrd's Fokker trimotor *America* made it across the Atlantic, but the flight ended with Byrd ditching his airplane off the coast of France; all the crew survived, but the ending was less than triumphal for the famed aviator. Chamberlin was more successful, even setting a new distance record. He crossed the Atlantic, with his sponsor Charles Levine as a passenger, landing near Berlin. Both Byrd and Chamberlin discovered that their aerial feats were largely ignored in the storm of publicity surrounding Lindbergh.

Lindbergh acquiesced to this popular mania on one level, deciding to exploit his unique status for the cause of aviation progress. He believed that the *Spirit of St. Louis* was a pathfinder for a global network of commercial air service. He returned to flying, not as a flamboyant stunt flyer, but as a high-minded apologist for aviation as a symbol of modernity.

▼ *Richard Byrd flew his trimotor* America *to France shortly after Lindbergh made his solo flight. Caught in difficult weather, Byrd and his crew ditched the plane off the coast of France, ending his involvement in the "Transatlantic Derby." He and Clarence Chamberlin, once considered favorites to win the Orteig prize, eventually slipped into relative obscurity, although Byrd later made flights to the South Pole.*

Fame became a cruel master, altering Lindbergh's daily life in dramatic and unanticipated ways. For the first time in his life, he could not enjoy the simple pleasures of attending a movie, taking a walk, or just appearing anonymously on the street. The press hounded his steps. His new life brought repeated meetings with kings, presidents, and captains of industry. Lindbergh never yearned to be part of the small circle of the rich and famous; in fact, he preferred a simple, even austere, lifestyle. His encounters with politicians and the financial elite often provided a context to promote aviation, however, so Lindbergh dutifully fulfilled his public commitments. No doubt there were many times when he desired to escape the klieg lights of celebrity, but he resisted the idea of sealing himself off from the outside world. Still, Lindbergh's strong drive for personal privacy shaped and limited all his contacts with the public, particularly the media.

Newspapers, magazines, and radio followed Lindbergh's movements with intense curiosity. Years after the flight, cars crowded the roads around his home near Hopewell, New Jersey, in the vain hope of capturing a glimpse of the air hero.

Lindbergh's photograph appeared in countless classrooms. Streets, and in one case a town, bore his name. Inspired by the Lindbergh flight and his vision of commercial airlines, municipalities clamored to build airports. James E. West, chief executive of the Boy Scouts of America, wrote a biographical treatment of Lindbergh, *The Lone Scout of the Sky*, which co-opted the Lindbergh persona as a fitting ideal for American youth. The 1928 book contained a special message from Lindbergh himself and "complete instructions on how to make a flying model of the *Spirit of St. Louis*."[6] No person had ever captured the popular imagination as Lindbergh had done in 1927.

Apart from the hoopla in popular culture, there was and continues to be some debate over how important his transatlantic flight of 1927 really was. This question, then and now, is an important aspect of the Lindbergh saga. In a narrow technical sense, the flight did not demonstrate anything new. The innovations in the engine and design of the *Spirit of St. Louis* had been evident to many before Lindbergh's flight. Lindbergh's stunning transatlantic flight confirmed his theory that one pilot in a single-engine airplane could make it from New York to Paris safely to win the Orteig prize. The historic achievement was not technical, but human: Alone he had faced and conquered the Atlantic Ocean.

In the wake of his flight was the "Lindbergh Boom." Aviation stocks and aircraft sales skyrocketed. New capital investment suddenly became available

▲ *A greeting card written by Raymond Orteig to Charles Lindbergh in December 1927. The French-born New York hotel owner spurred the progress of aviation by offering a $25,000 prize for the first nonstop transatlantic crossing, of which Lindbergh was the unexpected winner. Orteig had fulfilled his dream to be a patron of aviation, and he took great pride in Lindbergh's achievement.*

for the embryonic aviation industry. Airlines grew, and airport building became the *sine qua non* for municipal progress. And the numbers of applicants for air pilot's licenses at the aeronautics branch of the department of commerce mushroomed beyond anyone's expectations. While these factors were real, they did not originate with Lindbergh; his flight merely accelerated the inherent tendency for growth within the aviation sector of the economy. But Lindbergh himself would come to play a key role in shaping the future of aviation, using his fame to promote the development of commercial flight.

Amid all the coverage in newspapers and magazines, booksellers discovered a flurry of new books on Lindbergh. Some titles were frivolous and designed to exploit the popular fascination with the young Minnesotan, as in the case of *Plucky Lindbergh,* a hastily written account of "incidents in the life of Colonel Charles Lindbergh and a brief biography." The authors of this 1927 "biography" were Gerald R. Gage and James Lindbergh, who published the book under the pseudonym of "Gage Lindbergh." At first glance the book bore the earmarks of an authoritative account of the life of Lindbergh, written by a member of his family. But closer examination revealed that James

▲ *Lindbergh salutes, with French and American landmarks in the background.*

◄ *Lindbergh's flight ignited a flurry of newspaper and magazine coverage of aviation, including feature articles in the* New York Times *and the* Literary Digest. *In its aftermath there were a number of attempts to fly across the Pacific from the West coast of the United States to Hawaii. Interest in aviation also led to the "Lindbergh Boom," in which Wall Street stocks in aviation companies suddenly skyrocketed in value.*

• –◆– •

Lindbergh was not a relative, and his book was designed merely to exploit the Lindbergh name.

More serious in tone was the widely read *Sky High* (1929) by Eric Hodgins and F. Alexander Maguon, which had evolved from an article in the *Atlantic Monthly.* In addition to discussing Lindbergh and his epic flight, the authors set to chart out, in prophetic terms, the future course of aviation. Hodgins and Maguon were properly respectful of Lindbergh, but quick to point out that he was not the first to brave the skies over the Atlantic Ocean, reminding readers that Harry Hawker had attempted an east-west flight in 1919. Since Hawker crashed and was rescued at sea, however, his flight merely highlighted the success of Lindbergh and provided a cautionary tale of the dangers of transoceanic flying. In fact, by July 1929, the month *Sky High* went to press, only eleven of thirty-two aircraft attempting transoceanic flights had succeeded. Yet in their chapter "The Humbled Oceans," Hodgins and Maguon viewed Lindbergh as a new pathfinder, heralding a time when aircraft would routinely fly the Atlantic at 25,000 feet and at the unheard-of speed of three hundred miles per hour. In their imaginative future, passengers would board an airplane in the late afternoon in New York and arrive the next day for breakfast in London. Waxing prophetic, the authors affirmed that this aerial mode of transportation would come "as surely as the Wrights flew at Kitty Hawk."[7]

Harry Frank Guggenheim, son of the American industrialist Daniel Guggenheim, also shared this sense of promise in the future of aviation. Shortly after the New York–to–Paris flight, Guggenheim became

"I was astonished at the effect of my successful landing in France had on the nations of the world. To me, it was like a match lighting a bonfire." —Charles A. Lindbergh

Lindbergh's most important patron and friend. As the administrator of the Daniel Guggenheim Fund for the Promotion of Aeronautics, Harry Guggenheim was in an excellent position to influence the then-small American aviation industry. His dispersal of the Guggenheim fund, established by his father in 1926, had already done much to advance aeronautical technology. Guggenheim offered Lindbergh the financial and organizational backing to enable him to become a spokesman for aviation. He was Lindbergh's natural ally, and their friendship would only deepen in the following decade.

Guggenheim published his own book on aviation, *The Seven Skies* (1930), which attracted a wide audience. In the book, Guggenheim endeavored to provide "an authoritative and straightforward" record of how aviation had evolved. His analysis of the past was linked to an analysis of the major problems standing in the way of aviation progress. Guggenheim

▼ *A banner with American and French flags welcomes Lindbergh home in 1927. Later that year, on a forty-eight-state tour in the* Spirit of St. Louis, he *was greeted by enthusiastic crowds wherever he appeared.*

devoted an entire chapter to Lindbergh, in which he attempted to weigh the significance of the New York–to–Paris flight. Filled with optimism, he described that event as one that startled the world: "a deed as boldly conceived, as courageously performed and as skillfully executed as any heroic episode in legend or history."[8] While making a conscious contribution to the growing hagiography of his friend, Guggenheim nevertheless accurately assessed the meaning of Lindbergh's achievement: "Colonel Lindbergh's flight was one of the things which marked the end of the early pioneering period of aviation and the beginning of the industrial period."[9]

Almost immediately upon his landing at Le Bourget, public interest dictated that Lindbergh should prepare a book on his historic New York–to–Paris flight. Lindbergh agreed to collaborate on such a project, with reporter Carlyle MacDonald as the writer. This seemed to be the quickest way to get a book to the public.

But, wisely, Lindbergh did not forfeit his right to approve the final product. When he read MacDonald's first draft in late June 1927, he reacted negatively, finding the narrative filled with the sort of exaggerations and distortions that he so loathed in press reports about his life. Lindbergh then decided to write the book himself to ensure that the facts were presented to the public in an accurate way. Harry Guggenheim offered him the seclusion of the family's four-hundred-acre palatial estate, overlooking the Long Island Sound. Hurriedly written with a fountain pen on plain white paper, the book—now entitled *"We"*—expresses Lindbergh's own measured sense of his transatlantic flight. Its publication also signaled to the world that the young flyer from Little Falls, Minnesota, possessed an aptitude for writing.

By the end of June, Harry Guggenheim had another idea for Lindbergh: Why not an aerial tour of the forty-eight states in the *Spirit of St. Louis?* He would make $50,000 available from the Guggenheim Fund to cover the costs of the tour. Lindbergh jumped at the idea, and Guggenheim set to work on the details. Herbert Hoover, then secretary of commerce, offered to sponsor the tour jointly with the Guggenheim Fund. With Lindbergh as the central figure, the proposed tour would be an opportunity to promote aviation in a concrete way, to

▲ Welcoming program for Charles Lindbergh's visit to San Diego, September 21, 1927.

▼ One of Lindbergh's closest friends was Harry Guggenheim, who headed the Guggenheim Fund for the Promotion of Aeronautics. Guggenheim and Lindbergh pose at the center of this June 1928 photograph.

demonstrate dramatically the larger meaning of the New York–to–Paris flight for the future of commercial aviation.

The tour unfolded between July and October 1927. Lindbergh flew his beloved *Spirit of St. Louis* some 22,000 miles, involving more than 260 hours of actual flying. The itinerary called for him to visit eighty-two cities, with planned fly-overs of other towns along the way, where the famed aviator would drop messages by parachute. The arduous aerial trek allowed Lindbergh to make some 147 speeches.

The public response was spectacular in terms of the intensity of interest and the large numbers who crowded small airstrips to get a glimpse of Lindbergh. Exact figures are not available, but the number of people who saw him may have exceeded thirty million. Along the way the local and national press hounded Lindbergh, but he refused to answer any personal questions. Coinciding with the flight, the U.S. Post Office issued a special Lindbergh stamp, the first for a living aviation figure.

For Lindbergh the tour presented a physical challenge with its demanding itinerary, made worse by his own passion for precise planning and unerring punctuality. Soon he yearned for an end to the demonstration flights and the seemingly endless round of public ceremonies.

The Spirit of St. Louis in the Panama Canal Zone. Lindbergh made a highly publicized tour of Mexico, Central America, and the Caribbean in 1928.

Always disciplined, he had sacrificed a measure of personal privacy for the larger end of promoting aviation. One personal benefit for Lindbergh had been his exposure to the United States in all its geographical expanse and physical beauty. This positive image of America would linger in his memory and influence his interest in conservation later in life.[10]

Soon there was a siren call to extend the flying abroad, to Mexico, Central America, and the Caribbean. Lindbergh agreed to this overture, accepting an invitation from Dwight Morrow, then ambassador to Mexico, to fly to Mexico City. Such a flight, in Morrow's mind, would greatly enhance relations with America's southern neighbor, even as it would allow Lindbergh to extend the scope of his promotional flights with the *Spirit of St. Louis.* To demonstrate the range of his famed silver monoplane, Lindbergh made a nonstop 2,030-mile flight from Bolling Field in Washington, D.C., to Mexico City. The aerial trek prompted no small amount of concern for Morrow, in particular when Lindbergh did not arrive at the airport in Mexico City on time. Morrow was

▼ In the Spirit of St. Louis, *Lindbergh made 137 flights after his return to the United States on a huge pan-American tour. Lindbergh used his celebrity to increase interest in aviation and its commercial potential.*

there with the president of Mexico and a crowd of 150,000 people. As time passed all became concerned over the fate of Lindbergh, a pilot who took great pride in his punctuality. On the approach to Mexico City he got lost and, not knowing Spanish, had great difficulty in reading signs on buildings along the way. Still, his late arrival did not dampen the enthusiasm of the assembled crowd at the airport. During the next six weeks Lindbergh completed a series of survey flights in Central America and the Caribbean, spreading his own gospel of air-mindedness.

By February 1928, Lindbergh was back in St. Louis. It was in this symbolic locale that he decided to end the flying career of the *Spirit of St. Louis.* The sleek monoplane had responded to every challenge, flying across oceans, across the continental United States, and to remote places such as the Panama Canal Zone. With each sortie in his fabled airplane, Lindbergh heard people expressing concern: How long would it be before the plane was destroyed in a crash? After some conversations with the Smithsonian Institution, he decided to donate the historic flying machine to the nation. When Lindbergh flew the *Spirit of St. Louis* to Washington, D.C., on April 30, 1928, he used the event to signal an end to his tours and staged encounters with the public.[11] From the beginning, Lindbergh had been restive as a prisoner of his fame. He had been buffeted by the winds of popular acclaim and dutifully adapted to the endless rounds of public ceremonies, but now he sought a way to assert absolute sovereignty over his life.

The young aviator lived a private life that, to some, seemed boring and conventional. He didn't smoke and abstained from all alcohol. He paid his taxes. Even in the heyday of his barnstorming and military flying, Lindbergh had lived a rather ascetic life, one occasionally filled with pranks and horseplay, but a busy life of flying that seemed to preclude dating or womanizing. After the New York–to–Paris flight women often sought him out, but he reacted with real discomfort when any well-meaning—or not-so-well-meaning—member of the opposite sex engaged him in small talk as a way to introduce herself as a potential mate. Yet now, for the first time, the twenty-six-year-old Lindbergh was thinking seriously about marriage. In keeping with his character and personality, he approached this milestone with a precise set of criteria for an ideal mate, reflecting his interest in seeking out a wife with intelligence and solid heredity.

When Lindbergh visited Dwight Morrow in Mexico City over the Christmas holidays in

▲ *Letter by Charles Lindbergh to Frank Mahoney relating his desire to donate the Spirit of St. Louis to the Smithsonian Institution. Concerned about potential damage to the historic plane, Lindbergh gave it to the museum in 1928.*

December 1927, he was invited to dine with the Morrow family at their official residence.

At that family gathering he met the ambassador's daughter, Anne Spencer Morrow, then a student at Smith College, who had aspirations of becoming a writer. The fact that Anne did not aggressively seek out Lindbergh for small talk or, for that matter, even display any particular interest in the renowned aviator placed her in a special category. Her shyness and introverted character was matched with a striking physical beauty, which did not escape Lindbergh's notice. As he later confessed to a friend, she lingered in his memory for many weeks. Eventually, he sought her out for a date, but their contacts required staging and constant vigilance to maintain privacy. However, there were times to meet, to talk, and to begin a relationship.

Predictably, the press took a keen interest in Lindbergh's social life, asking about his dating life and plans for marriage. Lindbergh's every step, alone or with Anne, risked the probing cameras of the press or the relentless curiosity of celebrity seekers. Charles and Anne quickly adapted to the peculiar context of their courtship, composing their letters in code so as to shield their thoughts and movements from probing reporters. One interesting outing was Anne's first plane ride, an event that allowed Charles to introduce his future bride to his world of aviation.

the morrow family

Charles Lindbergh's marriage to Anne Spencer Morrow brought the young aviator into one of the most prominent American families, one known for its contributions to banking, politics, and diplomacy.

Dwight Morrow was born in Huntington, West Virginia, in 1873, the son of a college president and a member of a family of educators. He graduated from Amherst College, class of 1895, and then trained for a career in law. After a stint as a lawyer Morrow sought out a new career in international finance, joining the banking house of J. P. Morgan & Company in 1914. During World War I, Morrow served as a member of the Allied Transport Council and a chief civilian aide to General John J. Pershing, the commander of the American Expeditionary Force in Europe. During the decade of the 1920s, Morrow increasingly turned from banking to government service. His Amherst College classmate President Calvin Coolidge appointed him ambassador to Mexico in 1927, a post Morrow used effectively to foster better relations with Mexico. Later he served as a U.S. senator from New Jersey.

No less important, Morrow became a significant player in aviation in the same decade, at a time when the airplane ceased to be a novelty and began to rival railroads as a new mode of transportation. He served as the director of the Daniel Guggenheim Fund for the Promotion of Aeronautics, an influential private agency promoting the airplane as a legitimate and safe mode of travel. Morrow played a key role in shaping a new regulatory role for the federal government in aviation, serving as the head of an advisory board to President Coolidge and making recommendations that, in part, led to the Air Commerce Act of 1926.

Short in stature at five feet six inches, with unruly hair and a certain disheveled look, Morrow impressed his contemporaries with his innate intelligence and high energy. He

Portrait of the Morrow children: *(from left)* Elisabeth, Anne, Dwight Jr., and Constance

married Elizabeth Reeve Cutter in 1903. A graduate of Smith College, Elizabeth shared a midwestern background with her husband, having grown up in Cleveland, Ohio. Elizabeth also possessed an energy level equal to her husbands, with interests in poetry and women's higher education. They had four children: Elisabeth (1904), Anne Spencer (1906), Dwight Jr. (1908), and Constance (1913). Both parents were active members of the Presbyterian church, and they cultivated a strong moral and religious sensibility in their children.

Lindbergh talking to Anne Spencer Morrow, his future wife, and her family

Lindbergh spent Christmas 1928 with the Morrow family in Mexico City.

Dwight Morrow loved to read the classics and history and took steps to ensure that his children traveled widely with their parents in Europe. Elizabeth, as a mother, bequeathed to her children a love of reading and diverse cultural interests. Although the Morrow family resided in Englewood, New Jersey, they enjoyed the seashore, spending part of each summer at Martha's Vineyard or Cape Cod and, later, on the island of North Haven, off the coast of Maine.

Growing up in the genteel Morrow household offered unique opportunities, but with privilege came a strong sense of public service. Both of the Morrow parents served on numerous educational, charitable, and public-service boards. Anne Spencer Morrow, the second child, attended Smith College, where her mother was on the board of trustees. As a college student, the young Anne Morrow thrived in the humanities and aspired to be a writer. During her senior year she won several literary awards, clear indicators that she indeed possessed a flair for writing.

When Charles Lindbergh flew to Mexico City in December 1927, he was hosted by Dwight Morrow. As ambassador, Morrow had encouraged Lindbergh to visit the region to promote better relations between the United States and Mexico. While visiting the Morrow family, Lindbergh was taken with the demure Anne and began to court her. They were married on May 27, 1929.

Anne quickly adapted to the arduous and exciting lifestyle as the wife of Charles Lindbergh, learning to fly and participating with her husband in a series of survey flights to chart future airline routes. She served as copilot, navigator, and radio operator on long-distance flights in a Lockheed Sirius over

Mexican president Pascal Ortiz Rubio greets Dwight Morrow, the U.S. ambassador to Mexico, in 1930 before a Fourth of July ceremony in Mexico City.

Canada and the North Pacific to Asia. Anne later chronicled this 1931 survey flight in her book *North to the Orient*. Subsequent survey flights included a 33,000-mile aerial trek that spanned North America, Europe, the west coast of Africa, Brazil, and Central America. This extraordinary flight, which touched four continents, became the basis for another of her books, *Listen! The Wind*. Anne's interests in flying were real and significant, leading her to become one of the first women to obtain a glider pilot's license. She often used themes from her aviation life as the basis for her writing.

Dwight Morrow died suddenly in 1931. His widow recruited Harold Nicolson, the well-known English biographer, essayist, and diplomat, to prepare a biography of her late husband. Later, the link between the Morrow family and Harold Nicolson proved decisive: After the kidnapping and death of their first child, Charles and Anne escaped to England in 1935, taking up residence on the Nicolson estate in Kent.

◀ ▲ *Anne Morrow*
Lindbergh on her
honeymoon in May
1929. The Lindberghs
slipped away on a boat
off New England to
escape reporters.
▼ *Anne and Charles*
visit the Grand Canyon
in the early days of their
marriage.

While opposites in many ways, the two quickly established close romantic ties. They were married in a private ceremony on May 27, 1929. Their honeymoon, as with the wedding, had to be arranged with great secrecy. They managed to escape the swarm of reporters for a boat trip off New England.

The marriage of Charles Lindbergh and Anne Morrow fascinated Americans in the 1930s, as it would in later decades. The marriage endured over time—it was a real love story. But it was a relationship that ran a gauntlet of crises: the kidnapping and murder of the first of their six children, their self-imposed temporary exile to Europe, public ostracism, separation during the war, and the constant shifts in lifestyle and homes.

Writing from Martha's Vineyard in February 1942, Anne Lindbergh wrote a long letter to family friend Jim Newton, then considering marriage, on her own passage in 1929 from a college student to the wife of the world's most celebrated aviator. Her husband also had counseled Newton on marriage, briefly in conversation, but Anne chose to write so that her thoughts could be more orderly and focused. Given the Lindberghs' private natures, the letter offers a rare insight into a complex marriage.

Antigua. West Indies. Sep 22. 1929.

◆ *The Lindbergh
honeymoon and travels,
1929–33. Among their
many trips, the couple
traveled to the
American Southwest
and Antigua in 1929 and
Canada in 1931 and
took survey flights to
Greenland and
Newfoundland in 1933.
The Lindberghs shared
a love of the outdoors.*

◆

Lindberghs at Churchill
1931 Canada

Anne Lindbergh told Newton to follow his "inner voice," as she had done. Looking back on her state of mind as a twenty-two-year-old when she married, Anne admitted that "sheer logic and pure rationalism" had little to do with her decision. She had sketched out, admittedly in "a hazy way," the direction she wished her life to take, even the sort of husband she wanted. In her ideal, she had thought of an alignment of "mutual interests, outlook, and understanding" as the critical values shaping a marriage. "Charles," she admitted, "satisfied none of my conditions . . . a man with whom I had nothing in common but youth." Every rational argument suggested that she should not marry him, but she did. Summarizing this fateful decision in life, she

▼ *Anne Lindbergh played a crucial role in her husband's survey flights as a radio operator and navigator. In 1931 Charles taught her to fly. She earned her pilot's license and emerged as a major female pilot of the era.*

• ◆ •

told Newton: "I married him because of one overwhelming certainty in my mind. That I had never in my *life* come across any individual so fine, so clear, so true, so utterly good, so real."[12]

Mirrored also in the letter were other factors at play in the marriage, in particular the divergence in views between the couple. "Of course," she observed, "I disagree with him often and feel sometimes deeply grieved when the crystal clarity, the burning purity, the sheer goodness doesn't shine through to other people. But that doesn't change the feeling or belief in what he is."[13] Such was the dynamic that defined their marriage. And this understanding prompted Anne to make a concluding point, one that sustained her in the most difficult moments in this complex marriage: She did not believe that "happiness," as conventionally understood, was her primary motive. Instead she talked about the "pull of life": "Charles was life, real life, like pure sunshine or pure fire."[14] Implied in her commentary was the acknowledgment that her marriage, if lacking in some of the more conventional emotional satisfactions, did provide a sense of meaning and purpose. Anne Lindbergh wrote her letter in 1942 on the eve of her thirteenth wedding anniversary. Her marriage would face new challenges and crises in the decades ahead.

In this same letter, Anne Lindbergh gave voice to one of the essential character traits of her husband that, in retrospect, enable us to understand his turbulent life in the late 1930s, a time when he embraced certain principles at odds with a large segment of the American population. "There were no words," she noted, "between what he said and what he was. And it was true all the way through, right down to the bottom of him."[15] When facing any crisis in his public life, Lindbergh firmly stated his principled views, never trimming his sails or adjusting them to the expectations of others. He could not be bought with praise or high office, as President Roosevelt would discover at the onset of World War II. Lindbergh's stoicism, discipline, and inattention to popularity defined his public life. There was a stubbornness to Charles Lindbergh that often overrode common sense. Because of this settled and irreversible character trait, he frequently let rumor or deliberate acts of distortion pass without comment. His silence reflected his rectitude and personal serenity, but his unwillingness to defend himself often deeply distressed his family. His wife in particular had to contend with this reality, at once challenged to be supportive and to forge her own views on a wide variety of public-policy issues.

Anne Morrow Lindbergh's marriage catapulted her into the world of aviation. She learned to fly, mastered the subtleties of navigation and radio communication, and participated in a pivotal survey flight

▲ Anne Morrow Lindbergh takes a flying lesson from her husband in 1931 in a biplane.

▼ A writer at heart, Anne chronicled her travel experiences in her books. Her most famous book, North to the Orient (1935), is an account of the survey flight she took with Charles to the North Pacific in 1931.

to the Orient. The Lindberghs flew the Great Circle route from New York to Tokyo, flying a single-engine Lockheed Sirius airplane equipped with pontoons. The overriding goal of the flight was to pioneer a future commercial air route from North America to the Far East. They departed on July 27, 1931, from Long Island and followed an itinerary that included northernmost Canada, Point Barrow in Alaska, Kamchatka in Soviet Siberia, and Japan. They continued their survey flight to China, only to return home when news reached them that Anne's father, Dwight Morrow, had died. Two years later Anne joined her husband on an Atlantic survey flight, one that would take the flying couple to Labrador, Greenland, the Scandinavian countries, and the Soviet Union. But the initial survey flight across the North Pacific endured in her memory as the most dramatic, prompting her to write her highly acclaimed book *North to the Orient* (1935).

The survey flights for Charles Lindbergh reflected his larger vision for the American aviation community. His 1927 aerial tour of the United States, which was quickly followed by flights to Central America and the Caribbean, demonstrated his commitment to advance the cause of establishing new commercial air routes.

north to the orient

Beginning in 1931, Charles Lindbergh pioneered a series of survey flights to chart out future airline routes. Anne Morrow Lindbergh joined her husband on the inaugural survey flight over the Arctic Circle to the Pacific. Following the Great Circle route, they traveled from Hudson's Bay across upper Canada to the Seward Peninsula and Alaska, down the North Pacific across the Bering Strait to Japan, and then to the flood-ravaged Yangtze River in China.

The Lindberghs arrive at Point Barrow.

They flew in a black Lockheed Sirius with orange wings, specially fitted with pontoons. The Sirius was a state-of-the-art monoplane, equipped with two spacious cockpits, dual controls, and a sliding isinglass canopy.

Anne was not just a passenger. She had trained as a pilot and served as a radio operator and a navigator on this historic flight. She later recorded a moving account of aerial adventure in her hugely successful book *North to the Orient* (1935). In it, Anne stated that "... if flying, like a glass-bottom bucket, can give you that vision, that seeing eye, which peers down to the still world below the choppy waves—it will always remain magic."[16] Anne had caught the magic of flying, and her popular chronicle of the excitement and dangers associated with their first survey became a classic in aviation literature. That extraordinary flight offered a meaningful reward for the long hours she spent mastering Morse code and learning to fly an airplane.

With her husband, Anne faced the many dangers associated with the survey flight. On the approach to Point Barrow, Alaska, they flew through storm-tossed skies. Anne maintained tenuous radio links with distant Point Barrow, alerting the world via Morse code to their whereabouts and asking for the latest weather data. "Through the cockpit cover," she observed, "I could see fog on the water ahead, motionless piles of light gray cotton wool.... On for hours through the unreal shifting of soft mist. Here a cloud and there a drizzle; here a wall and there, fast melting, a

The Morrows bid the Lindberghs farewell.

hole through which gleamed the hard metallic scales of the sea. That was no mirage. That rippling steel below us was real.... At times we seemed to be riding on its scaly back and then, with a roar, up we climbed into the white blankness. No sight of land; no sight of sea or sky; only our instruments to show the position of the plane."[17] After passing through what seemed to be an endless purgatory of bad weather and radio silence, Anne finally received the reassuring news from the radio operator at Point Barrow that the fog was lifting, setting the stage for their successful landing on a lagoon in the half light of the Arctic night.

When Charles and Anne reached China—a nation then beset by a disastrous flood of the Yangtze River—they faced new

The Lindberghs arrive at Nemuro, Japan, in August 1931.

Map showing the route of the
Lindberghs' 1931 flight to the Orient

Anne Morrow Lindbergh at Karingawa, Japan, in
August or September 1931

dangers, ones not necessarily associated with the weather. After seeing the devastation of the Yangtze River flood, the destroyed crops, and the countless refugees, Charles decided to make his airplane available to fly a doctor and medical supplies to the stricken region. Upon making a river landing in the interior, he oversaw the process of unloading the medical supplies on a sampan. Soon a large crowd gathered. Thinking the cargo was foodstuff, the desperate onlookers swam to the sampan and overwhelmed the crew. The weight of the uncontrolled mob sank the sampan. As the chaotic scene unfolded, people then began to swim for the nearby Lockheed Sirius. Some actually reached the pontoons, attempting to board the aircraft. Fearing the Sirius might also be damaged or sunk, Charles took out a revolver and fired into the air to disperse the crowd. Only with great difficulty did he manage to start up the plane's engine, maneuver the aircraft away from the refugees in the water, and take off.

There were other adventures when Charles and Anne reached the mouth of the Yangtze River off Shanghai. Here the British aircraft carrier HMS *Hermes* offered hospitality and temporary shelter. However, the rescue effort by the Royal Navy nearly ended in disaster when the crew of the *Hermes* hoisted the Sirius out of the rapids of the churning Yangtze. Suddenly, the airplane lurched at the end of the pulley, swung around, and almost turned over in the water. Both Lindberghs were in the cockpit at the time, forcing Anne first and then Charles to leap into the water. Damage to the Sirius proved to be minor; the cables had only damaged the plywood fuselage. The famed aircraft would fly again; in fact, it would make subsequent survey flights and be renamed by the Eskimos of Greenland the *Tingmissartoq,* or "the one who flies like a big bird."

The Lindberghs' aerial excursion to the Far East ended abruptly on October 5, 1931, when Anne received a telegram relaying the news that her father, Dwight Morrow, had died of a cerebral hemorrhage. Charles and Anne then canceled the survey flight, returning home by passenger liner. Before his departure Charles made arrangements for the shipment of the Sirius to San Francisco by cargo ship. Upon reaching home, the Lindberghs faced a bittersweet homecoming; there was the painful loss of Anne's father, but also an emotional reunion with their young son, Charles Augustus Lindbergh Jr.

Lindbergh approached this work with high seriousness. Moreover, he was not content to return to his former life as an airmail pilot or to reenter the competitive world of record-breaking flights. Many of Lindbergh's contemporaries in the aviation world were slow to realize this dramatic shift in his life. Fame for Lindbergh was not an end, but a platform to accomplish his individual goals—never careerism in the narrow sense but a principled commitment to the future progress of aviation.

The promotion of commercial aviation offered Lindbergh in the 1930s an avenue to assure his financial well-being for the future. Henry C. Breckenridge, a friend of the Morrow family, earlier had volunteered to oversee Lindbergh's financial affairs. His work, especially with the growing consultation activities with aviation firms, established a solid stream of income for the young Lindbergh, a secure setting to allow the Lone Eagle to emerge as the spokesman for the new Air Age.

Lindbergh's first link with the fledgling airline industry came with his active involvement with Transcontinental Air Transport (TAT), the forerunner of Trans World Airlines. He served as a technical advisor for the pioneering airline, which blended rail and air transportation

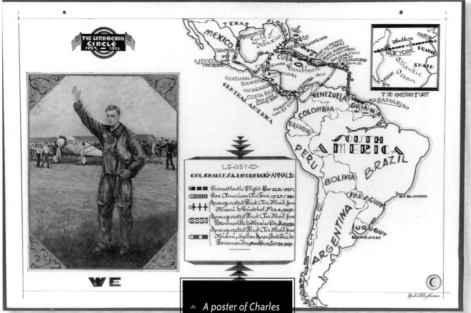

A poster of Charles Lindbergh and map of South America. Lindbergh was very popular in Central and South America, and his association with Juan Trippe and Pan American World Airways only deepened this tie.

An airmail letter flown by Lindbergh, February 21, 1928.

to provide a quick means to cross the country. Lindbergh promoted air travel as a safe and quick mode of transportation. For his services, he received an annual stipend and a healthy share in TAT stock. Later, Lindbergh joined with Juan Trippe to advance the interests of Pan American World Airways, an association that would endure for many years.

Lindbergh's larger-than-life role in the aviation community unexpectedly brought him into a fateful confrontation with President Franklin D. Roosevelt. Roosevelt assumed the presidency in March 1933 and soon presided over a vast new program of government legislation, the "New Deal," to contend with the Great Depression. In Washington there was a new climate of reform, with calls to root out past corruption, both real and imagined. Senator Hugo Black headed a senate committee to investigate the influence of big banking interests and Wall Street on the aviation industry. The thrust of this investigation prompted President Roosevelt in February 1934 to cancel the post-office contracts for airmail. The new president believed that monopolistic practices were apparent in the awarding of the contracts. In the aftermath of the cancellation order, Roosevelt called upon the U.S. Army Air Corps to deliver the airmail. Angered by the sudden change,

Lindbergh openly criticized the president, setting up a dramatic clash between a powerful political leader and a legendary aviator. Lindbergh predicted dire consequences if Roosevelt's arbitrary order was allowed to go forward. His analysis proved correct. Army pilots encountered many difficulties with the weather, and there were a large number of crashes and fatalities. For Roosevelt, then on the crest of a wave of his New Deal reforms, there was the humiliation of having to back down, owing in large part to Lindbergh's spirited lobbying. The airmail crisis, as Lindbergh later discovered, would linger in President Roosevelt's memory.

Charles and Anne Lindbergh's life spiraled into tragedy with the kidnapping of their firstborn son, Charles Jr., on the night of March 1, 1932. At the time of the kidnapping, the child was twenty months old, a chubby, blue-eyed toddler with golden locks of hair and the object of great interest in the popular press and among Lindbergh watchers. The child had been abducted from his second-story bedroom at the Lindbergh home, located on four hundred acres in the Sourland Mountain region of northern New Jersey. News of the kidnapping electrified the nation, with massive newspaper coverage and wild theories on the exact whereabouts of the child. Lindbergh took the lead in the investigation that followed, a step that brought him inevitably into the public arena he detested. Ransom money was offered and then delivered to a

▲ *Charles Augustus Lindbergh Jr., the firstborn child of Anne and Charles Lindbergh, was kidnapped on March 1, 1932, from their New Jersey home.*

▼ *Police examine the ladder used in the kidnapping.*

mysterious man in a Bronx cemetery. Hopes soared, only to lead to deeper despair with the passing of time and the failure of the kidnappers to return the child. Soon a circus atmosphere began to overwhelm the investigation. Countless letters came to the police from the lunatic fringe of society, some thirty-eight thousand letters in the first five weeks after the kidnapping. Some people offered arcane theories on how to capture the kidnappers; others reported on their psychic dreams about the location of the child; still others even offered their own children as substitutes to fill the void in the Lindbergh family. The constant media attention to the case, punctuated by wild reports and rumors, deeply offended the Lindberghs, even as they courageously maintained their vigilance and cooperated with the police on every reasonable tactic to find their child and solve the crime.

A breakthrough came on May 12 when the body of Charles Jr. was discovered near the family home. Two years later, the police arrested Bruno Richard Hauptmann, a German immigrant and carpenter. When the trial began in Flemington, New Jersey, in early January 1935, a swarm of reporters and photographers descended on the courthouse. The ensuing trial, with all its pandemonium and excesses, inevitably drew Charles and Anne Lindbergh into its vortex, compelling them to testify after walking through a gauntlet of reporters and onlookers.

trial of the century

The kidnapping of Charles Augustus Lindbergh Jr., the first-born son of Charles and Anne Lindbergh, took place on the night of March 1, 1932. At the time of the abduction, the child was twenty months old. A ransom note was discovered on the window-sill, demanding $50,000 for the safe return of the infant. A crude handmade ladder had been left at the scene of the crime. The New Jersey State Police assumed responsibility for finding the kidnappers in a climate of intense publicity. Great pains were made to follow every credible lead. Charles Lindbergh actively participated in the criminal investigation and even hired private investigators to seek out evidence. A second ransom note reached the Lindbergh family five days after the kidnapping, postmarked from Brooklyn, New York, but it led nowhere.

Numerous ransom notes followed in the spring of 1932 amid a flurry of publicity, false leads, and failed efforts to identify the kidnappers. At one critical juncture Dr. John Condon, a retired Bronx school principal, stepped forward, offering to serve as a go-between. Lindbergh approved Condon's initiative and

arranged for him to transfer money to the shadowy negotiators promising the return of the Lindbergh child. Then, on May 12, ten weeks after the kidnapping, the body of the child was discovered not too far from the Lindbergh home in Hopewell, New Jersey.

The crime sparked a broad investigation, eventually prompting President Franklin Roosevelt to order FBI director J. Edgar Hoover to centralize the federal government's investigation of the case under the Justice Department. Thousands of leads were followed in a massive effort to find the person or persons responsible for the murder. In September 1934, Bruno Richard Hauptmann, a German immigrant carpenter, was arrested for the crime. A thirty-five-year-old with a criminal record, including robbery and illegal entry into the

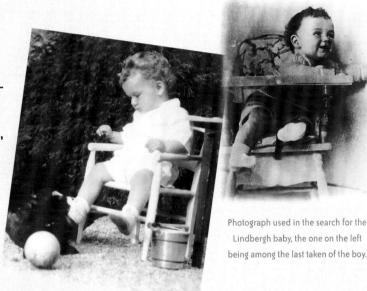

Photograph used in the search for the Lindbergh baby, the one on the left being among the last taken of the boy.

Wanted poster for the kidnapper of Charles Lindbergh Jr.

United States, Hauptmann claimed that he was innocent of the crime. He was indicted for murder in Hunterdon County, New Jersey, on October 8, 1934. Hauptmann was placed in the jail at Flemington for the trial, which began on January 3, 1935.

While the evidence was largely circumstantial, Charles Lindbergh and most Americans believed Bruno Hauptmann was in fact the kidnapper and murderer. Police discovered marked ransom money in the garage behind his house. There were other telltale bits of circumstantial evidence pointing to Hauptmann, such as

> If the kidnappers of our child are unwilling to deal direct we fully authorize "Salvy" Spitale and Irving Bitz to act as our go-between. We will also follow any other method suggested by the kidnappers that we can be sure will bring the return of our child
>
> *Charles A. Lindbergh*
> *Anne Lindbergh*

The Lindberghs signed a note to deliver to the kidnappers. At right, key players in the 1935 murder trial.

Charles Lindbergh never anticipated the sustained public interest that would dog his every step in life. That interest had never before

the fact that wood in the floor of the German immigrant's attic matched the wood of the ladder used to kidnap the Lindbergh child.

The Lindbergh kidnapping and the two-year investigation that followed became one of the most sensational events of the decade. The town of Flemington became a media circus in 1935, drawing huge crowds and national press coverage on an unprecedented scale. Countless reporters poured into the small New Jersey town. Celebrities vied with one another to gain seats in the courtroom. Souvenir vendors in the streets even sold small ladders to commemorate the crime. The flash of cameras, the milling crowds, and the jammed roads into Flemington made the whole trial scene one of chaos and frenzy. While Anne Lindbergh made only two appearances at the trial, Charles made many visits to the courthouse in Flemington to monitor the proceedings.

A verdict of guilty was returned on

February 13, 1935, and after his appeals were exhausted, Bruno Hauptmann was electrocuted on April 3, 1936. The crime engendered broad sympathy for the Lindberghs, who occupied a special place in national consciousness as celebrities. Its spectacle led the U.S. Congress to pass the "Lindbergh Law," making kidnapping a federal crime.

People continue to debate the merits of the case, some feeling that Hauptmann had been convicted on circumstantial evidence and that he lacked a competent defense. Yet Hauptmann never adequately explained how he obtained part of the ransom money or, for that matter, the physical evidence that implicated him in the crime. For the Lindberghs, the trauma of the six-week trial and the heightened concern for the safety of their second son, Jon, further isolated them from the public and diminished their willingness to tolerate intrusions into their personal and private lives.

been as intense as it was during the "Trial of the Century," which established precedents for subsequent decades. The cult of celebrity was no longer a phenomenon restricted to movie stars, sports figures, and politicians. All public figures, even in times of private grief and distress, were now subject to the glare of the media spotlight.

Anne Morrow Lindbergh leaves the courthouse with Ruth Schwarzkopf, who had testified at the Hauptmann trial.

Celebrities—movie stars, writers, and the rich—vied with one another to gain seats in the courtroom. Outside, peddlers hawked souvenir "kidnap ladders." Eventually, Hauptmann was found guilty and executed.

In the midst of these difficult months, the second Lindbergh son, Jon, was born. His safety quickly became an issue, and anonymous threats were made to kidnap or harm him. Seven years had passed since Lindbergh had made his dramatic landing at Le Bourget. The trauma of the kidnapping and the bedlam at Flemington, New Jersey, stood in stark contrast to the boundless optimism and sense of opportunity that followed the epic flight of 1927. Now only the earthly concerns for the safety of his family dominated Lindbergh's thoughts. Always determined in the face of any challenge, he decided with Anne to seek a new life in England as émigrés. In the British Isles, he reasoned, there would be sanctuary—and the chance to reorder his life.

The Lindberghs' new home in England was called Long Barn, an old remodeled cottage on the estate of Harold Nicolson and his wife, Vita Sackville-West. The Nicolsons had invited the beleaguered Lindberghs to their English estate, believing the

▲ Anne Morrow Lindbergh with her third son, Land, and her mother, Elizabeth Cutter Morrow.

▼ During the Lindbergh's stay at Long Barn, Anne, pictured here in her bedroom, would write her book Listen! The Wind and give birth to her third son, Land.

large picturesque cottage situated in the lovely countryside of Kent offered a unique precinct of privacy. Long Barn was a rambling affair, set amidst terraced gardens. It offered a unique chance for Charles to pursue his scientific interests and for Anne to begin writing a new book, which later became *Listen! the Wind*, her account of the survey flight of the North Atlantic. Most of all, Long Barn afforded security. Here their second and surviving child, Jon, was genuinely safe, beyond the reach of celebrity-seekers and the probing cameras of news reporters.

While in England, Charles and Anne were delighted by the kindness and reticence of their hosts and new neighbors. It appeared that everyone in the rolling countryside of Kent understood their recent travail and allowed them peace and anonymity. Anne Morrow Lindbergh's diary account of their arrival at Long Barn on February 20, 1936, captures their new sense of beginning: "It was suddenly very quiet as we stepped out and opened the gate. There were lots of birds singing. We tiptoed around to the back and found the two arms of the low house made a court and then looking down the hill—over gardens to fields and hills and farms—all quiet, all country, all still."[18]

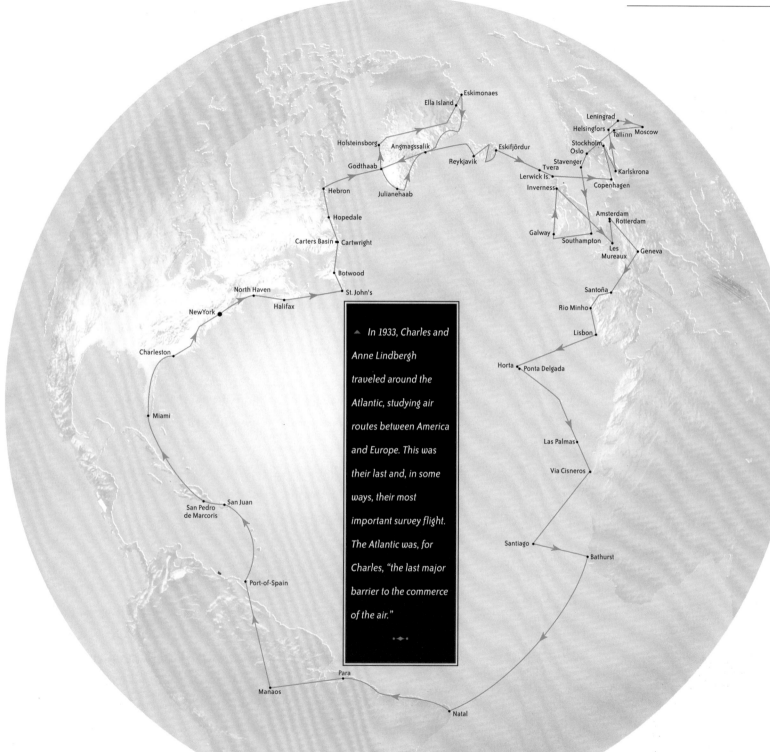

In 1933, Charles and Anne Lindbergh traveled around the Atlantic, studying air routes between America and Europe. This was their last and, in some ways, their most important survey flight. The Atlantic was, for Charles, "the last major barrier to the commerce of the air."

alexis carrel

Charles Lindbergh met French-born scientist and Nobel laureate Alexis Carrel in November 1930. From that moment until Carrel's death in 1944, Lindbergh expressed deep respect for his brilliant, if eccentric, mentor. Carrel was profoundly influential in shaping Lindbergh's interests and views, redirecting the famed aviator's energies to a remarkable set of scientific experiments and redefining his philosophical outlook. To Lindbergh, Carrel was a teacher, a collaborator, and a friend.

Carrel was born in Lyons in 1873, attended a Jesuit-run academy for his early formal education, received his medical degree at the University of Lyons in 1900, and joined the staff of the Rockefeller Institute (now University) in New York City in 1906. Working as a surgeon at the Institute, Carrel impressed his contemporaries with his brilliant mind and extraordinary skills. He was awarded the Nobel Prize in 1912 for his pioneering advances in the suturing of blood vessels. He was the first scientist working in the United States to receive such an honor in this field of scientific endeavor. During World War I, he developed a special method for the treatment of war wounds, prompting additional praise for his original research and experimentation. The Allied governments, including the United States, showered Dr. Carrel with awards for his wartime efforts.

While Carrel's brilliant work as a surgeon and clinician won wide praise, his eccentric style and unconventional views as a scientist prompted widespread criticism. Carrel's assistants were required to wear black robes with hoods and to work in rooms with the walls painted black. Carrel himself opted for exotic garb, often wearing his distinctive white cap and black jacket festooned with brass buttons. Vestments aside, Carrel's hard-driving approach, frequently punctuated with temperamental outbursts and impatience with his subordinates, alienated many of his colleagues.

He also attracted attention from his controversial writings for popular magazines on a variety of topics. Carrel, a theist, took a keen interest in philosophical and religious issues, believed in the afterlife, extrasensory perception, and miracles, and expressed an abiding concern over the fate of civilization. His belief in the supernatural and the nonrational aspects of reality, even the efficacy of prayer, placed Carrel outside

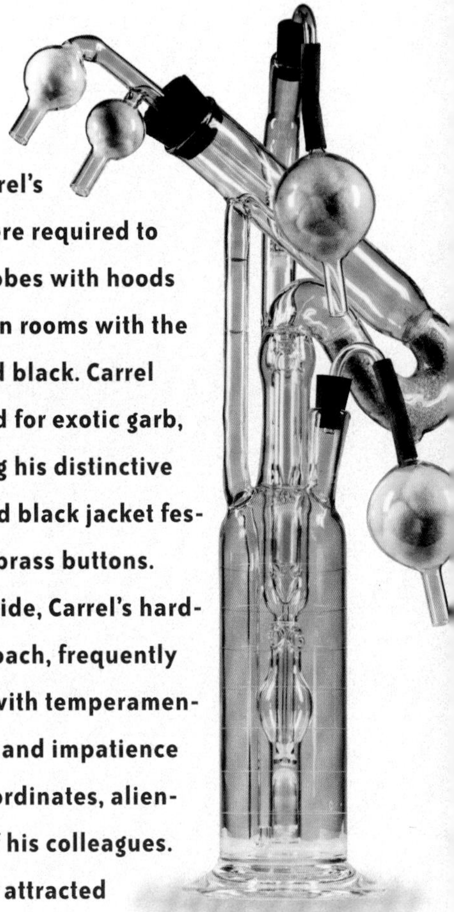

The perfusion pump invented by Lindbergh and Carrel

Lindbergh with Nobel Prize winner Dr. Alexis Carrel, November 1936

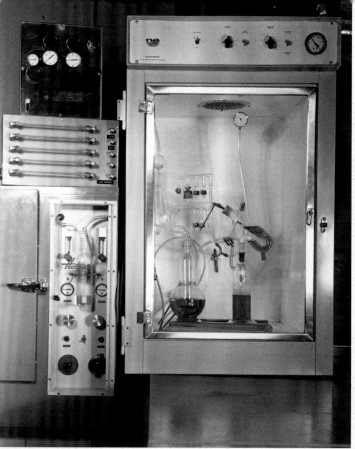

The artificial heart pump, successor to the perfusion pump, designed by Carrel and Lindbergh

the conventional bounds of the scientific community of his day.

As with many in his generation, Carrel studied eugenics and race and advanced his own theories of "elitism," the idea that a small, creative minority are responsible for human progress. Linked to his elitism was his belief that human capacity and behavior are profoundly influenced by genes or genetic endowment. Carrel articulated his ideas on the fate of civilization and humanity for a popular audience in his book *Man, the Unknown* (1935), which sold over 900,000 copies. The book gave expression to his wide-ranging views on science, society, metaphysics, and human nature. But its thinly veiled critique of democracy, along with his interest in eugenics and his idiosyncratic concept of elitism, was controversial.

Charles Lindbergh's association with Alexis Carrel grew out of a family crisis. Lindbergh's sister-in-law, Elisabeth Reeve Morrow, had suffered as a child from rheumatic fever, which led to the development of a lesion in her heart. This condition severely restricted her activities as an adult, and she faced the possibility of heart failure. Her doctors said that the condition was incurable and explained that it was inoperable because the heart could not be stopped temporarily to allow any surgical procedure. This prompted Lindbergh to seek a possible cure.

Lindbergh's quest led him to the Rockefeller Institute, where he sought out Carrel for a new invention that would allow for operations on the heart. He knew little of the anatomical and bio-logical aspects of the problem, but he did possess the mechanical and technical skills to assist Carrel in his laboratory at the Institute with his work on designing an improved pump. Elisabeth died in 1934, long before the art and technology of open heart surgery was perfected. However, her ailment served as a catalyst for the Lindbergh-Carrel collaboration on a prototype for an artificial heart.

Even at the Rockefeller Institute, Lindbergh learned that he could not escape the media, who hounded his every step and asked the staff about his curious work in Alexis Carrel's laboratory. Even the staff and technicians sought out the famed aviator,

Lindbergh inspects an artificial heart pump at the National Naval Medical Center in April 1965.

peering into windows and shadowing Lindbergh down hallways. Many of Carrel's scientific colleagues at Rockefeller resented the intrusion of such a celebrity, and they openly questioned his fitness to contribute to scientific research. For his labors, however, Lindbergh received no pay or compensation, and his modesty and manifest talents quickly won over the research staff. Throughout this project, Carrel expressed confidence in his

collaborator from the world of aviation. Carrel and the entire Rockefeller staff maintained a strict discipline toward the press, never revealing any details of Lindbergh's research activities.

Lindbergh collaborated closely with Carrel on the design of a new prototype mechanical heart pump. He applied his considerable practical skills to the enterprise and, like Thomas Edison, worked tirelessly with various models until he found a solution. Five years of experiments and testing led to the creation of a workable glass perfusion pump, one that would allow Carrel to keep organs alive and sterile for study. The so-called Lindbergh pump debuted in April 1935. It demonstrated that a whole organ, in this case the thyroid gland of a cat, could be cultivated in vitro. The purpose of the apparatus was to sustain organs in isolation, in conditions approximating the natural environment of the body. Such a breakthrough led Carrel and Lindbergh to continue experiments on other organs, such as spleens, hearts, and kidneys of test animals. The results with the pump were officially publi-

cized in the magazine *Science*. And, before the end of 1935, news of the innovation landed Lindbergh and Carrel on the cover of an issue of *Time* magazine. Later, Lindbergh and Carrel published *The Culture of Organs* (1938), which gave detailed analysis of their collaborative research.

Alexis Carrel and his wife, Anne-Marie, became close friends of the Lindberghs. Carrel divided his time between his scientific labors in America and his second home in France. As a scientist, he was known for his extraordinary energy and discipline, which offered only modest amounts of time for social contacts with his wide circle of friends in America and his native France. In the spring of 1938, Charles and Anne Lindbergh purchased a home on the small island of Illiec, near the Carrel residence at St. Gildas, on the northern coast of France. Situated on the rocky and storm-tossed coastline, Illiec offered a primitive locale, but one that ensured privacy. At low tide, the Lindberghs could walk from Illiec across the rocky shore to the mainland. At nearby St. Gildas, Lindbergh made many visits to the Carrel home to discuss biological experiments or Carrel's proposed "Institute of Man." With Charles Lindbergh's decision to return to the United States in the spring of 1939,

A 1934 issue of *Literary Digest*, profiling Lindbergh's scientific achievement.

however, there was a parting of ways. The advent of the war and Carrel's decision to remain in occupied France ended his collaboration with Lindbergh.

Throughout the 1930s, Carrel had been outspoken on a number of political issues. He viewed the Nazi movement as a threat to civilization and feared that his native France was ill equipped to resist the advance of Nazi Germany. With the coming of World War II, he looked upon Hitler as a modern-day incarnation of Genghis Khan, a conqueror intent on world domination. Carrel, unlike Lindbergh, was quick to call for the intervention of the United States in the struggle against Nazi Germany.

Carrel and his wife spent the war years in occupied France, living in difficult circumstances at St. Gildas on the Brittany coast. He persisted in his studies of hypnosis, extrasensory perception, and mental telepathy. These austere years also provided a context for Carrel to complete his last major book, *Reflections on the Conduct of Life* (1950), a treatise on human behavior that called for curbs on the exercise of unfettered free will, among other issues. In the wake of the liberation of Paris by the Allies, many in the French media accused Carrel of being a Nazi sympathizer for his views on race and eugenics, a charge that greatly depressed him in the last months of his life. He died on November 5, 1944.

Centennial celebration of Carrel's birth, Georgetown University, 1973

APRIL 3, 1936

Bruno Richard Hauptmann is executed by electrocution in Trenton, New Jersey, state prison for the murder of the Lindberghs' first-born son.

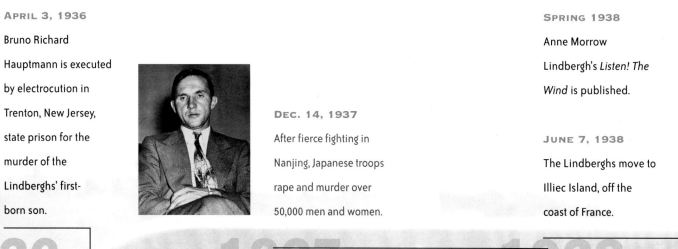

DEC. 14, 1937

After fierce fighting in Nanjing, Japanese troops rape and murder over 50,000 men and women.

SPRING 1938

Anne Morrow Lindbergh's *Listen! The Wind* is published.

JUNE 7, 1938

The Lindberghs move to Illiec Island, off the coast of France.

OCT. 18, 1938

Lindbergh accepts the Service Cross of the German Eagle from Hermann Goering during a diplomatic dinner at the U.S. Embassy in Berlin.

1936   1937   1938   19

JULY 28, 1936

Charles Lindbergh flies to Berlin for the first of his five visits to Nazi Germany, 1936–39.

MAY 12, 1937

The Lindberghs third son, Land, is born.

FALL 1938

Lindbergh and Carrel's *The Culture of the Organs* is published.

FALL 1938

Lindbergh attends the Lilienthal conference in Munich, his third visit to Nazi Germany for the United States government.

NOV. 9, 1938

Kristallnacht: Nazi storm troopers strike out against German Jews after the assassination of a German diplomat in Paris. Nearly a hundred Jews are killed, hundreds are injured, and some 7,500 businesses and 177 synagogues are gutted.

APRIL 8, 1939

Lindbergh sets sail for New York and, later, relocates his family back to the States.

MAY 1940

The Germans invade and occupy France and the Low Countries.

OCTOBER 1940

Anne Morrow Lindbergh's book *The Wave of the Future* is published.

APRIL 17, 1941

Lindbergh officially announces that he has joined the America First Committee and explains why.

39　　**1940**　　**1941**　　**1942**

SEPT. 1, 1939

German forces invade Poland, marking the beginning of the war in Europe.

SEPT. 15, 1939

Lindbergh makes his first radio address, "An Appeal for Isolation," opposing U.S. intervention in the war in Europe.

OCT. 13, 1939

Lindbergh makes his second radio address, "What Our Decision Should Be."

NOV. 1939

Lindbergh publishes his essay "Aviation, Geography, and Race" in *Reader's Digest*.

MARCH 1940

Lindbergh publishes a follow-up essay, "What Substitute for War?," in *The Atlantic Monthly*.

OCT. 2, 1940

The Lindberghs' first daughter, Anne, is born.

OCT. 30, 1940

Lindbergh delivers his first speech before the America First Committee at Yale University.

APRIL 25, 1941

Lindbergh resigns as a colonel in the U.S. Army Air Corps Reserve after a personal attack by President Franklin Roosevelt.

attaché's apprentice

In the spring of 1936, the American embassy in London delivered a special letter to Charles Lindbergh, then living in the English countryside. When Lindbergh opened it, he encountered a most unusual request. The letter, postmarked May 25, came from Major Truman Smith, the American military attaché in Berlin. Major Smith was inviting Lindbergh to come to Nazi Germany for an inspection tour of air bases, aviation factories, and research facilities. In his brief and courteous letter, he assured Lindbergh that the invitation came with the blessing of Hermann Goering, the head of the German air force, or *Luftwaffe*. More important, the German Air Ministry had assured Smith that Lindbergh would be granted access to a variety of aviation facilities hitherto sealed off

A German officer assists Lindbergh in retrieving his luggage from a Miles Whitney Straight, a British two-seat monoplane
that Lindbergh flew to Germany on his first visit in 1936.

from foreigners: "From a purely American point of view," Major Smith observed, "I consider that your visit here would be of high patriotic benefit. I am certain they will go out of their way to show you even more than they will show us."[1] Smith needed Lindbergh's help in evaluating the recent German air rearmament, and he boldly asked the reclusive air hero to come to Nazi Germany to assist him in this intelligence-gathering operation.

The invitation came shortly after Charles and Anne Lindbergh's embrace of self-imposed exile in England. For the Lindberghs, the desperate passage into exile meant escape from the frenzy and the inherent dangers that came with celebrity status, a chance to rebuild their lives after the travail of the kidnapping and murder of their first-born child and the Bruno Hauptmann trial. Smith's letter, appearing out of the blue, gave Lindbergh the option to serve his country again, if remotely and clandestinely as Smith's assistant. But to visit Nazi Germany also meant the abandonment, at least temporarily, of his new lifestyle of anonymity.

Lindbergh promptly responded to Major Smith's extraordinary offer. In a letter dated June 5, he stated that he would be "extremely interested in seeing some of the German developments in both civil and military aviation." But he added, "What I

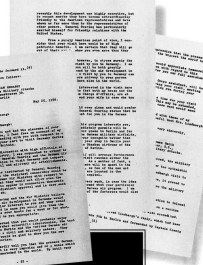

am most anxious to avoid is the sensational and stupid publicity which we have so frequently encountered in the past; and the difficulty and unpleasantness which invariably accompany it. . . . As a matter of fact I thoroughly dislike formal functions and have not attended one for several years."[2]

Smith had anticipated Lindbergh's need for privacy in his original letter of invitation. Now he faced the daunting task of keeping the Lindbergh trip on a relatively low key, at a time when the Germans would, no doubt, exploit the aviator for their own propaganda purposes. Once word of the visit reached the outside world, the old press hysteria over Lindbergh might also be re-ignited. Throughout the entire tour there would be a need to conceal his actual work for the U.S. government.

Lindbergh accepted the invitation for an inspection tour of Nazi Germany with a certain relish, but in 1936 he couldn't foresee the consequences of his decision for him and for his country. Lindbergh made a total of five visits to Nazi Germany between 1936 and 1939: the first three tours in close cooperation with Truman Smith, and the last two organized by Lindbergh in association with French government officials. During those three years he fulfilled his intelligence-gathering tasks superbly, but the exposure to Nazi Germany gave birth to new interests and priorities that soon led him into controversy.

▲ Major Truman Smith's letter of invitation to Lindbergh to inspect German aviation facilities set the stage for an important American intelligence operation on the eve of World War II.

▼ Lindbergh and son Jon build a treehouse at Long Barn in 1937.

"The other great danger aviation brings is the ember of war, fanned by every new military weapon, flaming today as it has never flamed before." —Charles A. Lindbergh

Before the decade ended, Lindbergh's life would be reordered in ways he never could have imagined. The inspection tours catapulted him into the public arena again, where he became a spokesman for nonintervention in any future European war. Lindbergh began his visits to Germany in 1936 with his broad popularity in America still intact, but by 1939 he abandoned his work there under a cloud of suspicion as a defeatist, widely reviled by many of his countrymen for his alleged Nazi sympathies. These years of tumult and eventual public ostracism mimicked the fate of his congressman father, who had stubbornly refused to support America's entry into World War I.

Perhaps the most positive aspect of Lindbergh's work in Nazi Germany was his interaction with Major Truman Smith. With time, both men grew to respect each other and develop an enduring friendship. Smith began his odyssey in Nazi Germany in August 1935, when he reported to the American embassy in Berlin as the new military attaché. His arrival coincided with Hitler's massive program of military rearmament, then at full stride and the object of great consternation

▼ *Anne Morrow Lindbergh with her third son, Land, at Long Barn, England, in 1937. While in England, Charles and Anne found safety and normalcy for their sons Jon and Land. Three children were born after their return to the United States: Anne (1940), Scott (1942), and Reeve (1945).*

throughout Europe. Tall and handsome, Major Smith possessed a gregarious personality, high energy, fluency in German, and a real aptitude for ferreting out military secrets. His wife, Katharine (or Kay), no less an engaging figure, soon caught the attention of the diplomatic community with her lively personality and outspoken views. Truman and Kay Smith spent nearly four years at the Berlin embassy, abandoning their post for home only when Truman developed diabetes and faced mandatory retirement. Among all their myriad diplomatic activities, there was one episode that gave the Smiths' tenure in Berlin special meaning: their relationship with Charles and Anne Lindbergh.

In his first year in Berlin, Major Smith launched a systematic program to assess the fighting capabilities of Hitler's army, sending American army officers to inspect German infantry, artillery, and other specialized regiments. Always attentive to the technical side of military intelligence, he took pains to provide his superiors at the war department in Washington, D.C., with highly detailed descriptions of new equipment and technical advances, along with data on

German army organization and methods of training. Wherever Smith discovered new tactics or new leadership, he endeavored to gauge the meaning of each change on the evolving German army. Military intelligence work in totalitarian Nazi Germany often became an exercise in "looking through a glass, darkly," but Smith's clever tactics routinely brought excellent results.[3]

With all his breakthroughs in gathering data on the German army, Major Smith remained unsatisfied because the intelligence mosaic remained incomplete: The *Luftwaffe* still awaited analysis. As the newest branch of the German armed forces, the *Luftwaffe*—operating in greater secrecy and autonomy—offered fewer avenues for penetration. Hermann Goering, a close associate of Hitler and a World War I aviator, headed this new air arm. Outside Germany the *Luftwaffe* became the most feared weapon of the Third Reich, prompting apocalyptic visions of Hitler unleashing a vast air armada to destroy the major capitals of Europe. Winston Churchill, in a speech before Parliament on November 28, 1934, gave voice to the Nazi air menace. The *Luftwaffe*, he charged, represented an "illegal" air force, at odds with the restrictions laid down in the peace settlement following World War I. Looking to the future, he argued that Hitler's air arm would soon be on a par with the Royal Air Force. In three years, he prophesied, the *Luftwaffe* would be double the size of Britain's air arm: "Beware," Churchill warned, "Germany is a country fertile in military surprises."[4]

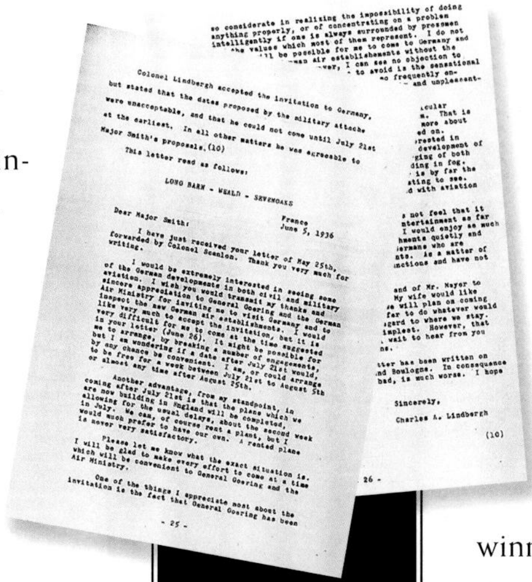

▲ The military report of Lindbergh's first visit to Germany.

▶ Adolf Hitler, Hermann Goering, and other Nazi officers on the march.

Lindbergh offered an avenue to confirm or discount Churchill's grim prophesies. Major Smith realized that he and his assistant, Captain Theodore Koenig, lacked the necessary credentials to negotiate their way into the secret world of German aviation. As nonflying regular army officers they had demonstrated some success in winning the respect of their counterparts in the German army, but they were aliens when it came to military aviation. Moreover, neither Smith nor Koenig possessed the technical background to exploit fully any opportunities to inspect *Luftwaffe* aircraft and facilities. At the time the *Luftwaffe* and the entire German aviation sector were controlled by the Air Ministry, which occupied a huge modern structure in downtown Berlin, a monument to Nazi architecture and Goering's power within Hitler's inner circle. To gain entrance to this sealed-off world, Smith sought out Charles Lindbergh as a tour guide.

Major Smith's decision to recruit Lindbergh as his special air attaché arose in a most unlikely place—at the breakfast table in early May 1936. That morning in his apartment in Berlin, his wife noticed an article in a Parisian newspaper describing a visit by Colonel Charles Lindbergh to a French aviation factory. When Smith read the piece he quickly

▲ Postcard showing the insignia of the commanding officer of the Luftwaffe. It includes a quote from the commander, Hermann Goering: "Achievement is having your opponent not only acknowledge you but fear you."

realized that Lindbergh's celebrity status opened many doors, particularly in the aviation world. The French gave him unique access to their aviation facility, and they were flattered that the pilot of the *Spirit of St. Louis* agreed to tour the factory. The seed was planted. And as the days passed, Smith began to think more concretely about how Lindbergh might be recruited to assist his intelligence-gathering operations. Why not invite Lindbergh to come to Berlin? Perhaps, as a reserve officer in the U.S. Army Air Corps, he could be convinced to serve as an informal intelligence agent. If major German aircraft factories, research institutes, and air bases were suddenly opened to the famed aviator, there might be an intelligence bonanza for his office.

A brilliant scheme, for certain, but Smith faced some real obstacles in executing his plan. First, he had never met Lindbergh. Smith even lacked a direct address for him, although he knew the famed aviator had moved to England. Any approach to the reclusive Lindbergh would require careful planning and considerable sensitivity to the fact that he would, no doubt, want to avoid any itinerary that involved crowds or endless rounds of receptions. And there would be the daunting task of gaining the cooperation of German air commander Hermann Goering before any invitation could be advanced to Lindbergh. Smith also faced certain procedural problems at the embassy, where the current ambassador, William E. Dodd, might not approve of the idea. Throughout his tenure as ambassador to Berlin, Dodd had displayed only a polite interest in military affairs.

◆ *Scenes at Long Barn. The residence of Harold Nicolson and Vita Sackville-West provided a welcome respite from the press for the Lindberghs in the mid-1930s, which was soon to be broken by Charles's work for the United States in Nazi Germany.*

◆———◆

His indifference toward the work of the military attaché had meant isolation for Smith. Dodd's thinly disguised loathing of the Nazi regime also precluded any systematic effort by the senior diplomatic staff to secure favors from such men as Goering. Smith would have to wing it.

Rather than get ensnared in a thicket of clearances from his superiors in Berlin and also in Washington, Smith decided to press ahead on his own, to make Lindbergh's visit to Germany a *fait accompli*, reasoning that the American aviator's wide popularity, his technical expertise on aeronautics, and his status as an officer in the air corps reserve would carry the day. To Smith's delight, officials at the German air ministry quickly agreed to the proposed visit, even promising to show Lindbergh the latest aircraft designs and hitherto off-limits facilities. There was a risk that the Germans would use the visit for propaganda purposes, but the trade-off would be decisively in favor of Washington. At this juncture, fate seemed to smile on the project: Ambassador Dodd returned to the United States on leave. This timely departure excluded Dodd from the planning process and allowed Smith to work with the more cooperative *chargé d'affaires,* a man named Ferdinand Meyer. Smith would need to maintain contact with the war department in

▲ *Lindbergh's letter accepting the invitation to visit German military aircraft bases.*

▼ *Field Marshal Hermann Goering inspires schoolchildren with a demonstration of Germany's air power.*

Washington, but he believed that he could act independently of Washington on the project. Moreover, he enjoyed a warm and cooperative relationship with the G-2 division (military intelligence), a branch of the war department that shared his keen interest in intelligence on the *Luftwaffe*.[5]

Lindbergh flew to Nazi Germany on July 22, 1936, landing at Berlin's Tempelhof Airport in his own private plane, a Miles "Whitney Straight." Anne joined him on this historic journey. In the highly organized ten-day tour, the Lindberghs were introduced to the elite of the German air establishment. The reception party at Tempelhof included the top echelons of the German aviation world—high-ranking members of the air ministry, the leadership of Lufthansa (the civil airline), representatives of the *Luftwaffe*, and the president of the Air Club of Germany. Truman Smith, accompanied by his assistant for aviation, Captain Theodore Koenig, represented the American embassy.

After a reception at the air ministry, with hosts State Secretary for the Air Ministry General Erhard Milch and famed German World War I ace Ernst Udet, Lindbergh followed an intense schedule of inspections of the various aviation facilities. To Major Smith's delight the Germans kept their word, allowing Lindbergh to inspect the Heinkel factories at

Rostock and Warnemunde, the once-secret Junkers factory at Dessau, and other major aviation sites. They allowed Lindbergh to see up close the Junkers Ju-87 Stuka dive bomber, destined to play a cutting-edge role in the early days of the Blitzkrieg in World War II. He even took the controls of a Junkers Ju-52 transport, the same aircraft that flew Hitler to Nuremburg for the annual Nazi party rallies. Flying the Ju-52 set a precedent for Lindbergh to fly other German aircraft. The German hosts, from Hermann Goering down to the workers on the bustling factory floors, found themselves enthralled with the renowned conqueror of the Atlantic. The inspection tour, an intelligence coup of the first order, exceeded Truman Smith's highest hopes.

Lindbergh met with Smith and Koenig each morning at the attaché's office to set the agenda and to plan the most optimal ways to exploit their rare opportunity to garner information on the *Luftwaffe*. Koenig, if a talented army officer, lacked technical insights into modern aircraft, so he allowed Lindbergh to take the lead. Throughout the tour, a nervous Smith attempted to limit the social agenda as much as possible. But there was great pressure from German officials and the press to meet with the famous American aviator. One reception was held at the American embassy, and Smith and his

▲ *One of the modern German fighters flown by Charles Lindbergh was an early variant of the Messerschmitt Bf-109. Shown here is the Bf-109G, which became the standard German interceptor in World War II. Lindbergh's pre-war report on the Bf-109 offered the United States an intelligence coup, a rare look at one of the most advanced fighters in the world.*

wife arranged for visits to museums in Berlin. Another magnet that drew a reluctant Lindbergh from the aviation itinerary was the Olympic Games, then in progress in Berlin. At the personal invitation of Goering, Charles and Anne Lindbergh made a brief appearance at the Olympic stadium. Goering also sponsored a special luncheon for the Lindberghs, held on July 28 at his official residence on Wilhelmstrasse. For this special event Goering invited high-ranking aviation figures, including crew from the "D.O.X." eight-engine flying boat—the same crew that had just completed a highly publicized round-trip flight across the Atlantic.

Smith's report to Washington, made in the immediate aftermath of the first Lindbergh inspection tour, confirmed that the Germans were expanding their air force at a rapid rate, with bold plans, in the words of Milch, "to create an air force second to none."[6] Lindbergh was impressed with the overall technical sophistication of the German program. The inspection of the Heinkel factory at Rostock revealed Germany's new medium bomber, the He-111, which pointed to the future. But Lindbergh also reported areas of backwardness. While visiting the Richthofen wing, he was surprised to see that this crack fighter group was flying He-51 biplanes, considered obsolete given their lack of streamlining.

truman smith

Major Truman Smith

Charles Lindbergh's association with Truman Smith, the American military attaché to Berlin from 1935 to 1939, became a pivotal episode in the life of the famed aviator. Smith recruited Lindbergh to assist him in the assessment of German air power, a vital arena for American military intelligence in the late 1930s. The resulting intelligence reports, at the time considered highly valuable and informative, ultimately led to controversy for both men. Smith regarded Lindbergh as a friend and patriot. In time he embraced many of Lindbergh's political views, which cast a shadow over his military career.

Truman Smith was born at West Point, New York, on August 25, 1893, the son of a regular army officer. At the age of seven, his father was killed in action in the Philippines in the Spanish-American War. The young Smith grew up in Stamford, Connecticut, where he lived with this mother. He graduated from Yale in 1915. That same year he attended the

Plattsburg military camp, which afforded him a first-hand glimpse at military life. This pivotal event prompted Smith to consider the military as his own career path. Subsequently, he joined the Twelfth Infantry Regiment of the New York National Guard, even as he pursued graduate work in history at Columbia University. His regiment was called up in 1916 to serve on the Mexican border. The following year he was commissioned a second lieutenant in the regular army, setting the stage for his service as an infantry officer in World War I. For his heroism in combat, he received the Silver Star in 1917.

In the postwar years, Smith served as a political adviser with the U.S. Army's Office of Civil Affairs in Coblenz, Germany. His fluency in German led to additional assignments with the American diplomatic corps in postwar Germany, including assistant military attaché. While in Germany in the early 1920s, Smith was one of the first

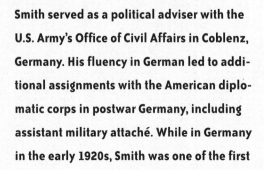

Lindbergh visits a German air force base.

Americans to interview Adolf Hitler, then an obscure nationalist politician in Bavaria.

Truman Smith married Katharine Alling Hollister in July 1917. They had one child, a daughter, and the marriage became a close one, with Katharine (or Kay) playing an influential role in her husband's turbulent three decades in the American military. After Smith left Germany, he won a prestigious appointment to the army's command and general-staff school at Fort Leavenworth in Kansas. At Fort Leavenworth, Smith met General George C. Marshall, who became an important mentor and supporter in subsequent years. Throughout Smith's career, even in moments of political controversy, Marshall remained loyal and supportive, always appreciative of Smith's talents.

Lindbergh greets German reception committee.

Assuming his post as military attaché in Berlin in 1935, Smith organized a systematic effort to assess the growing military power of Nazi Germany. His recruitment of Charles Lindbergh to assist in intelligence gathering on the *Luftwaffe* proved highly effective, because Lindbergh's name opened avenues for the inspection of *Luftwaffe* facilities and the latest military aircraft. Smith dutifully reported back to the war department with detailed estimates on German air strength. On the eve of America's entry into World War II, some attacked Truman Smith for making exaggerated estimates of German military power, and some even accused him of being a Nazi sympathizer. Despite the

attacks, Smith's expertise on German affairs was widely valued in the war department, in particular by General Marshall and his staff.

When France fell to Nazi Germany in May 1940, opponents of Lindbergh such as Secretary of the Interior Harold Ickes and columnist Drew Pearson argued that prewar estimates of German air power had contributed to a climate of defeatism. These charges focused on Lindbergh but also implicated Smith, who had made the formal reports. Smith always defended the essential accuracy of his intelligence reports.

In 1939 Smith became ill with diabetes, which forced his return to the United States. By 1941 he had retired from the army. But in the aftermath of Pearl Harbor, General Marshall brought Smith back to Washington to work in the intelligence division of U.S. Army General Staff. Smith unsuccessfully ran for

Lindbergh greets German General Erhard Milch.

congress in 1946. During his retirement years he began to write about his experiences in Germany before the war. Finding his own notebooks and personal memory often incomplete, Smith gathered many archival records and conducted extensive correspondence with former military colleagues to clarify his thinking. He endeavored to redeem his name and to establish the integrity of his military intelligence work. In the ongoing debate on America's entry into World War II, many defended Smith for his honest reporting and professionalism, while others saw him as a partisan foe of Franklin Roosevelt and controversial advocate of American neutrality.

Having forged their friendship with the Lindberghs in Berlin in the late 1930s, Truman and Kay Smith remained close with Charles and Anne Lindbergh in the decades that followed. Truman Smith died in October 1970.

Both Lindbergh and Koenig were puzzled by the large number of Ju-52 transports, a trimotor design known for its minimal range and lumbering cruising speed. Why did the Germans continue to use these obsolete aircraft? While the Ju-52 had been hurriedly adapted as a bomber in the Spanish Civil War (1936–39), it was not suitable as a standard bomber for the *Luftwaffe*. Lindbergh concluded that the Junkers Ju-52 had been retained for its durability to serve strictly as an air transport. Nonetheless, the Heinkel and Junkers factories impressed Lindbergh and demonstrated Germany's growing capacity to build modern military aircraft in large numbers.

Lindbergh collaborated with Truman Smith on two additional inspection tours in 1937 and 1938. For these junkets, Captain Albert G. Vanaman replaced Koenig, but the script remained the same. Both of these formal tours were keyed to international conferences sponsored by the Lilienthal Society in Munich, which allowed Lindbergh to meet a wider spectrum of German scientists and industrialists. The Lilienthal conferences also brought to Germany many pivotal American aviation figures, including the renowned aeronautical engineer Igor Sikorsky.

In October 1938, at the Rechlin flight test center on Lindbergh's third visit, the Germans permitted him to take the controls of Germany's most advanced fighter, the Messerschmitt Bf-109. The Bf-109 had made a dramatic appearance in the Spanish Civil War, winning air supremacy for Francisco Franco, the leader of the nationalist forces. In 1940, this same fighter would fly as an escort for German

▶ *Major Truman Smith (right) greets Charles Lindbergh (center) at a German airfield. Smith employed Lindbergh to gather data on the German air force. Lindbergh's fame won him unique access to German air bases, factories, and research facilities, as well as a chance to fly late-model German military aircraft.*

"LINDY"

bombers in the epic Battle of Britain. Lindbergh performed a series of flying maneuvers in the advanced Messerschmitt fighter. His impressions became a vital dimension of Smith's ongoing reports on the *Luftwaffe*.

Lindbergh was now a familiar figure at many German factories and research institutes. He moved with relative ease in his inspection tours, asking technical questions, examining German manufacturing techniques, and occasionally flying the latest-model aircraft. His analysis extended to a wide range of German aircraft, from the Dornier Do-17 bomber-reconnaissance plane and the He-111 bomber to the sleek four-engine transport, the Focke Wulf FW-200.

It was on this third trip, in October 1938, that Lindbergh found himself caught up in controversy, one where his natural stubbornness and disinclination to pander to public perceptions eventually made matters worse. On this visit Hugh Wilson, the U.S. ambassador, sponsored a reception to enlist the aid of Hermann Goering in getting the German government to moderate its anti-Semitic policies. In the middle of the reception Goering, suddenly and without forewarning, presented Lindbergh with a special medal, the Service Cross of the German Eagle, a large white cross festooned with smaller Nazi eagles and swastikas. The medal was offered in recognition of Lindbergh's transatlantic flight of 1927. Lindbergh accepted the medal, as he had taken custody of many awards, not realizing the implications of his action. Later, after Lindbergh

▲ Charles Lindbergh inspects the cockpit of a Messerschmitt aircraft.

▶ Adolf Hitler in front of Germany's four-engine transport, the Focke Wulf FW-200 Condor. Lindbergh was given the unusual permission to fly this aircraft, which later was used as a bomber against the Allies in World War II.

returned to his apartment, Anne looked at the medal and remarked prophetically, "The Albatross."

News of the Service Cross medal soon reached newspapers in the United States. Although there was no particular negative reaction initially, this changed after the night of November 9–10, 1938, when anti-Semitic riots took place all over Germany, in which many Jewish synagogues and business establishments were destroyed. *Kristallnacht,* as it came to be known, was a violent reminder of Hitler's racist policies. Back home, American newspapers denounced the pogrom and criticized Lindbergh's earlier acceptance of the Service Cross medal. Adding his voice to the chorus of criticism, Harold Ickes, the secretary of the interior, questioned Lindbergh's patriotism in a speech in

Cleveland, a dress rehearsal for his later opposition to Lindbergh during the great debate over American nonintervention in World War II. Typically, Lindbergh did not respond to such criticism, being confident that he had behaved properly. His silence on the darker side of Nazi Germany—in particular his silence on anti-Semitic policies, which he privately found abhorrent—only fueled the growing impression that he was either pro-Nazi or a Nazi dupe.

Lindbergh's actual posture toward Nazi Germany was an amalgam of positive impressions and nagging doubts. When he and Anne first arrived in Berlin in 1936, they were favorably impressed with the outward vitality of the "New Germany"—the economic renewal, the apparent end of unemployment, the well-dressed populace, the new sense of order. Anne, in a letter to her mother, wrote: ". . . [T]here is no

▲ The Service Cross of the German Eagle, presented to Charles Lindbergh by Field Marshal Hermann Goering. The award was for his historic 1927 transatlantic flight, but many interpreted Lindbergh's uncritical acceptance of the medal as a telltale sign of Nazi sympathies.

question of the power, unity and purposefulness of Germany. It is terrific. I have never in my life been so conscious of a *directed* force. It is thrilling when seen manifested in the energy, pride, and morale of the people—especially the young people."[7] They reacted only privately to the less-desirable aspects of the Nazi regime as isolated events, failing to see clearly the evils of the Nazi New Order.

In this context, Lindbergh forged his viewpoint on the question of Nazi Germany and the specter of a future world war. He felt any war would be a catastrophe for Europe, perhaps even for civilization itself. In a struggle between Nazi Germany and the Western democracies, Lindbergh was convinced that Germany would win. Even if Germany won such a war, Lindbergh argued, this would not be the worst-case scenario; the real threat to civilization was the Soviet Union. Germany stood as a bulwark against the Soviet Union, which was associated with an alien revolutionary ideology that, if not held in check, would dominate all Europe. As with many of his contemporaries, Lindbergh often thought in racial terms, seeing the fate of the white race caught up in this geopolitical struggle: The Soviets could be the wedge for Asiatic hordes to once again threaten Western civilization. Given these grim prospects, he preferred to see a war between Germany and Russia. Any effort by the United States in alliance with Britain and France to defeat Germany might hasten a Soviet occupation of central Europe. Whatever the future might hold, Lindbergh ardently believed that the United States

should be rearmed for its own survival. The more Lindbergh saw of Europe, the more he endorsed the traditional American foreign policy of isolationism, first articulated by George Washington.

Lindbergh shared with many people at the time the notion that the Western democracies were under siege. The totalitarian regimes of Nazi Germany and Soviet Russia appeared ascendant and threatening. World War I had left a legacy for a future war, with the Treaty of Versailles offering defeated Germany not a just peace but humiliation. Stalin, at the helm of the communist revolutionary regime, posed a dire threat to the West. Italy and Germany embraced new radical regimes, also at odds with the democracies. Called "Fascist," they engaged in a titanic struggle with communism for the future of Europe, an ideological struggle that projected itself into the Spanish Civil War. By contrast, the democracies—even the United States—appeared to be on a retreat, seemingly incapable of solving the social and economic challenges of the time. Much of Lindbergh's analysis was shaped and conditioned by these political trends.

Throughout his tenure as military attaché, Truman Smith had observed the rapid remilitarization of Germany with alarm. Both Smith and Lindbergh viewed the German military juggernaut as a lethal force, fully capable of destroying the air forces of Great Britain and France. The advent of World War II in September 1939 gave ample evidence of the striking power of the *Luftwaffe*, a key component in Nazi

▲ This wartime German postage stamp portrays the Luftwaffe's dreaded Ju-87 Stuka dive bomber. Flying at the cutting edge of the German Blitzkrieg, the Stuka struck terror in the enemy. As the war progressed, however, it proved to be slow and vulnerable to Allied fighters.

▶ Adolf Hitler at Nuremberg Nazi Party rally, September 1938.

Germany's rapid victory over Poland. With the fall of France, Norway, and the Low Countries in 1940 and the narrow victory of the Royal Air Force over the *Luftwaffe* that same year, one could point to the essential accuracy of their prewar assessment of the German air arm. They had warned of the growing menace of the German military. However, what Smith and Lindbergh failed to comprehend were the strategic weaknesses of the *Luftwaffe*. Once caught up in the demands of a total war, the German war industries were dwarfed by the expansive manufacturing output of the Allies. The *Luftwaffe* looked invincible in the late 1930s; only in 1945 were Germany's inherent weaknesses fully apparent.[8]

As Robert Graves wrote in his social history of the interwar years, Hitler "seemed only an unpleasantly dynamic element in the world, ultimately manageable if the proper tactics were adopted."[9] As with fascist Italy, Germany—in its early years—became the object of praise by such luminaries as Arnold Toynbee and Lloyd George, not to mention emulation by Oswald Mosley and his group in England. Lindbergh was never alone in his praise of certain aspects of the "New Germany." He would be judged harshly in later decades for his moral indifference regarding the Nazi regime.

Some pundits arose to accuse both Smith and Lindbergh of being Nazi dupes, suggesting that their positive evaluations of the *Luftwaffe* reinforced defeatism and fueled the process of appeasement. These charges are largely unfounded, although Lindbergh did influence the thinking of Joseph Kennedy, then the American ambassador to Great Britain. The roots of appeasement were deeper, reflecting a broad-based sentiment in Europe that a negotiated peace was preferable to the carnage of another world war. Appeasement, in fact, possessed a certain moral appeal in those years; there were still vivid memories of the ten million casualties in World War I. A policy favoring negotiation over war, in the minds of many Europeans, was a noble undertaking, not an act of cowardice.

Lindbergh and Smith were both later attacked for what some called exaggerations in their intelligence work. While Lindbergh was disinclined to answer his critics, Smith was not. Writing in the 1950s, Smith fully acknowledged some errors, exaggerations, and omissions contained in his reports, but he affirmed that these intelligence reports had served the best interests of the United States, providing accurate data on German air rearmament. Smith's own retrospective critique of the shortcomings of these reports pointed to the failure of his staff to discern clearly German research on jet-aircraft development and rockets.[10] Both Smith and Lindbergh forcefully argued for the expansion of the American air forces as the logical policy spin-off from these reports.

While German affairs were at the epicenter of Lindbergh's life in the late 1930s, there were other important changes that defined his life. In the spring of 1938 he purchased a new home on

▲ Charles Lindbergh (center), *in formal garb, greets one of his German hosts at a reception. Although Lindbergh attended such events, he spent most of his time inspecting* Luftwaffe *facilities.*

Illiec, a small island off the coast of Brittany near the home of his mentor Alexis Carrel. With Carrel, Lindbergh completed his work on the book *The Culture of Organs*, and Anne finished her writing of *Listen! The Wind*. The association with Carrel was pivotal for Lindbergh in the development of his own philosophy of life, one that mirrored a growing interest in mystical and religious questions.

While in Berlin, Charles and Anne stayed with the Smiths, who occupied a large suite of rooms in their apartment in the Hotel Esplanade. Such proximity allowed a close friendship to develop, one where the Smiths provided a bridge to the German social and political scene. Kay Smith left perhaps the best description of the Lindberghs, as they appeared in the late 1930s. "I do remember," she recorded in her unpublished memoir, "that I found out very quickly Charles was not a person with whom one made light conversation, remarks simply to fill silences as one does in society."[11] She discovered that when you asked him a question, he would pause, meditate on the matter, and then answer in a deliberate way. He gave you, she remembered, "a genuine opinion," not his personal stream of consciousness. Typically, he rubbed his hand over his cheek and eyes in the course of a conversation. He discouraged trivialities or mindless chatter. When he asked questions he was direct and highly focused, always thoughtful and courteous in manner. He did have certain mannerisms that she remembered vividly: his tendency in conversation was to stand with his hands in his pockets, with one foot slightly forward for balance, his eyes narrowed "as he peered

ahead as though scanning the future, rather as one does on shipboard when searching the horizon."[12]

There were other aspects of Lindbergh that caught Kay Smith's attention, in particular his personal appearance. She felt he was "disdainful of usual social forms."[13] He wore blue or blue-gray suits invariably, except on rare occasions that required formal attire. She was surprised to see him once in a gray suit. Most of the time, he preferred informal clothes. Kay Smith remembered that he routinely kept a comb in his upper breast pocket and combed his hair before entering a building or a house, perhaps his only concession to personal appearance. He preferred black shoes, of a sturdy type to allow a chance for walking.

As a hostess for the Lindberghs, Kay Smith discovered that Charles did not drink any coffee, tea, or liquor, the latter a challenge in a world of festive dinners with numerous toasts. He explained that his abstinence was based on a personal goal of never being addicted to anything. He did drink a lot of milk, she remembered, and enjoyed eating cheeses and sweets, but for the most part he appeared "indifferent to food." He was always in excellent physical shape—for Lindbergh a necessary aspect of life, to allow him to walk away from any crash.

When Lindbergh first came to Berlin, both Truman and Kay Smith were apprehensive, having heard that he was "difficult" and aloof. Lindbergh's handshake, as she remembered, was firm, and always offered at some distance, even as he leaned forward slightly. He always sought out eye contact with whomever he was talking. Without fail, he was "very

▲ Anne Morrow Lindbergh on the cover of Life magazine.

◄ Charles and Anne Lindbergh are greeted by Ernst Heinkel (center) upon their arrival in Germany in July 1936. Heinkel would later open his aircraft factory to Lindbergh for inspection.

"Lindy" soft drink

polite, his manners excellent." He never enjoyed close bodily contact: "I recall that as we drove from the airport when we first met them at Tempelhof, we sat three in the back seat, he in the middle. It was a little cramped. I could feel him shrink away from me towards Anne. This was characteristic."[14] As a guest he was most considerate, always asking if any request was burdensome.

Lindbergh's typical facial expression was one of high seriousness, as Kay Smith remembered him in Berlin in the late 1930s. However, this façade could give way in an instant to a smile, his face aglow and his eyes vivid and twinkling. On occasion, Lindbergh's altered mood led to his legendary interest in pranks performed on his close friends. Once when Truman and Kay visited England, they drove in a car with the Lindberghs. Truman was seated in the back seat reading a newspaper spread out across his lap. Reaching back from the front seat, Lindbergh took a match and set the paper on fire at the center fold. Soon the flames moved up the paper, to the horror of Smith, who worked desperately to put out the flames. The prank prompted great laughter from Lindbergh.[15]

With Anne Lindbergh, Kay Smith developed a close relationship, one that endured over the years. "Anne had lovely brown eyes," according to Kay, "dark brown, slightly wavy hair, a very pointed chin, retroussé nose, a slight sideway twist to her lips while speaking."[16] She toyed constantly with her wedding ring, slipping the ring off and on repeatedly. The attaché's wife also noticed Anne's shyness,

A crowd of 10,000 gather in Chicago to hear Charles Lindbergh and other speakers for the America First Committee speak out against the United States entering the European war, April 23, 1941.

but there was an accompanying appreciation for her physical strength and resilience, notwithstanding her small stature. She was not fragile but rather a determined person, given to bouts of independence. When Charles was around and in the midst of a conversation, Anne was prone to silence. She was an excellent conversationalist, which was demonstrated more than once on the trips to Germany.

While hosting the Lindberghs, both Truman and Kay Smith were reminded of the peculiar burdens and hazards that came with celebrity. No sooner had the Lindberghs landed at Tempelhof than they were deluged with letters, most asking for money or special favors. When Kay Smith translated some of the letters written in German, she encountered several threats. At first, she paused and asked Charles if she should continue. He insisted that she read them in their entirety. Such letters were always retained, Charles told her, in case of some violent act against him or his family. "It gave me a sudden pang," Kay Smith recorded in her memoir, "to realize that he and Anne had to live all the time with this horrible experience and had to be prepared for a repetition. It was not until several years later that the kidnapping was mentioned between us."[17]

The winter of 1938–39 became a time of decision for Charles Lindbergh. His intelligence-gathering work for Truman Smith had been completed with his third and final inspection tour in October 1938. On his own, without the knowledge or assistance of Smith or his staff, Lindbergh arranged two additional trips in

▲ Charles and Anne Lindbergh shared the celebrity limelight in the 1930s. Both were well known for their promotion of aviation, in particular the development of commercial airlines. Anne learned to fly and became a licensed female glider pilot. The couple's lives were dramatically altered by the kidnapping and murder of their son, Charles A. Lindbergh Jr., in 1932.

December 1938 and January 1939 in an ill-fated attempt to arrange the purchase of German aero engines for the French. Launched in the eleventh hour, these trips expressed Lindbergh's vain hope that greater economic ties between the Western democracies and the Third Reich would foster peace. His efforts fell prey to hostile forces within the French government.

Even as these activities consumed Lindbergh's time and attention, the Munich crisis unfolded. German demands for the annexation of the Sudetenland, then part of Czechoslovakia, brought Europe close to war. Only at the last moment did the British and French relent, sacrificing the territorial integrity of Czechoslovakia for peace. Following this diplomatic triumph, Hitler quickly occupied the entire territory of Czechoslovakia in early 1939. Now Hitler could count a sequence of territorial annexations at the expense of his adversaries: the Rhineland in 1936, the integration of Austria into the Third Reich in 1938, and finally the Sudetenland in 1939. The only remaining objective was the Polish corridor, which separated Germany proper from East Prussia. Any move against Poland, many feared, would bring war.

Lindbergh observed these events with alarm, believing that war was near at hand. Now concerned about America's defenses, Lindbergh decided to return home in the spring of 1939, taking up temporary residence at the Morrow family home in Englewood, New Jersey. Lindbergh acted on principle.

franklin delano roosevelt

When Charles Lindbergh made his transatlantic flight in 1927, Franklin Delano Roosevelt was the governor of New York, already a national figure trumpeted as a future candidate for president. Roosevelt joined other Americans in welcoming Lindbergh home, even asking for a photograph of the new air hero. Later, in 1932, then-governor Roosevelt mobilized his state police to seek out the kidnappers of the Lindbergh child. These warm and positive gestures on the part of Franklin Roosevelt contrasted sharply with his negative stance toward Lindbergh later in that same decade, when, as president of the United States, he openly clashed with the Lone Eagle in the great debate over America's neutrality.

The Roosevelt-Lindbergh clash on the eve of World War II is remembered for its partisan rancor and mutual recrimination, but the origins of the conflict run deeper than the debate over nonintervention. The first sharp encounter between the two men occurred in 1934, at the time Roosevelt was entering the second year of his presidency and was at the height of his popularity. That year, Roosevelt decided to cancel existing airmail contracts with civilian carriers. His actions were based on the alleged fraud and

Charles Lindbergh *(center)* at an America First rally

corruption in awarding airmail contracts. A senate committee under the chairmanship of Hugo Black (who later became a Supreme Court justice) had exposed a widespread pattern of monopolistic practices in the infant aviation industry. Roosevelt was angered at this situation and decided to act, in this case in an arbitrary fashion. He ordered the army air corps to deliver the mail. With no experience, army air corps pilots assumed responsibility for flying twenty-seven airmail routes.

Roosevelt faced widespread criticism for his action, and Lindbergh quickly joined the chorus of critics. He sent a telegram to the president complaining of the unfairness of the cancellation order. Lindbergh was alarmed that all the commercial airmail carriers had been assumed guilty without a trial. Moreover, the Lone Eagle—once an airmail pilot himself—warned of disaster if untrained military pilots were suddenly asked to fly the airmail on an emergency basis.

Lindbergh's warnings proved prophetic. On the first day of the army airmail service, February 19, 1934, the northern states were hit with snow, rain, and fog. Flying in open cockpits in this unusually severe winter weather, the inexperienced army pilots proved unequal to the task. A series of unfortunate crashes, with numerous fatalities, followed. An angry Roosevelt eventually had to reduce and then end the army's involvement in the airmail and turn its delivery over to commercial airlines and contractors.

For Roosevelt, this defeat—and the role of air hero Charles Lindbergh as one of his most vocal critics—was deeply resented. Neither man ever forgot the acrimonious days of the airmail crisis of 1934.

President Franklin D. Roosevelt speaking on a pre-invasion Fireside Chat radio program

MBS NBC

He felt that the existing American air strength was totally inadequate when compared with Nazi Germany's. Deeply committed to a policy of nonintervention in the event of a European war, Lindbergh also remained a strong advocate of an American military buildup, one that would assure an adequate defense against any potential enemy. While on the boat on his return voyage to the United States, Lindbergh received a radiogram from General H. H. "Hap" Arnold, then chief of the U.S. Army Air Corps, requesting a meeting as soon as possible. Upon arrival, Lindbergh gave Arnold and his staff a detailed briefing on the *Luftwaffe*, covering a gamut of topics from personnel and equipment to operational plans. So impressed was Arnold with the Lindbergh report that he encouraged Lindbergh to go on active duty in order to play an influential role in shaping the development of American air power. Lindbergh declined, for fear such status would require him to remain silent on critical issues of war and peace. By the fall of 1939, Europe was at war. Lindbergh's embrace of nonintervention ran counter to President Roosevelt's policy of informal support of Britain and France. For Lindbergh, there was now a challenge to find a way to retain his links with the air corps even as he opposed the Roosevelt policy.

On September 15, 1939, less than two weeks after Europe went to war, Lindbergh delivered his first speech calling for the United States to remain neutral. He gave the

▼ In September 1939, Lindbergh took to the airwaves to call for American neutrality in the conflict. His crusade for nonintervention consumed great energy, and in the end led the famed aviator into partisan politics and controversy.

speech over radio from Washington, D.C. "We must band together," Lindbergh stated, "to prevent the loss of more American lives in these internal struggles of Europe. We must keep foreign propaganda from pushing our country blindly into another war. . . . We should never enter a war unless it is absolutely essential to the future welfare of our nation."[18] In November 1939, Lindbergh expanded his commentary on the issues at stake in an article in *Readers' Digest*, "Aviation, Geography, and Race." Aviation, he argued, had altered notions of time and distance, placing "a premium on quickness of thought and speed of action." There were dangers facing the Western nations, with Asia pressing against them at the Russian border. For Lindbergh, it was necessary for Western civilization to defend itself against either a "Genghis Khan or the infiltration of inferior blood." He compared the internal conflicts of the West with those of ancient Athens and Sparta, where a whole civilization found itself in peril because of its lack of unity.

This article pushed Lindbergh's foreign policy posture disastrously into a new realm, one with racist overtones. Lindbergh had grown up in a cultural context where such ideas were common. Aviation, in particular, seemed defined by certain racial ideas. The U.S. Army Air Corps, for example, barred blacks from pilot training because of the widely held notion that blacks lacked the aptitude to fly, a product of their racial makeup. General Billy Mitchell stated in his book *Skyways* that "breeding and environment have a great deal to do with the individual making a good pilot or a poor one. Just as the Anglo-Saxons and Scandinavians made the best navigators the world has ever seen, so the people of Anglo-Saxon and Norse stock make excellent pilots."[19] Lindbergh shared this widespread Anglo-Saxon ethnocentrism and adapted it to his evolving posture on nonintervention.

Seeking an outlet to rally his countrymen, Lindbergh, by nature not a joiner, associated himself with the America First movement. Organized in September 1940, the America First Committee eventually drew a national following of 800,000 members, all dedicated to keeping the United States neutral. A diverse group of national figures were drawn to the movement: politicians such as senators Bennett Champ Clark, Burton K. Wheeler, Gerald Nye, and William E. Borah; university presidents such as Alan Valentine and Robert Maynard Hutchins; business leaders such as General Robert E. Wood; political activists such as perennial socialist candidate Norman Thomas; and an array of pacifists, lawyers, students, and foreign-policy traditionalists. This broad-based alliance was held together by a simple proposition that American democracy could be preserved only by keeping the country out of a foreign war and building impregnable defenses at home.

Lindbergh, for certain, did not share a common set of values with many members of

▲ *Members of the America First Committee. America First was a broad coalition of Americans with over 800,000 members. Even on the eve of the Japanese attack on Pearl Harbor on December 7, 1941, a vast majority of Americans favored nonintervention rather than war.*

America First, but he was willing to coordinate his own work with the larger noninterventionist movement. His many speeches between 1939 and 1941 did much to advance the cause of American neutrality. In radio addresses and rallies, Lindbergh made his rounds as a crusader for nonintervention. On September 11, 1941, in a speech in Des Moines, Iowa, Lindbergh sparked real controversy. There he argued that three groups were pressing the United States to enter the war: the British, the Roosevelt administration, and Jewish activists. By mentioning the Jews, Lindbergh appeared to have crossed a line into racial bigotry. While he couched his charge with qualifiers and sympathies for the plight of Jews in Germany, Lindbergh's Des Moines speech prompted a torrent of criticism. No less important, many began to abandon the aviator for his alleged anti-Semitism. Wisely, Anne Lindbergh had urged him to omit any reference to Jews in his speech, for in her opinion making such reference would be like "lighting a match next to a heap of excelsior."

President Roosevelt viewed Lindbergh's activism as a real threat. He sincerely believed that support of Great Britain was essential to American security, if not to civilization itself, but was constrained by the Neutrality Act of 1935, which required an arms embargo in any state of belligerency. Support of neutrality was widespread prior to Pearl Harbor. Even as late as the summer of 1941, the Selective Service Act passed by only one vote.

WHY THE AFC?

The overwhelming majority of Americans — 80 to 90 per cent — are strongly opposed to going to war in Europe or Asia. The America First Committee was organized and has grown to give expression to this sentiment.

Americans are concerned with solving American problems first. The America First Committee was organized and has grown to express the yearnings of Americans for a better American democracy.

The America First Committee is not trying to sell anything to the people or impose anything on them. It is the spontaneous expression of the majority of the people against participation in foreign war.

WHO IS BEHIND IT?

You are behind it. You and numberless thousands of patriotic Americans like you. The America First Committee was organized because you wanted and needed such an organization. It has grown and become powerful because you have supported it with your effort and your money.

The leaders of the America First Committee are respected Americans from all walks of life who have served and are serving their country valiantly on the battle-grounds of war and peace. They are leaders in whom the people have confidence.

The America First Committee is American from top to bottom. It has no truck with totalitarians of any kind—nazis, fascists, communists. It is opposed to them and opposed to Americans who will not defend democracy.

So long as you are behind it, there will be an America First Committee.

WHAT DOES IT DO?

The activities of the America First Committee are based on the democratic principle that the people rule.

The people—who are opposed to war—have the right and the duty to make their voices heard. They must organize. They must write (and sign petitions) to their President, their Senators, their Congressmen. They must hold meetings. They must write to their newspapers. They must talk to their friends. They must make their voices heard.

The members of the America First Committee do all these things. It is the American way. When you join the America First Committee and take part in its activities, you are making democracy work.

The people still rule. If you are pushed into war against your will, you will have only yourself to blame.

"THE PATH TO WAR IS A FALSE PATH TO FREEDOM"

America First literature

america first

Charles Lindbergh returned to the United States in early 1939, and he soon found himself caught up in the great debate over American neutrality. War broke out in Europe in September of that year, and then in late spring of 1940, the Germans advanced into the Low Countries and France, decisively defeating the British and French armies. Britain now stood alone. President Roosevelt desired to assist the beleaguered British, but he still presided over a nation favoring neutrality. After the election of 1940, Roosevelt became more open in his support of the Allied cause, winning congressional support for material aid with the Lend Lease Act and taking overt steps, short of war, to demonstrate American opposition to Nazi Germany.

Many Americans expressed alarm at the United States' gradual drift toward war, either as a belligerent or informally as a supplier of arms to the embattled Allied forces. Behind this sentiment was an older tradition of American isolationism. But there was also a diverse group of Americans who fervently desired to avoid any repetition of World War I, where American human and material sacrifices had not led to an enduring peace. Even on the eve of Pearl Harbor, a majority of Americans favored nonintervention.

The America First Committee became the major voice calling for the preservation of America's neutrality. It was

Charles Lindbergh speaks to an antiwar rally in Minneapolis on May 10, 1941.

formally organized in September 1940, with a broad coalition of participants drawn from the entire spectrum of American politics. At its zenith, America First had over four hundred chapters and some 800,000 members, including politicians, academics, prominent businessmen, peace activists, and common citizens opposed to the war. Robert S. Wood, president of Sears Roebuck, led the movement. The advent of America First prompted the formation of a counter organization, the Committee to Defend America by Aiding the Allies.

Lindbergh's popularity and fame soon pushed him to the forefront of the noninterventionist forces as a spokesman for the America First Committee. He made his debut as a speaker on October 30, 1940, at Yale University. Lindbergh had feared open hostility at Yale, but he was gratified with the warm response, even the thunderous applause of his audience. Emboldened by the experience, he joined the ranks of America First, an alliance of citizens whose bipartisanship and

Antiwar demonstrators march through Times Square in New York City.

separation from radical fringe elements he found appealing. Lindbergh's advocacy of non-intervention in numerous speeches, radio addresses, and articles soon won him many enemies, including the hostility of Harold Ickes, the secretary of the interior, who accused him of being the "No. 1 Nazi fellow traveler."

The Japanese attack on Pearl Harbor on December 7, 1941, abruptly ended the great debate on the war. The America First Committee quickly dissolved, with most of its members actively supporting the war effort against the Axis powers.

President Franklin D. Roosevelt signs a bill into law.

From 1939 to 1941, Lindbergh delivered numerous public addresses about nonintervention and neutrality. The following are excerpts:

We must band together to prevent the loss of more American lives in these internal struggles of Europe. . . . Modern war with all its consequences is too tragic and too devastating to be approached from anything but a purely American standpoint. We should never enter a war unless it is absolutely essential to the future welfare of our nation. . . .

These wars in Europe are not wars in which our civilization is defending itself against some Asiatic intruder. There is no Genghis Khan nor Xerxes marching against our Western nations. This is not a question of banding together to defend the white race against foreign invasion. This is simply one more of those age-old struggles within our own family of nations—a quarrel arising from the errors of the last war—from the failure of the victors of that war to follow a consistent policy either of fairness or of force.
—September 15, 1939

With an adequate defense, no foreign army can invade us. Our advantage in defending America is as great as our disadvantage in attacking Europe. From a military geographical standpoint, we are the most fortunate country in the world. There is no other nation in this hemisphere strong enough to even consider attacking us, and the Atlantic and Pacific Oceans separate us from the warring armies of Europe and Asia. . . . As far as invasion by air is concerned, it is impossible for any existing air force to attack effec-

tively across the ocean. . . . America stands today where the road divides, at the signpost of war and peace.
—June 15, 1940

There is a policy open to this nation that will lead to success—a policy that will leave us free to follow our own way of life, and to develop our own civilization. It is not a new and untried idea. It was advocated by Washington. It was incorporated in the Monroe Doctrine. Under its guidance, the United States became the greatest nation in the world. It is based upon the belief that the security of a nation lies in the strength and character of its own people. It recommends the maintenance of armed forces sufficient to defend this hemisphere from attack by any combination of foreign powers. It demands faith in an independent American destiny. This is the policy of the America First Committee today. It is a policy, not of isolation, but of independence; not of defeat, but of courage. It is a policy that led this nation to success during the most trying years of our history, and it is a policy that will lead us to success again.
—April 23, 1941

The three most important groups who have been pressing this country toward war are the British, the Jewish and the Roosevelt administration. . . . These war agitators comprise only a small minority of our people; but they control a tremendous influence. . . .

It is obvious and perfectly understandable that Great Britain wants the United States in the war on her side. England is now in a desperate position. Her population is not large enough and her armies are not strong enough to invade the continent of Europe and win the war she declared against Germany. . . .

The second major group I mentioned is the Jewish. It is not difficult to understand why Jewish people desire the overthrow of Nazi Germany. The persecution they suffered in Germany would be sufficient to make bitter enemies of any race. No person with a sense of the dignity of mankind can condone the persecution of the Jewish race in Germany. But no person of honesty and vision can look on their pro-war policy here today without seeing the dangers involved in such a policy both for us and for them. . . .

I am not attacking either the Jewish or the British people. Both races, I admire. But I am saying that the leaders of both the British and the Jewish races, for reasons which are as understandable from their viewpoint as they are inadvisable from ours, for reasons which are not American, wish to involve us in the war. We cannot blame them for looking out for what they believe to be their own interests, but we also must look out for ours. . . .
—September 11, 1941, known as the Des Moines speech

Roosevelt's program to make the United States the "arsenal of democracy" advanced with considerable opposition. Lindbergh's attack on Roosevelt's clandestine moves to support the British—Atlantic patrols against submarines, the "shoot on sight" policy, and arming merchant ships in the European war zone—greatly alarmed the administration.

Roosevelt initially offered Lindbergh the sub-cabinet-level position of secretary of air on the condition that he refrain from speaking out openly against the administration. Lindbergh summarily refused to accept the offer, a reminder to Roosevelt that he could not be bought. Now viewing Lindbergh as an implacable enemy, Roosevelt unleashed a campaign to discredit him. The cynical tactics employed anticipated the smear campaigns and spin artistry in subsequent decades of American history. Secretary of the Interior Harold Ickes led a group of Lindbergh critics both within and outside the Roosevelt administration. Ickes referred to Lindbergh's political views as pro-Nazi and unpatriotic and called him a "ruthless and conscious fascist."[20] The campaign also included efforts at wiretapping and surveillance and even an investigation by the attorney general of the finances of the America First Committee. Finally, Roosevelt himself voiced his open opposition to Lindbergh in April 1941, accusing the aviator of being a "copperhead" in American politics.

▲ *Secretary of the Interior Harold Ickes became the Roosevelt administration's most outspoken critic of Charles Lindbergh. With a flair for invective, Ickes painted Lindbergh as a Nazi sympathizer.*

◄ *President Roosevelt signs the Selective Service Act in 1940, establishing a pool of men eligible for military service in case of war.*

Lindbergh himself stoically endured the many slurs that came his way in the great debate over intervention—being charged as a traitor, a fascist, Hitler's *gauleiter* for America—but the president's charge of being a "copperhead" moved him to a fateful decision: He decided to resign his reserve commission in the air corps. Throughout this bitter debate, in the words of Anne Lindbergh, "he wrote his own speeches and, to the dismay of friends and foes alike, took no one's advice."[21] She realized, too, that her husband was no politician, a man ill-equipped to handle the darker side of partisan politics. Consistently, Lindbergh remained principled and incorruptible, even as public perception of him became more negative.

The great debate over intervention in the war came to a sudden and dramatic conclusion Sunday, December 7, 1941, when the Japanese navy attacked Pearl Harbor. History had overwhelmed Charles Lindbergh. His crusade for nonintervention was now irrelevant. On December 8, through the America First Committee, Lindbergh issued a statement in support of a vigorous prosecution of the war.

Charles Lindbergh had promptly committed himself to the war, a conflict thrust on the United States by an aggressive adversary. The question now was whether the hero of the Atlantic and the ardent defender of traditional American noninterventionism would be welcomed into the war effort.

MAY 1942

Japanese conquer the northern shore of New Guinea. This sets the stage for the Fifth Air Force to participate in liberation of the area.

DEC. 7, 1941

The Japanese attack Pearl Harbor; two days later, the United States officially enters World War II.

JUNE 1942

The Battle of Midway

1941

1942

1943

DEC. 1941

General "Hap" Arnold, chief of the U.S. Army Air Corps, ignores Lindbergh's appeal to rejoin the corps.

JAN. 12, 1942

Lindbergh appeals to the secretary of war, Henry L. Stimson, about his commission and is again rebuffed.

APRIL 1, 1942

Lindbergh departs for Detroit, Michigan, to work for Ford Motor Company, testing B-24 Liberator bombers.

APRIL 18, 1942

Colonel James Doolittle leads B-25 bombers in bold mission over Japan, bringing the war to Japan's home islands.

AUGUST 7, 1942

American marines establish beachhead on Guadalcanal, signaling the long drive to Japan.

AUGUST 12, 1942

The Lindberghs' fourth son, Scott, is born.

APRIL 18, 1943

American P-38s intercept and kill Admiral Isoroku Yamamoto, the Japanese navy commander.

JULY 22, 1943

The Italian government of Benito Mussolini falls as Allied armies near victory in the Italian campaign.

MAY 1944

Japanese finally driven from outposts in New Guinea.

JUNE 19–20, 1944

The Battle of Philippine Sea

OCT. 25–26, 1944

The Battle of Leyte Gulf

NOV. 5, 1944

After suffering from a serious heart attack in August, Alexis Carrel dies in Paris.

AUGUST 6, 1945

In response to Japan's refusal to respond to the demands of the Potsdam Declaration, the United States destroys the Japanese city of Hiroshima with an atomic bomb. Three days later, a second bomb is dropped on Nagasaki.

1944   1945   1946

JAN. 24, 1944

Lindbergh leaves San Diego for the South Pacific to fly some 50 combat missions as a civilian technical assistant.

MAY 8, 1945

V-E Day: President Truman and Prime Minister Churchill declare the end of war in Europe.

MAY 30, 1945

Besieged in his bunker in Berlin, Hitler commits suicide.

SEPT. 2, 1945

Japan's foreign minister signs documents on board the U.S.S. *Missouri*, officially ending the war in the Pacific.

OCT. 2, 1945

The Lindberghs' second daughter, Reeve, is born.

Pearl Harbor—December 7, 1941—signaled the abrupt transition from peace to war for the United States. For Charles Lindbergh, the Japanese attack on the American bases in Hawaii ended his two-year campaign to keep America out of war. "I believed," Lindbergh

shadow warrior

wrote retrospectively in his memoir *Autobiography of Values*, "that a second world-wide conflict within a quarter-century would result in the decline, if not the destruction, of our Western civilization."[1] To avert such a catastrophe, Lindbergh gave speeches, spoke on the radio, wrote magazine articles, and even testified before congressional committees of the House and the Senate in a vain quest to preserve America's neutrality. Never a pacifist or defeatist, he had advocated the complementary policies of building up America's armed forces to ensure national security

General Robert Wood *(right)*, national chairman of the America First Committee, looks on as Colonel Charles Lindbergh makes his maiden speech to 10,000 people there to express support for a policy of isolationism and an end to all aid to Britain.

and using American influence to bring about a negotiated peace in Europe. Yet, in Lindbergh's words, "the prowar forces were too great and influential. Step by step, the United States was maneuvered into a position that inevitably brought war. When the Japanese attacked Pearl Harbor . . . we had no practical alternative but to enter the fighting."[2]

Lindbergh's first instinct in the aftermath of Pearl Harbor was to find a way to reorient his life toward the new war emergency. Having been one of the most visible public figures in opposition to war, he felt compelled to affirm his patriotism and his desire to serve his country. On December 8, 1941, through the auspices of the America First Committee, he issued an unambiguous statement calling for national unity and common purpose: "Our own defenses and our own military position have already been neglected too long. We must now turn every effort to building up the greatest and most efficient army, navy, and air force in the world. When American soldiers go to war, it must be with the best equipment that modern skill can design and modern industry can build."[3]

Given his past military service and intelligence work for the war department, Lindbergh believed naively that he could quickly reestablish his links with the air corps. To hasten the process, he decided to seek out an interview with General H. H. "Hap" Arnold, the air commander. But he soon learned

▲ A patriotic poster calling for victory against the Axis powers, in this case Japan.

▼ View of Battleship Row in Pearl Harbor on December 7, 1941. In the foreground, the USS Arizona bellows smoke from its sunken hull. Of the crew of 1,731 men, 1,177 perished in the attack.

General Arnold, once a most accessible and friendly contact, was now an elusive figure in Washington. When Lindbergh personally approached Arnold's staff for a meeting, he encountered only vague promises, the telltale evidence of a runaround. He then sent General Arnold a personal note, offering his services. In this same note, Lindbergh made reference vaguely to the "complications" of the recent past, his way of saying that he would like to get past the partisan rancor of recent years. Eventually Arnold responded with a note of appreciation, but nothing more.

Later, when Arnold mentioned Lindbergh's offer on the radio, the issue became public for the first time. A flurry of commentary followed, much of it emotional and partisan in character. In an editorial comment, the *New York Times* struck a positive note and endorsed Lindbergh's overture as "a symbol of new-found unity and an effective means of burying the past."[4] Most of the American press, however, did not share this spirit of reconciliation, with some columnists again attacking Lindbergh for his alleged fascist sympathies, anti-Semitism, and borderline treason. The debate over Lindbergh—coming as a sort of aftershock in the earthquake of Pearl Harbor—would prove to be a momentary issue for an American public now overwhelmed with the reality of a world war. No less important, the America First Committee, the erstwhile major voice for nonintervention, had dissolved itself voluntarily, and many of its most prominent members rushed to support the war mobilization effort. For Lindbergh, though, there was still the daunting problem of finding his place in the scheme of things.

At this point in his life, Lindbergh still maintained an optimistic outlook. Having been rebuffed by Arnold, he decided to go to the top, to appeal to Henry L. Stimson, the secretary of war. Stimson met with Lindbergh on January 12, 1942. Impatient with the many delays, Lindbergh pressed Stimson on his proposal for service with the air corps. Now compelled to be candid for the first time, Stimson told Lindbergh that he could not ignore the prewar debate on intervention. Moreover, he acknowledged his reluctance to put Lindbergh in any position of command, fearing he would not "carry on the war

▼ President Franklin Roosevelt shakes hands with his newly appointed secretary of war, Henry L. Stimson, on July 10, 1940. Stimson opposed Lindbergh's reentry into the U.S. Army Air Corps, arguing that his prewar statements on Nazi Germany raised serious questions about his fitness to lead in the American military.

with sufficient aggressiveness."[5] Lindbergh tried in vain to put forward his essential argument that once America was at war, he stood behind his country. In response, Stimson only offered to refer the matter to Robert Lovett, his assistant secretary for air, to explore the possibility of Lindbergh taking on some noncommand function. Within a short period of time this gesture proved to be an empty one, a way to deflect Lindbergh from the war department.

Unbeknown to Lindbergh at the time, President Roosevelt had received memoranda from cabinet members on the matter of Lindbergh's reenlistment in the air corps. Lindbergh's old nemesis, Harold Ickes, predictably took an extreme viewpoint, encouraging Roosevelt to deny Lindbergh any avenue for war service. Among its many charges, Ickes's letter accused Lindbergh of being a "loyal friend of Hitler" and a ruthless enemy of American democracy. Secretary of the Navy Frank Knox echoed Ickes's firm opposition, if not the invective of the Ickes letter, suggesting a novel way to handle Lindbergh. Knox proposed to the president that he give Lindbergh the humiliating offer of enlisting again as an air cadet. Roosevelt himself retained vivid memories of his past struggles with the Lone Eagle on issues as varied as the airmail crisis to the great debate on American neutrality. His intention to punish Lindbergh became evident in a conversation with some senators when he remarked candidly, "I'll clip that young man's wings."[6] Even at

"I have seen the science I worshipped, and the aircraft I loved, destroying the civilization I expected them to serve." —Charles A. Lindbergh

the highest echelons of power, Charles Lindbergh learned, there would be no Lincoln-style generosity toward former adversaries.

Frozen out, Lindbergh now realized his personal contribution to America's effort would have to be made as a civilian in the shadows and outside the imprimatur of the Roosevelt administration. However, when he turned to several old friends in the civilian sphere, there was evidence that Roosevelt's hostility had a chilling effect on those predisposed to help him. Even Juan Trippe, a longtime associate and the head of Pan American World Airways, felt intimidated. He offered Lindbergh a job, only to withdraw it once he discerned the extreme negative reaction of the administration. Now anyone with a major government contract realized that the famed aviator had become a persona non grata.

Among all the industrialists mobilized for the war, Henry Ford alone possessed the power and independence

▼ Lindbergh with Edsel (left) and Henry Ford (right). Lindbergh's close ties with Henry Ford proved helpful with the coming of World War II, when Ford hired him to assist in bomber production.

to resist the Roosevelt campaign to cast Lindbergh into outer darkness. Boldly, Ford extended a timely offer to Lindbergh to join him at his Willow Run plant in Michigan as a technical advisor in the manufacture of the B-24 Liberator bomber. Ford's overture suddenly extended legitimacy to the beleaguered aviator, offering not only meaningful work in military aviation but a platform from which to seek out future avenues of war service. Ford's hiring of Lindbergh went unchallenged by the administration, which was preoccupied by other, more compelling, priorities. Ford was too essential to the war effort to be unduly pressed on the matter, however unacceptable his actions appeared to some in Washington.

Ever a maverick, Ford had acted on personal principle, and Lindbergh deeply appreciated his gesture. Lindbergh and Ford had forged their friendship in 1927, when Lindbergh landed the *Spirit of St. Louis* in Detroit on his forty-eight-state tour. On that stop, Lindbergh took Ford up for his first airplane ride. Lindbergh recalled, "He sat, with obvious delight, on one arm of my pilot's seat, hunched into a low and narrow cockpit that had been designed for me alone. Previously, he had refused to fly with anyone, even in the trimotor passenger planes his own company was building."[7] Ford now wanted his former pilot around to advise him on how best to design his massive bomber plant.

Lindbergh considered Ford to be a genius, if an eccentric one. Ford took great pride in his past achievements, in particular his factories' manufacturing low-cost cars for millions. Now, for the production of the B-24 bomber, he presided over a vast factory complex of assembly lines, machinery, jigs, and thousands of workers. Often he invited Lindbergh to join him for inspection tours, beginning with the blast furnaces and rolling mills at "The Rouge" and continuing to some of his smaller factories in the countryside. "Sometimes," Lindbergh wrote in his memoirs, "he would come to my office, sit on my desk in his favorite leg-swinging position, and talk about creating a Parliament of Man to prevent war in the future. His vice president Harry H. Bennett and I would head it."[8]

Working on the B-24 project, even with the welcoming environment, presented certain problems for loner Charles Lindbergh. The hierarchical organization and tight regimentation that went with the twenty-four-hour, seven-day-a-week factory operations did not suit his preference for solitary action.

▲ *Lindbergh notes opposition from the Roosevelt administration in a letter to his friend William Robertson.*

▼ *Male and female workers at the Ford Willow Run plant in Dearborn, Michigan, install an engine in a B-24 Liberator bomber.*

Grappling with technical problems or test-flying the B-24 brought satisfaction, but Lindbergh yearned for alternative modes of work. One meaningful avenue for special work came from the Mayo Clinic in Rochester, Minnesota, where Lindbergh volunteered to be tested in a one-man altitude chamber to see how low atmospheric pressure affected breathing, mental acuity, and body temperature. His study of these effects at several simulated altitudes represented a major contribution to flight medicine. While in Michigan, Lindbergh also served as a test pilot with the Republic P-47 Thunderbolt fighter, working on flight emergency procedures and the redesign of the aircraft's hatch. On one test flight at high altitude, he suffered oxygen deprivation and lost consciousness temporarily, the first of many narrow encounters with death in the war years.

Being at the Ford Willow Run plant required an extended period of work in the Detroit area, so Charles took great pains to find a suitable rental residence for Anne and his four children. (His youngest son, Scott, was born in 1942.) They found a rental home in Bloomfield Hills, which became the Lindbergh home for the duration of the war. Charles's mother still lived in the Detroit area, so the shift in residence to Michigan afforded a rare opportunity to live in close proximity to Evangeline Lindbergh, a woman still actively engaged in teaching during the 1940s. Since returning to the United States in 1939, Charles and Anne had not enjoyed a permanent home.

henry ford

Lindbergh flew the *Spirit of St. Louis* to Ford Airport in Dearborn, Michigan, in August 1927. Less than three months had passed since his epic transatlantic flight. Now a global celebrity, Lindbergh encountered an enthusiastic crowd of 60,000 people when he landed at nearby Detroit, the city of his birth.

Landing at Dearborn allowed the young Lindbergh to meet the automobile pioneer Henry Ford for the first time. Ford himself had diversified his empire by manufacturing his own trimotor airliner. But this venture into the new world of commercial aviation expressed his business instincts, not any personal love of flying—in fact, the terrestrial-bound Ford had refused to fly, even in one of his own planes. Caught up in the moment, however, Ford agreed to go for a plane ride with the famed aviator. Despite his fears, he enjoyed the flight, even when forced to hunch down in the crowded cockpit next to Lindbergh. A friendship between Ford and Lindbergh developed as a result of this remarkable flight in the summer of 1927.

While interested in commercial aviation as a new arena for manufacture, Ford never let the temptation move him away from his first love, the manufacture of automobiles. Lindbergh attempted to enlist Ford's support in the late 1920s in the development of an air transportation system. Ford had experimented with the development of a commercial airliner in the mid-1920s, with the design of the Ford Tri-Motor. The Ford all-metal, high-wing monoplane with its distinctive corrugated skin became a popular airplane, purchased by several fledgling airlines. The Tri-Motor mirrored the Ford emphasis on simple and durable construction, a sort of Model T of the air. Edsel Ford, the son and heir to Henry Ford, aimed to manufacture two thousand of these "flivver planes," but his proposal was rejected by his father, thus ending the Ford Motor Company's endeavors in aviation. Edsel Ford, however, did prevail on one point: He instructed Ford dealerships across the country to paint the names of their hometowns on the roofs of their garages as a navigation aid to pilots.

Many years passed after the celebrated ride of Henry Ford with Charles Lindbergh, but the two men met again in 1942. This encounter came in an altered context, at a time when the United States was at war and Ford's Willow Run plant had been converted to manufacture B-24 Liberator bombers. Because of his prewar views on nonintervention, Lindbergh found himself isolated and denied any formal avenue to contribute to the war effort. Ford came to his rescue, offering the embattled aviator a consulting job on the B-24 project. Ford's timely gesture offered legitimacy and a concrete way for Lindbergh to demonstrate his patriotism. The interlude at Willow Run

Passengers board a Ford Tri-Motor.

The Ford Flivver was the prototype for a mass produced airplane for the common man, but it was never put into production.

proved to be redemptive for Lindbergh, and he profoundly appreciated Ford's helping hand at a critical moment in his life.

Detroit possessed a special significance for Lindbergh, being the place of his birth and the hometown of his mother, Evangeline Lindbergh. Beginning in 1922 his mother taught at Cass Technical High School, a position she would hold for twenty years. Ford considered Lindbergh to be a hometown boy. With the offer to join the B-24 team, Lindbergh moved to Detroit with his family.

The B-24 Liberator was a huge four-engine bomber destined to play a critical role in America's strategic bombing campaign in World War II. The mass production of the B-24 Liberator at Willow Run struck Lindbergh as a "giant ant hill," but he found a way as a civilian consultant to contribute to the project. Lindbergh felt deeply loyal to Ford for his friendship and timely offer of a job when most avenues to participate in the war effort had been closed to him.

Working with Henry Ford in 1942 and 1943 only deepened Lindbergh's assessment of the automobile pioneer as a maverick and a genius. Ford's mass-production techniques had revolutionized the auto industry, making reliable and inexpensive vehicles available to the common man. In the context of war mobilization, Lindbergh appreciated the impact of Ford's techniques; the United States quickly emerged as a military power, waging war on two fronts and becoming for the Allied cause the "Arsenal of Democracy." Like Ford, Lindbergh was largely untutored, a self-taught engineer, but a person at home with all sorts of technology.

Lindbergh was less impressed with Ford's social views, considering his call for a "Parliament of Man" eccentric and impractical. Ford, in fact, had invited Lindbergh to become part of this visionary ruling body that would guarantee future peace. He had sympathized with Lindbergh in the great debate on neutrality in the prewar years, which offered another common bond between the two men. One consequence of this posture had been a significant degree of public ostracism. Ford was often criticized in the prewar years for his highly controversial views, in particular his overt anti-Semitism and his stubborn opposition to labor unions. Even if they shared common political adversaries, Ford and Lindbergh often pursued separate goals in life, and they were quite different men. However, they discovered that their interests at times did intersect, and there was a feeling of mutual admiration between the two men.

Will Rogers (left) and Lindbergh peer out the cockpit of a Ford Tri-Motor.

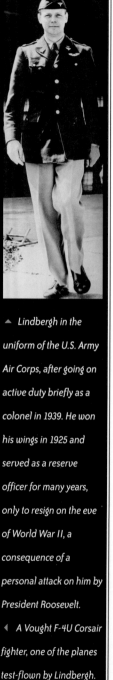

▲ *Lindbergh in the uniform of the U.S. Army Air Corps, after going on active duty briefly as a colonel in 1939. He won his wings in 1925 and served as a reserve officer for many years, only to resign on the eve of World War II, a consequence of a personal attack on him by President Roosevelt.*

◄ *A Vought F-4U Corsair fighter, one of the planes test-flown by Lindbergh.*

His constant travel, first as a lecturer for nonintervention and then as an aviation consultant, put strains on the marriage, although there was never a time when Charles had so eagerly sought out closer emotional ties with his wife and family. A lifestyle of constant movement and forced separation, so evident in the war years, established a fateful precedent for the duration of their married life.

As the year 1942 drew to a close, Lindbergh began to make a series of trips to East Hartford, Connecticut, to assist United Aircraft in testing their new navy/marine fighter, the Vought F-4U Corsair. The sleek, gull-winged fighter was destined to make a dramatic impact on the air war in the Pacific. As a test pilot, Lindbergh enjoyed flying this highly maneuverable airplane. His mastery of the Corsair was tested in a mock gunnery contest one day with two of the marines' best pilots. The forty-one-year-old Lindbergh, to the surprise of his younger adversaries, carried the day, outperforming them in both maneuver and gunnery.[9]

Work with United Aircraft in Connecticut extended into July 1943, with some eight separate trips from Michigan. Technical consultation on the F-4U Corsair increasingly commanded Lindbergh's time and his soul. Going back to his air corps days he had identified himself as a fighter pilot, and his work for United Aircraft brought him close to that reality in the war context. In January 1944, Lindbergh approached U.S. Marine Corps General Louis Wood to explore new avenues for his work, already prized by United Aircraft and gaining note with the prime customer for the Corsair, the marines. These discussions

with General Wood opened the
way for Lindbergh to inspect
marine air bases in the states and
later in the Pacific.

While in California on his
way to the Pacific Theater,
Lindbergh visited the marine
squadron of a young pilot named
John Glenn. The future astronaut found Lindbergh's
skills as a pilot of the highest order, a harbinger for
the positive reaction of military pilots in the Pacific to
Lindbergh's work as a civilian pilot-consultant.
Without the knowledge or approval of Frank Knox,
the secretary of the navy, Lindbergh departed from
San Diego on April 24, 1944. For his work at the
marine air bases, "technical representative" Lindbergh
purchased standard navy uniforms, which he wore
without any insignia of rank.

For those who fought there in the 1940s (a time
when air travel was uncommon), the Pacific Ocean
was a vast and featureless part of the world. Piston-
powered aircraft of those times lacked range. Knowing
the whereabouts and the intent of your enemy was
never a certainty. Meteorology and radar were still in
their infancy. There were also the rigors of climate.
At the equator the noontime sun was intense and
debilitating, with temperatures reaching 130 degrees
Fahrenheit. Both the Japanese and the Allied naval
forces, in alternating advances and retreats, moved
across this enormous ocean with its island chains and
atolls, many separated by hundreds, even thousands,
of miles. Many islands were primitive and isolated and

▲ *Report of combat mission to Kavieng on June 3 1944, a mission in which Charles Lindbergh flew as an active participant with other pilots of the 475th Fighter Group.*

▲ *Charles Lindbergh (center) with Corsair fighter pilots in the Pacific Theater, 1944. Lindbergh flew actual combat missions with navy and marine airmen. He also helped the navy to adapt Corsairs to carry augmented bomb loads against the enemy.*

covered with tropical rain
forests, an inhospitable environment of hardwood trees,
vines, swamps, and insects.

Along the shoreline of
the huge and largely unex-
plored island of New Guinea were small settlements
such as Milne Bay, Finschhafen, Wewak, and Hollandia,
all outposts of civilization and points of entry into the
inhospitable interior. The Japanese had occupied and
built defensive positions on the north shore, where they
struggled in vain to hold on in the face of the American
military might. General Douglas MacArthur decided to
clear this area of Japanese forces as a prelude to his
westward advance to the Philippines.

Lindbergh's arrival in the
Pacific Theater followed the

Allied invasion of Hollandia on the north shore of New Guinea. While working with the marines, he flew a total of fourteen patrol missions to Rabaul in the Solomon Islands, then the main Japanese naval base. While technically a civilian liaison for United Aircraft, he was allowed to participate in actual combat, his marine hosts defining his gunnery and strafing activities as practice shooting. On May 29, Lindbergh dropped a five-hundred-pound bomb on Kavieng, north of Rabaul, destroying buildings and an anti-aircraft battery. Throughout his brief interlude with the marines, Lindbergh never encountered a Japanese plane. Initially, there had been some resentment among the Marine aviators to his arrival, some even questioning his age and competence to fly their

▼ *Lindbergh poses with pilots on Emirau Island in the South Pacific in May 1944. As a test pilot with United Aircraft he became a highly skilled flyer of the Corsair, which at the time was a major fighter in naval air operations. One of Lindbergh's final missions in the Pacific was his experiment in arming the Corsair to carry larger bomb loads. Lindbergh tested this technique in actual combat missions.*

airplanes. Quickly, though, Lindbergh won them over, earning their respect with his flying skill.

For Lindbergh, however, there was yet one more aircraft that he yearned to fly—the twin-engine P-38 Lightning, then assigned to air units of the Fifth Air Force. He wanted to test fly the P-38 and compare it with the Corsair. Gaining access to the P-38 would also bring Lindbergh, an old air corps pilot, back into contact with army aviation. General Ennis Whitehead, a friend, responded to his request to fly the P-38 by sending him to Hollandia, to join the 475th fighter group, the "Satan's Angels." Upon arrival, Colonel Charles MacDonald welcomed the "civilian observer" and assigned Major Thomas B. McGuire, the army air forces' second-ranking ace, to fly on his wing. In the days that followed, Lindbergh quickly mastered the P-38 and was flying with pilots of the 475th on various bombing and strafing missions.

Colonel MacDonald's unit flew out of Biak, a small island located off the northwest coast of New Guinea. The unit occupied a former enemy airfield, which had been battered into rubble. Personnel of the 475th lived in tents along a coral reef. Conditions were primitive, with few amenities. Biak was the forward edge of the Allied advance toward the Philippines. From here, the 475th flew combat sorties to distant island strongholds of the enemy, some hundreds of miles across open ocean. All pilots in the unit were attentive to the rate of fuel consumption of their P-38s, always anxious that there would be sufficient reserves to make it home to Biak.

Typically, pilots of the 475th flew six- or seven-hour missions, which meant they were operating at the outer edge of the P-38's range. When Lindbergh joined the air unit, he impressed both ground crews and pilots with his economical fuel consumption. When asked to explain his method, he stated that he ran the P-38's Allison engines at 1,600 revolutions per minute (rpm), set the fuel mixture at "auto-lean," and raised the manifold pressure slightly. For pilots instructed to keep their engines at a minimum of 2,000 rpm, Lindbergh's formula for fuel-saving appeared suicidal, a technique that would result in damage to the cylinders and lead to disaster. Lindbergh argued that the military engines fitted on the P-38 were durable and designed to take punishment. Impressed with Lindbergh's innovation, Colonel MacDonald decided to employ it. Soon pilots of the 475th were flying nine-hour missions.

Richard Kirkland, who flew with the 475th in the summer of 1944, was one of the first to fly with Lindbergh on sorties out of Biak. On one fighter sweep of Piroe Bay, led by Major Thomas McGuire, Kirkland remembered how surprised he was with Lindbergh's skillful flying of the P-38: "There was a skill to leading as well as flying wing, and he had it. Lindbergh was right on target for the join up. He arched across McGuire's first circle and brought us sliding up into a perfect element formation without a bobble. . . . I'm sure everyone in the flight was surprised, too: I knew they were all watching. I couldn't help wondering what was going on in their thoughts as they watched the 'old man' handle the P-38 like he'd been born to it."[10] On that same mission, Kirkland and his fellow pilots mimicked Lindbergh's reduced-rpm technique on the critical return leg. They were pleased and reassured when their Allison engines did not blow up on route home. "All clouds of uncertainty and doubt about him," Kirkland observed, "just seemed to dissolve away."[11]

Lindbergh himself flew over fifty combat missions while in the Pacific. While officially a technical advisor or civilian liaison, he actually functioned as a regular combat pilot at Biak. On July 28, Lindbergh downed a Mitsubishi 51 Sonia reconnaissance plane on the return leg of a mission to Amboina, a Japanese-held island near Cebu. The Sonia had attacked Lindbergh's P-38 in a head-on pass. Both planes fired simultaneously, with Lindbergh banking away at the very last moment. The enemy airplane fell into the sea. On another occasion a Zero attacked Lindbergh's P-38, only to be shot down by others in Lindbergh's formation. That incident, Lindbergh later confessed, was the closest he came to being killed in air action.

Living on Biak, Lindbergh saw firsthand the merciless nature of the

▲ Lindbergh in the cockpit of a Corsair fighter in the Pacific in 1944.

▼ Map of the South Pacific during World War II. From 1942 to 1944, the Allies sought to expel the Japanese from New Guinea and the Solomon Islands. Lindbergh participated in the decisive campaigns north of New Guinea.

Pacific war. In a jeep, he and several officers of the unit made their way across a bombed-out area where a major battle had taken place. Writing decades later, Lindbergh still remembered vividly their slow and meandering passage through a debris field, where "the smell of souring rice and unburied bodies" lingered in the air.[12] The whole region was littered with abandoned or destroyed equipment of both armies, American K-ration boxes, shells, and the bodies of ten or twelve dead Japanese soldiers. Some skulls of the dead Japanese had been crushed to extract gold tooth fillings. No one took time to bury the enemy dead, so they remained decomposing in the heat of the tropics, partially devoured by ants and other insects. When the party reached the cliff caves, they were greeted by the sight of the propped-up, decapitated body of a lone Japanese soldier. Passing this gruesome sentry, Lindbergh took a flashlight to explore the dark and wet interior of some of the cliff caves, once the habitat of the Japanese defenders in their final hours. To his horror, he viewed a labyrinth of dead bodies, many half submerged in the water and mud on the floor of the cave. The dome of the cave was filled with stalactites, which dripped water on scattered cases of ammunition, food, and clothing. These wartime impressions of Biak made an indelible imprint on Lindbergh.

▼ *Biak, the largest of the Schouten Islands of Indonesia, is bombarded by air units of the Fifth Air Force just before its occupation by American forces. Lindbergh flew out of Biak with members of the 475th Fighter Group. Located off the northwest coast of New Guinea, Biak was the scene of heavy fighting from May 27 to June 20, 1944.*

While in the Pacific, Lindbergh had a rare opportunity to speak to General Douglas MacArthur, a meeting that took place on August 22, 1944, in Brisbane, Australia. The two men chatted for two hours. MacArthur was curious about Lindbergh's unofficial work as a combat pilot, asking the renowned aviator how many Japanese aircraft he had shot down. When Lindbergh told him he had downed one enemy aircraft off Ceram, MacArthur congratulated him warmly, knowing full well that the famed pilot had been in combat flying without proper authorization.

Lindbergh's last tour of duty in the Pacific took him to the Kwajalein and Roi Islands, where he joined the marines for some dangerous experiments in augmenting the bomb load on Corsair fighters. In action over Wotje and other enemy-held islands and atolls, Lindbergh flew Corsairs specially equipped to handle ordnance weighing four thousand pounds, four times the standard bomb-carrying capacity of the fighter. Flying such an overladen aircraft, especially in marginal weather, posed real hazards. On one mission, Lindbergh dropped this enormous bomb load on a Japanese fortified position on Wotje. The attack proved successful, completely destroying the enemy position. Again, Lindbergh had applied his considerable engineering skills to improve the operational effectiveness of American military aircraft in the Pacific.

By September 1944, Lindbergh had spent four months in the Pacific Theater. He was ready to return home, having completed a remarkable sequence of flying activities as a civilian consultant. Wherever Lindbergh worked, he won the affection and respect of the military. His interlude in the combat zone had been triumphal in every respect. His decision to return home did not signal an abandonment of his wartime service, only the conclusion of one phase of it.

The passage home for Lindbergh called for the improvised use of military and civilian transport—first a military flight from Kwajalein to Hawaii on September 16, then one to San Francisco and Los Angeles. For the final leg to the east, he took a regular scheduled TWA airliner flying cross-country to Pittsburgh. After a night in Pittsburgh, Lindbergh boarded a train for New York City. No sooner had he reached New York than reporters sought him out, cameras flashing, following him every step of the way. Lindbergh adamantly refused to give interviews. This grim reminder of the haunting presence of the media greatly angered him, suggesting that nothing had changed, even with the distraction of the war and the anonymity of his work in the Pacific.

Anne Lindbergh eventually met her husband at Westport, Connecticut, where they had secured a new home. Throughout most of the war years and during Charles's four-month interlude in

▲ *A captured Japanese battle flag given to Lindbergh by Colonel Charles MacDonald, commander of the celebrated 475th Fighter Group, dubbed "Satan's Angels."*

▼ *Americans make a surprise attack on Japanese airfield on Selaroe Strip, New Guinea. Lindbergh participated in the air campaign against enemy strongholds in the New Guinea theater.*

the Pacific, Anne had lived with their four children in Bloomfield Hills, Michigan. There she had attended to child-rearing, dealing with wartime shortages and rationing, and whenever free, taking art and sculpture classes. Anne had not abandoned her writing, but the war had not been an ideal setting to keep that aspect of her life vital and on track. The war had been disruptive for the Lindberghs, as it had been for countless American families.

The reunion of Charles and Anne in the fall of 1944 marked an important milestone in their lives, providing a new context for the couple to establish a more settled existence as World War II drew to a close. Their second daughter, Reeve, was born on October 2, 1945. But this return to normalcy proved to be incomplete, with renewed calls for Charles to participate in a series of conferences on fighter-aircraft design and maintenance. Then and in the future, such consultation work, on both military and civilian projects, would continue to define the peripatetic lifestyle of Charles Lindbergh.

With the death of President Roosevelt in April 1945, official Washington began to change, even in its attitudes toward Charles Lindbergh. No longer a persona non grata, Lindbergh was now actively sought out as a consultant. He soon found himself openly recruited for a special technical mission to defeated Germany—one that would cast a long shadow over the emerging Cold War.

Charles Lindbergh began his writing career in 1927 when he wrote *"We,"* his first account of the remarkable saga of the *Spirit of St. Louis.* This writing assignment had been an expedient, since Lindbergh discovered that journalists seeking to tell the story of the transatlantic flight had been prone to exaggeration. Getting the proper tone and recording history accurately were uppermost in Lindbergh's mind.

In subsequent decades, Lindbergh took a pen in hand on more than one occasion to record his evolving outlook on life. *Of Flight and Life* (1948), *The Spirit of St. Louis* (1953), and *Autobiography of Values* (published posthumously in 1978) represent the most important of these writings. The publication of *The Spirit of St. Louis* was something of a literary event. Readers marveled at Lindbergh's engaging writing style and his capacity to convey in vivid prose an epic moment in the history of aviation. The book quickly emerged as a bestseller, won a Pulitzer Prize, and prompted Warner Brothers to adapt the story into a major motion picture. Lindbergh's diaries, in particular *The Wartime Journals*

(1970), and his occasional magazine articles dating back to the 1930s round out his substantial literary legacy.

Whereas writing was for Charles one part of a life full of diverse interests and activities, it was for Anne a deeply felt calling and a lifelong occupation. Her first book, *North to the Orient* (1935), is a beautifully written account of the Lindbergh survey flight across the Great Circle route over Canada to the North Pacific in 1931. In the same genre she published *Listen! The Wind* (1938), which provides an account of flying from Africa to America, with a preface by famed aviator and writer Antoine de Saint-Exupéry. Along with her published poems and letters, Anne wrote a total of thirteen books.

One of Anne's most controversial books was *The Wave of the Future: A Confession of Faith* (1940), published during the great debate on nonintervention, at a time when her husband was at the epicenter of political controversy. In her small book, Anne clearly opposed Nazi tyranny but

appeared to be saying the Nazis represented an irresistible tide. Later in life Anne confessed that she and Charles were often blind to the evils of the Nazi movement, and this was most apparent in her controversial book.

Perhaps Anne's most memorable book is *The Gift from the Sea* (1955), an essay on the changing role of women in society. Also in the postwar years, she made a significant contribution to historical literature with the publication of her diaries and letters in five volumes: *Bring Me a Unicorn* (1972); *Hour of Gold, Hour of Lead* (1973); *Locked Rooms and Open Doors* (1974); *The Flower and the Nettle* (1976); and *War Within and Without* (1980). In these candid and revealing books, Anne supplemented the historical record, even revealing things about the Lindbergh saga that her husband was less inclined to share with the outside world.

Anne and Charles Lindbergh in Bavaria after World War II

THE TRUSTEES OF COLUMBIA UNIVERSITY
IN THE CITY OF NEW YORK
TO ALL PERSONS TO WHOM THESE PRESENTS MAY COME GREETING
BE IT KNOWN THAT

CHARLES A. LINDBERGH

HAS BEEN AWARDED
THE PULITZER PRIZE IN LETTERS
- BIOGRAPHY -
FOR "THE SPIRIT OF ST. LOUIS"
IN ACCORDANCE WITH THE PROVISIONS OF THE STATUTES OF THE
UNIVERSITY GOVERNING SUCH AWARD
IN WITNESS WHEREOF WE HAVE CAUSED THIS CERTIFICATE TO BE
SIGNED BY THE PRESIDENT OF THE UNIVERSITY AND OUR CORPORATE
SEAL TO BE HERETO AFFIXED IN THE CITY OF NEW YORK ON THE
THIRD   DAY OF   MAY   IN THE YEAR OF
OUR LORD ONE THOUSAND NINE HUNDRED AND FIFTY FOUR

Grayson Kirk
PRESIDENT

CUP

SUMMER 1946

Lindbergh joins the Chicago Ordnance Research (CHORE) Committee as a consultant.

SPRING 1954

Lindbergh wins the Pulitzer Prize for his book *The Spirit of St. Louis.*

FALL 1955

Anne Morrow Lindbergh's *Gift from the Sea* is published.

1946

1956

NOV. 1947

Lindbergh becomes a special advisor to the newly independent U.S. Air Force and assists with the organization and development of the Strategic Air Command.

DEC. 1947

Lindbergh becomes the second recipient of the annual Wright Brothers Memorial Trophy.

AUG. 23, 1948

Lindbergh's *Of Flight and Life* is published.

SEPT. 1953

Lindbergh's book *The Spirit of St. Louis* is published.

JAN. 25, 1954

Lindbergh receives the Daniel Guggenheim Medal for "pioneering achievement in flight and air navigation."

APRIL 7, 1954

With a nomination from President Eisenhower and the approval of the U.S. Senate, Lindbergh is appointed a brigadier general.

APRIL 11, 1957

The movie *The Spirit of St. Louis,* starring Jimmy Stewart, premieres at the Egyptian Theatre in Hollywood.

OCT. 4, 1957

The Soviet Union launches the first man-made satellite, *Sputnik,* into orbit around the earth.

OCT. 1, 1958

NACA (the National Advisory Committee for Aeronautics) is reorganized into the National Aeronautics and Space Administration (NASA).

APRIL 12, 1961

Yuri Gagarin becomes
the first man in space.

MARCH 19, 1968

Lindbergh addresses the
Alaska legislature on
environmental issues,
his first public speech in
over ten years.

JAN. 1, 1970

The National
Environmental Policy
Act is signed into law.

OCT. 1972

Upon a routine
examination, Lindbergh
is diagnosed with
lymphatic cancer and
begins radiation
treatments.

1966

1976

SEPT. 1962

Lindbergh becomes
involved with the World
Wildlife Fund and
eventually accepts an
invitation to join the
board of trustees.

SEPT. 1962

Rachel Carson's *Silent
Spring,* the touchstone of
the environmental
movement, is published.

MARCH 1967

Lindbergh completes a
redesign of his perfusion
pump to withstand
colder temperatures
and to accommodate
larger organs.

SUMMER 1969

The Lindberghs begin to
build their home on
Maui, Hawaii.

JULY 16, 1969

At the request of
astronaut Neil
Armstrong, Lindbergh
and his son Jon attend
the launch of Apollo 11
at Cape Canaveral.

JULY 1970

The Environmental
Protection Agency is
established.

AUG. 26, 1974

Lindbergh dies on Maui
at the age of 72.

new horizons

Returning home from the Pacific War, Charles Lindbergh entered a new phase of life, one that would lead to new intellectual interests and fresh opportunities for national service. The war years, spent in the wilderness of official Washington disapproval, allowed Lindbergh a context to rethink old priorities, in particular his attitude toward science and technology. Where he had once thought of science in uncritical terms, as the chief means to advance the quality of life, he now began to ponder its darker side, even speculating on the notion that science without a moral compass could actually threaten civilization itself. Where he had once been the evangelist for aviation as the cutting edge of modernity, he now began to see the airplane in more neutral terms, with a powerful capacity for good or evil, depending on how humans chose to use it.

Charles Lindbergh in 1972, at a time in his life when he devoted his energies to conservation and the preservation of wildlife.

World War II, in Lindbergh's opinion, had opened the way for the Soviet Union to emerge as a superpower, expanding the influence of communism to the very heart of Europe. He had warned of this dire consequence in the prewar debate on intervention. The course of the war had fulfilled his prophetic sense of the future, that the global conflict with its extraordinary devastation would not bring peace. Now the United States found itself engaged in a new global struggle, the Cold War. To contend with this new threat, Lindbergh openly called for a new strategy and an aggressive program of weapons development for national security. Such a posture meant the abandonment of his older idea of the United States as a sort of armed and self-regarding loner in world affairs, what his enemies called an irresponsible form of isolationism. For Lindbergh the shift was tactical; it did not represent a change in his core beliefs. In fact, he viewed his prewar ideas as largely vindicated by the course of history. After 1945, on his own and without apologies, Lindbergh adjusted to a new international reality, one where the United States now faced the formidable challenge of the Soviet Union in a nuclear age.

Lindbergh's wartime service had been exemplary—a testament to his personal patriotism and sense of duty. By 1945, many officials in Washington appreciated his contributions to the war effort. Moreover, within the war department there was a renewed interest in hiring Lindbergh on as a technical consultant, not in some shadowy arrangement, but openly. With the death of President Roosevelt in April

▲ *Charles Lindbergh as a "shadow warrior" in the Pacific in World War II, where as a civilian consultant he flew with navy and army pilots.*

▼ *Navy CPO Graham Jackson tearfully plays "Goin' Home" on the accordion while President Roosevelt's body is carried from the Warm Springs Foundation, where he died of a stroke on April 12, 1945.*

1945, the estrangement with Washington abruptly ended. The new Truman administration, echoing this new openness to Lindbergh, displayed little interest in sustaining Roosevelt's campaign to "clip the wings" of the Lone Eagle.

Just as the war in Europe was coming to an end, the war department offered Lindbergh a place on a new Naval Technical Mission, organized to study Nazi Germany's jet and rocket technology. Lindbergh quickly accepted the position as a civilian representative. On May 11, 1945, he joined the mission, less than a week after the collapse of the Third Reich. Participation on the Naval Technical Mission allowed Lindbergh to see Germany in the immediate aftermath of the war, making his way through bombed-out cities, around hundreds of thousands of refugees seeking safety, and into the once-secret Nordhausen facility, the site of Nazi Germany's rocket program.

Reaching Paris, the headquarters of the Naval Technical Mission, Lindbergh and the team donned G.I. uniforms with pistols (for defense if they encountered resistance elements) and then flew to Munich in a C-47 transport. The work of the mission consisted of confiscating technical documents, interrogating German technical personnel, and seeking out hidden jet and rocket facilities. Lindbergh joined a team that drove a jeep and trailer across roads clogged with refugees and columns of surrendering German soldiers. Some of the units made their surrender still armed and with their discipline intact. As Lindbergh recalled, "I remember approaching a crossroad that held an entire Wehrmacht regiment on the march—trucks, cannon,

"If our civilization is to thrive, we must surround our people with physical security, bodily vigor, and spiritual peace that come from close contact with earth and sky." —Charles A. Lindbergh

and thousands of rifled infantrymen strung out at right angles to our line of travel. A seemingly endless column of green-clad German soldiers moving in one direction; a single American jeep rolling up against it, like a fly buzzing at the body of a serpent."[1]

Munich brought to the surface many old memories for Lindbergh. It had been the locale for the Lilienthal conferences that he attended in the heyday of German air rearmament. The Bavarian capital was now largely in ruins, with vast sections of the city reduced to rubble by the Anglo-American strategic bombing campaign. The physical contrast between the past and present moved Lindbergh. The devastation at the end of the war gave witness to the efficacy of modern air power. There was also a visit to Hitler's retreat at Berchtesgaden. Lindbergh walked around the bombed-out shell of Hitler's former residence, atop a mountain with its many dramatic vistas. Lindbergh gazed out the gaping hole that had once been a picture window framing the spectacular Alps in the distance. He had seen Nazi

▼ When Charles Lindbergh reached Germany at the close of World War II, he witnessed the surrender of German troops amidst the ruins of the war. He inspected former German jet and rocket facilities as a member of the Naval Technical Mission.

Germany at its zenith and warned of its considerable military power, and now he contemplated its demise.

In his private journal, Lindbergh recorded his impressions of the Third Reich from the perspective of 1945. While he had never met Hitler, Lindbergh had been impressed with the early material achievements of the Nazi regime, though not its oppressive political rule. Now, he saw clearly how one man with enormous political power could do great evil. The legacy of Adolf Hitler was apparent to Lindbergh: " . . . the best youth of his country dead; the cities destroyed; the population homeless and hungry; Germany overrun by the forces he feared most, the forces of Bolshevism, the armies of Soviet Russia; much of his country . . . rubble—flame-blacked ruins."[2] There were also vivid memories in Lindbergh's mind of Hitler at the zenith of his power at the Olympic stadium in 1936, reviewing his huge army and receiving the applause of the adoring crowds. In his memoirs, he mused on the inexplicable appeal of Hitler: "Some irrational quality of the man, his actions, and his oratory enticed the entire German nation to support his ideas." For Lindbergh, Hitler's fate in the rubble of bombed-out Berlin was derived from the sheer independence he enjoyed as a ruler, the fact that "his orders were issued without the need to listen or persuade freely elected representatives of the people."[3]

While in occupied Germany, Lindbergh sought out an old acquaintance, Willy Messerschmitt, who had survived the war but had lost everything. He was destitute and slept in a barn loft. Messerschmitt's fate offered a poignant reminder of how the once-proud air establishment now shared the ignominious fate of the Third Reich. If Messerschmitt's melancholy circumstances prompted pity, Lindbergh took special notice of the plight of Germany's many homeless and hungry children, the most vulnerable to the war's cruel dislocation. The brutality of the European war now merged with his still vivid memories of the dead Japanese he had seen at Biak in the Pacific.

Eventually the Naval Technical Mission made its way to Nordhausen, where Lindbergh had his first opportunity to examine the V-2 factory carved into the recesses of the Harz Mountains. The tunnel complex, with its many assembly lines and storage rooms filled with partially assembled rockets and scattered debris, bore evidence of the last chaotic days of the war. Years later, Lindbergh contrasted these images of Nordhausen with the rocket experiments of Dr. Robert Goddard before the war: "What a contrast

▲ *View of the bombed section of Stuttgart, Germany, at the end of World War II. Lindbergh was stunned at the material damage to German cities with the strategic bombing campaign, in particular Munich and Berlin.*

▶ *An early enthusiast for rocketry, Lindbergh is shown here with Robert Goddard (third from left) at a test site in Roswell, New Mexico.*

it was to the scientific dreams I had listened to at the Goddard home in Worcester sixteen years before. Professor Goddard was dead. World War II had placed a nightmare of time between me and the hours we spent together while he was carrying on his pioneer work."[4]

Lindbergh's friendship had been critical in moving Goddard from a visionary to an actual experimenter with liquid-fueled rockets. As early as 1929 Lindbergh had approached Goddard, then a professor at Clark University in Massachusetts, to learn of his ideas and experiments. The speed of Goddard's small liquid-fuel rockets, in Lindbergh's mind, was a harbinger of the future—perhaps a moon

landing at some distant point in time. To free Goddard from his teaching duties so he could experiment on a full-time basis with his rocket experiments, Lindbergh recruited his close friend Harry Guggenheim to lead the effort to underwrite Goddard's work. Guggenheim was able to secure two two-year grants of $50,000. With these sizable grants Goddard was able to move to Roswell, New Mexico, and set up a new laboratory and test stand. For the first time, Goddard had the resources to fund the salaries of his staff and to purchase vital components such as Duralumin, steel tubing, liquid oxygen, and various supplies for the manufacture of his rockets. Lindbergh himself actually visited the Roswell site and, in the years that followed, shared Goddard's enthusiasm for rocketry and space travel.

▲ *Charles Lindbergh (right) recruited his close friend Harry Guggenheim (left) to provide the necessary funds for physicist Robert Goddard (center) to begin his rocket research in New Mexico. Without this intervention, Goddard would not have had the released time from teaching to experiment with rockets.*

At Nordhausen, Lindbergh met Wernher von Braun, another rocket pioneer and a leading engineer for the V-2 rocket program. Later in life, at Cape Canaveral, he met von Braun again in a dramatically altered context, where the former German rocket specialist had assumed a leading role in America's own missile program. While at Nordhausen, the Naval Technical Mission examined closely the V-2 rocket, part of a program that would eventually lead to the transfer of V-2 rocket technology to the United States for further testing. "How those Nazi rockets reminded me of Professor Goddard's," Lindbergh later observed, noting that Goddard's record altitude had been between eight and nine thousand feet, in contrast to a V-2 with a one-ton warhead traveling sixty miles above the earth.[5] The difference in performance, in Lindbergh's mind, related to the enormous funds Hitler allocated to build rockets for war.

Adjacent to the Nordhausen factory was Camp Dora, part of the Bergen-Belsen concentration-camp system. Here Lindbergh and his fellow inspectors saw firsthand the slave labor camp that had been organized to support the Nordhausen rocket production. Lindbergh inspected the barbed-wired enclosure in all its horror. Two cremating furnaces, situated side by side, gave witness to the machinery of mass extermination at Camp Dora. "Steel stretchers for holding bodies stuck out like tongues from open mouths," Lindbergh observed grimly in his *Autobiography of Values*.[6] While at Camp Dora he and his colleagues met a seventeen-year-old Polish boy, reduced to a mere skeleton after three years of slave labor. The young prisoner showed

Lindbergh and his party the camp, including a large pit where the ashes from the furnaces had been dumped. Lindbergh was struck with the organic ties between Camp Dora and the Nordhausen rocket facility: "The height of human accomplishment and the depth of human degradation were there at the underground tunnels of Nordhausen; the two had somehow joined together to show the catabolic tendency of our civilization's science, which had produced Hitler's hellish V-2 rockets."[7] For Lindbergh, the tour of Camp Dora with all its stench and degradation showcased the Nazi capacity for inhumanity.

Many anticipated that Lindbergh would apologize for his prewar views on Nazi Germany. But he did not—neither in 1945 nor in the decades that followed. The reasons are complex, perhaps stemming from an odd mix of personal stubbornness and principle. Lindbergh believed that he had pointed to the objective achievements and the growing military power of the Nazi state. In his view, he never endorsed Nazi ideology or condoned the inhumanity of Hitler. Camp Dora and the wider context of national ruin could be explained by Hitler's misuse of power. The war brought great physical destruction to Europe, millions of men and women lost their lives in the fighting, and Western democratic institutions appeared to be in an irreversible decline. And Lindbergh's most apocalyptic fear had come true: Soviet Russia now occupied most of eastern Europe, threatening the West with its

Charles Lindbergh saw firsthand the German slave labor camps, including Camp Dora, which had been set up to provide needed labor for the German rocket program. Pictured here is a U.S. congressional delegation inspecting the infamous Camp Dora facility.

revolutionary ideology and its enhanced military power. Civilization itself remained in great peril, despite the illusory triumph of World War II. History, in Lindbergh's opinion, appeared to vindicate the essential thrust of his prewar views.

Yet, for Lindbergh, these were altered circumstances that dictated new methods and a renewed vigilance on matters of national security. The end of World War II had given birth to a new reality, one where the oceans no longer offered the protection and luxury of insularity. The Soviet Union emerged as an aggressive and expansionist power, and this challenge would have to be met worldwide. Lindbergh now fervently defended the new Truman Doctrine, which called for an active opposition to Soviet expansionism across the globe. For Lindbergh, the Cold War represented a critical struggle, one where the United States found itself in danger and compelled to be the defender of Western values.

In the postwar years, Presidents Truman and Eisenhower offered Lindbergh many avenues for national service. The focus of his consultation work was as a technical adviser for the U.S. Air Force. Lindbergh had been struck by the potency of nuclear warfare, the reality that a city could be destroyed by a single bomb. Accordingly, he felt the whole equation of national defense had been dramatically and irrevocably altered and called on American military planners to fashion a whole arsenal of new weapons.

Charles Lindbergh established a warm and enduring friendship with Igor Sikorsky, the renowned Russian-born aviator and aircraft designer. Sikorsky had established himself as a prominent aviation designer in his native land, pioneering the development of large multi-engine airplanes. He won a medal from Tsar Nicholas II and built bombers for the Russian air force during World War I, only to be threatened with execution by the communists who took power in 1917. Sikorsky decided to emigrate, first to France and then to the United States. He reached America in 1919, and after some difficult years, he emerged as a major figure in the American aviation industry during the interwar period. Sikorsky displayed great versatility and creativity as the designer of seaplanes and the VS-300, the prototype for modern helicopters.

Sikorsky S-35 trimotor, 1926

Always a private person, Lindbergh was slow to develop close associates, and it is noteworthy that a sense of shared values cemented his friendship with Sikorsky despite differences in their age and background. By the early 1930s, Sikorsky and Lindbergh had become close friends with many shared interests. They participated together in long-distance flights to Central America, attended the international Lilienthal conferences in Germany, and worked to assure the development of commercial aviation.

Charles Lindbergh with Igor Sikorsky

Sikorsky was a talented aircraft designer with an appreciation for the role of intuition in the creative process of aircraft design. His honesty and personal integrity greatly impressed Lindbergh. Moreover, Sikorsky took a keen interest in the pressing political issues of the interwar era, in particular the threat of communism to the West. In time, Lindbergh accepted Sikorsky's assessment of Soviet Russia. Few aviation figures matched Sikorsky's eclectic interests in both technology and the humanistic fields of philosophy and religion. Lindbergh saw in Sikorsky a kindred soul.

When Igor Sikorsky died on October 26, 1972, Charles Lindbergh wrote a letter to his widow, Elizabeth, concerning their friendship. This remarkable letter says as much about Lindbergh as its does about his departed friend. Written within two years of Lindbergh's own death, it sheds unusual light on his own thoughts about the human intellect and spirit.

"When I start to write about Igor," he wrote, "it is hard to know where to begin for he was such a great man and his life covered such a broad expanse of the intellectual and spiritual worlds. . . . His scientific designs gained from his spiritual awareness just as his spiritual awareness was enhanced by his scientific knowledge. . . . Igor had a relationship with spirit, matter, time, and space that surmounts the incident named 'death.' Death is a rigid point in time only for those whose perception and penetration has not extended far beyond it . . . and the transition from life to death must have seemed hardly a transition at all to him."[8]

These words, in many ways, capture Lindbergh's own sense of life and death in his last years.

In practical terms, this meant the creation of an immense nuclear retaliatory capability, one that would allow the United States to endure a surprise attack from the enemy and then strike back with a decisive counter blow.[9]

Part of this consultation work involved a reorganization of the Strategic Air Command (SAC), the strike force mandated to deliver a nuclear blow against any enemy. At SAC headquarters, working with scientists and engineers, Lindbergh observed, "I felt myself a demonic god as I watched plastic discs being laid down on maps of target cities to show the area that one bomb of the latest kilotonnage could destroy."[10] He also flew on simulated missions with SAC, an experience that highlighted the vast changes in air power since World War II. Lindbergh found himself at the center of America's Cold War military planning. In April 1954, President Eisenhower approved Lindbergh's promotion to brigadier general in the U.S. Air Force Reserves. A driving force behind the promotion was General Robert Scott, who ardently believed that Lindbergh had been unfairly treated in the past and was worthy of the star. Keeping with his newly won status as a senior military advisor, Lindbergh also served on the Air Force Academy Site Selection Committee in 1954. By this juncture, the old suspicions of Lindbergh as a defeatist or potential traitor, at least in the armed forces, had largely evaporated.

▲ Charles Lindbergh served as a consultant for the newly independent U.S. Air Force after World War II, seen here on a 1948 inspection tour.

▼ Lindbergh poses with air force servicemen from the Sixty-fifth Bomber Squadron, stationed in Alaska, 1948.

One of Lindbergh's hidden talents—his remarkable skill as a writer—found expression in the decades after World War II. In 1953 he published *The Spirit of St. Louis,* which became a bestseller, garnered a Pulitzer Prize, and even prompted Hollywood to adapt the story of the 1927 transatlantic flight into a feature-length film starring Jimmy Stewart. Lindbergh spent many years and no small amount of time revising the manuscript for the book, writing a lively narrative in the present tense and offering the reader numerous asides to share details of his life. He dedicated his memoir to Anne, who contributed her considerable talents with thoughtful commentary as the project progressed. The book struck many as a literary achievement, even prompting the *Saturday Evening Post* to serialize the story in a condensed version, entitled "33 Hours to Paris." Picked up by the Book of the Month Club, it reached a vast audience in its first printing.[11] The popular acclaim for *The Spirit of St. Louis* seemed to suggest the transcendent nature of Lindbergh's historic flight in 1927; no amount of personal tragedy or political controversy, it seemed, could dampen the universal appreciation for Lindbergh's heroism. No aviator since the Wrights had garnered such a revered place in the American pantheon of heroes.

While *The Spirit of St. Louis* attracted a large readership, it focused more on the past than the present. Lindbergh's evolving worldview found expression in *Of Flight and Life* (1948).

In this short book, his first serious literary effort in the aftermath of World War II, Lindbergh attempted to articulate how he had changed in his intellectual outlook, his shift in values prompted by his diverse experiences since making his debut on the world stage in 1927. The mood of the book was grim, pointing to the many dangers now facing humanity. In the past, Lindbergh had confessed that he had thought of science as the all-powerful tool to transform the quality of life on the planet. Now he had profound doubts, seeing in science certain destructive forces that, if allowed to go unchecked, would undermine civilization. He also noted that while he had devoted his life to aviation, he no longer believed in the limitless future offered by the airplane. His most controversial stand had been on nonintervention, and in *Of Flight and Life* he once again stated that he felt his views had been essentially correct, although now in the postwar environment he was ready to acknowledge that his noninterventionist crusade had been a decisive failure, opening the way for all sorts of partisan attacks on his motives and loyalty. Looking to the future, Lindbergh warned of new dangers, such as a belief in scientific materialism, which, he thought, could bring many dire consequences to civilization. He had once worshipped science; now he argued for humans to exert a moral control of it: ". . . [W]e must learn to apply the truths of God to the actions and relationships of men, to the direction of our science. . . . We must draw strength from the forgotten virtues of simplicity, humility, contemplation, prayer . . . beyond science, beyond self."[12]

▲ *Jimmy Stewart poses before a replica of the* Spirit of St. Louis, *based at Guyancourt Airport. Stewart portrayed Charles Lindbergh, the famed "Lone Eagle," in the film* The Spirit of St. Louis, *based on Lindbergh's historic nonstop transatlantic flight in 1927. Location shots were filmed at Guyancourt, which was revamped to look as Le Bourget Airport did twenty-eight years before the filming, when Lindbergh landed there at the conclusion of his epic flight.*

In the postwar years, Lindbergh gave increased attention to what one could call the mystical or nonrational side of life. This emphasis underscored his conclusion that science alone could not explain all things or provide a moral sensibility for humankind. Many perceived a radical reorientation in Lindbergh's posture toward science and modernity, although many of these ideas could be traced to the prewar context. Lindbergh's postwar intellectual posture expressed, no doubt, more continuity than change in this thinking— a renewed effort on his part to speak out on matters of great importance for the survival of civilization. In these years, Lindbergh gave full expression to his own brand of theism, an affirmation of God, but one outside the realm of organized religion. Lindbergh believed humans possessed the capacity—even the imperative—to assert a moral standard to control the darker potential of science. His philosophical and religious musings were based on his reading of an eclectic body of literature. As a youth, he had been indifferent toward college, and in his mature years, he harbored a certain disdain for the academic world. But Lindbergh was a highly sophisticated commentator on a range of issues, a consequence of his intense reading and self-study. Nonetheless, these shifts in intellectual outlook, it should be noted, gave the last third of his life a different hue and purpose.

Always on the move, Lindbergh visited many parts of the world, sparking a new awareness of the fragility of the planet's environment and the vulnerability of wildlife to human advances. Increasingly, he spoke out on environmental issues.

the spirit of st. louis, the film

The film adaptation of Charles Lindbergh's book *The Spirit of St. Louis* debuted in movie theaters in the spring of 1957. For this Warner Brothers epic, Jimmy Stewart played the lead role, supported by a talented group of actors that included Murray Hamilton, Patricia Smith, Bartlett Robinson, Marc Connelly, Arthur Space, and Charles Watt. Billy Wilder directed the movie, an assignment he took on with high seriousness and a fervent desire to achieve historical accuracy. Leland Hayward served as producer, and he shared Wilder's belief that

Actor Jimmy Stewart in the 1950s

the film offered them a rare chance to capture on the screen one of the most remarkable acts of heroism in the twentieth century. Franz Waxman composed a highly regarded music score, which greatly enhanced the dramatic plot and the remarkable photography associated with the film. Interestingly, Jimmy Stewart lobbied to get the coveted role as the Lone Eagle, which allowed him to express his life-long admiration for Lindbergh and his personal interest in flying.

As a youth, Jimmy Stewart intently followed Charles Lindbergh's historic flight from New York to Paris on May 20–21, 1927. He made a model of the *Spirit of St. Louis* and took pride in the fact that his father showcased a map of the Lindbergh flight in the window of their family-owned store in Pennsylvania. Later in Hollywood, Stewart pursued his youthful interest in aviation by earning his pilot's license. These skills set the stage for his participation in World War II as a bomber pilot in the Eighth Air Force.

When Warner Brothers finally cast Stewart in the starring role, there was the problem of his age—at the time of the filming he was forty-eight years old, nearly twice the age of Lindbergh in 1927. One footnote to the film was the fact Hayward and Wilder had considered the young John Kerr for the lead role, but interestingly, Kerr had declined the offer because he disapproved of Lindbergh's purported pro-Nazi sympathies on the eve of World War II. Warner Brothers felt the film required a well-known actor to play the lead role, so

Stewart received the nod to depict his youthful hero.

Billy Wilder appeared to many as the most unlikely director for a film on Charles Lindbergh, given the political controversy and charges of anti-Semitism surrounding the famed aviator. A German Jewish émigré, Wilder appeared quite distant in cultural background and political outlook from Lindbergh. Despite these factors, he had remained throughout his life an admirer of Lindbergh. Wilder took his assignment with great seriousness, especially the screenplay, for which he deluged Lindbergh with questions on historical and technical details. On one occasion, Wilder flew with Lindbergh on a commercial airliner to the Smithsonian Institution in Washington, D.C., to examine the historic aircraft up close. To assure authenticity, Wilder hired Lindbergh's old barnstormer friend Bud Gurney. At the time

Parallel images of Charles Lindbergh and actor Jimmy Stewart

Gurney was a commercial pilot, and to assume this consulting role he had to take leave from his duties with his airline. Gurney was a wise choice for Wilder in many respects, since he knew Lindbergh well and could reinforce the drive for historical accuracy. Gurney, like Lindbergh, reacted negatively to any display of wild hyperbole in telling the story of the *Spirit of St. Louis.*

Stewart knew from his own experience in the cockpit that Lindbergh's transatlantic exploit represented genuine piloting skill and personal bravery. In the 1930s, Stewart had been profoundly moved by the personal tragedy faced by Charles and Anne Lindbergh in the kidnapping and murder of their firstborn child. No less important, he had expressed sympathy for Lindbergh when he fell under criticism for some of his controversial views. Both men were general officers in the U.S. Air Force Reserves. Stewart, who also starred in *Strategic Air Command,* shared Lindbergh's Cold War posture on a strong military establishment to thwart any potential aggressor. Playing Lindbergh offered the Hollywood actor—then at the top of his career—a unique opportunity to blend acting with his personal values.

The fact that Wilder and Stewart openly collaborated on this highly sympathetic portrayal of Lindbergh reflects the dramatic shift in public opinion in the 1950s. The Pulitzer Prize–winning *The Spirit of St. Louis* had reintroduced Americans to Lindbergh and his historic flight of 1927. Readers of the memoir expressed admiration for Lindbergh's literary skills. Few had doubted Lindbergh's flying skills, but now they had reason to applaud his considerable expertise as a writer. During the Eisenhower years, Washington displayed a keen interest in rehabilitating Lindbergh's career, promoting him to brigadier general in the U.S. Air Force Reserves and placing him on numerous commissions related to military affairs. The timing for the movie appeared ideal. Both Wilder and Stewart found compelling the saga of one individual making a solitary passage across the Atlantic in a single-engine airplane, and they were keen to bring the story to the silver screen. The producers of the film realized that a new generation of Americans were largely ignorant of the Lindbergh exploit, one of the most heroic and transforming episodes in the history of aviation.

Maurice Chevalier *(left),* Jimmy Stewart, and Billy Wilder *(right)* during the filming of *The Spirit of St. Louis*

Filming began in 1955 and lasted for eight months. For the dramatic flying sequences, Warner Brothers financed the building of three copies of the original Ryan-built *Spirit of St. Louis* airplane. Other planes were acquired to handle the airmail scenes associated with Lindbergh's formative aviation career in the 1920s. While most of the filming was done in California, at the Santa Monica Airport, there was a need to complete costly aerial photography in Cinemascope along the original flight path of the *Spirit of St. Louis* over New England, Nova Scotia, the North Atlantic, Ireland, England, and France. For the Le Bourget sequences, thousands of extras had to be recruited to capture the frenzy that accompanied Lindbergh's landing. Warner Brothers spent no small amount of funds to achieve Wilder's goal of historical authenticity.

Despite all these favorable factors, the movie version of *The Spirit of St. Louis* proved to be a financial failure. The book had been published in 1953, and Warner Brothers had paid a reported $200,000 plus ten percent of the gross for the movie rights, although rumors circulated that Jack Warner had paid a million dollars for the film rights. The budget for the film, in the final analysis, exceeded six million dol-

A movie poster for *L'Aquila Solitaria*, the Italian-language version of the film *Spirit of St. Louis*. Below, a parachute scene from the movie.

lars. Such a rare and admirable display of historical accuracy on the part of Hollywood producers proved an expensive undertaking and one not rewarded at the box office.

The film—to the surprise of Wilder and Stewart—failed to match its pre-production projections as a blockbuster. Only a modest number of filmgoers filled theater seats in 1957, prompting Jack Warner to view the effort as a colossal failure for his studio. Viewed in broad perspective, the younger generation in the 1950s were fully accustomed to commercial airliners crossing the globe, with the new jets then entering service further dwarfing the Atlantic as a natural barrier: The small and fragile *Spirit of St. Louis* flying the Atlantic appeared to many as something unremarkable. The manifest heroism of Lindbergh, portrayed in Cinemascope on film, did not spark the same popular enthusiasm that the actual flight did in 1927.

Jimmy Stewart suffered only a modest setback from the failure of the film. There was frustration on Stewart's part, because the film truly embodied some of his most cherished ideals. However, Stewart enjoyed exalted status in the 1950s as a major Hollywood star. Before his film portrayal of Lindbergh, he had appeared in the highly regarded thriller *Rear Window*. The decade

Jimmy Stewart, left, depicting Charles Lindbergh in *Spirit of St. Louis*

remained a creative and lucrative interlude in Stewart's fabled acting career.

In retrospect, Billy Wilder's approach to the filming of the Lindbergh flight may have been a contributing factor to its failure, despite the excellent music score and breathtaking aerial photography. Wilder decided to concentrate on the 1927 flight as the core story, with flashbacks as a way to capture the Lindbergh persona. Sustaining audience interest, even with all the drama of Lindbergh's flying career, proved to be problematical. Wilder later admitted that the film should have been focused on Lindbergh's entire life, not just the transatlantic flight from New York to Paris. Some movie-goers wrestled with the fact that Stewart, a middle-aged actor, had been cast as the twenty-five-year-old Lindbergh of 1927. Still, the impressive efforts of makeup artists to erase Stewart's telltale marks of aging made the film more plausible, and the actor's own knowledge of flying certainly enhanced his capacity to portray Lindbergh in a sensitive and convincing manner.

The failure of the film at the box office could not be traced to any lack of commitment to proper publicity at Warner Brothers. In fact, the studio exerted great energy and spent no small amount of money to make the Jimmy Stewart big-screen epic a success. They endeavored to promote it in an aggressive manner, with a highly publicized opening at the Hollywood Egyptian Theater, an event that drew many celebrities. The film then premiered throughout the country with a wave of studio-induced publicity to generate maximum public interest. A deal was even struck with Kellogg's cereal company to pack a small toy *Spirit of St. Louis* in each box of Rice Krispies. Well-known companies with links to aviation such as Standard Oil and Goodrich tied the debut of the movie to their own advertising campaigns. Despite the concerted efforts at promotion, the film failed to attract huge audiences, to the disappointment of Wilder and Stewart, not to mention Jack Warner and executives at Warner Brothers.

Lindbergh insisted on playing no part in the promotion of the film. However, on one lazy afternoon, Charles, Anne, and the Lindbergh children showed up at the Radio City theater in New York City to see it. There were a few instances where the story departed from historical reality for dramatic effect, but Lindbergh was generally pleased with Billy Wilder's rendition of his epic journey across the Atlantic in 1927.

He testified before government officials in Alaska and Montana, as well as political figures in distant Indonesia and Taiwan; lobbied in Peru and elsewhere for a ban on whale killing; promoted the preservation of the Amazon in Brazil; and endeavored to convince the Philippine government to come to the aid of an endangered species of eagle. The defense of the environment prompted Lindbergh to abandon his lifelong policy of refusing membership in organizations, working directly with the World Wildlife Fund and other private groups striving to conserve the earth's natural areas.[13]

Making survey flights and visiting remote areas of the world had influenced Lindbergh to think differently about the forces shaping the globe. He grew concerned that the gradual disappearance of wilderness areas would soon deny humans any real contact with nature. The growth of cities, in particular, struck him as one of the most powerful and visible forces redefining how humans lived. Lindbergh had visited Los Angeles as a teenager in 1916, at a time when the city was small, nestled between the ocean and mountains, and surrounded by farms and open spaces. Fifty years later, the whole area had been transformed into a sprawling urban complex, one that spread from the Pacific coast to the edges of the mountains. For Lindbergh, the rapid growth in California and elsewhere reflected in part the influence of technology. The mechanization of agriculture had reduced the need for farm labor, allowing for a migration to the cities. As a result, the footprint of cities expanded

▲ Charles Lindbergh in a boat in May 1967, holding the oar. Lindbergh's love of the outdoors only deepened his concern for the plight of the environment after World War II. He noted with alarm the rapid and uncontrolled growth of urban areas and the accompanying threats these trends had on wildlife and natural areas of the globe.

▶ In 1967, Lindbergh visits the Philippines with the Tamaran Conservation Program.

dramatically. There were transformations in more remote areas, too. Lindbergh had observed up close the logging and road-building that had transformed vast stretches of the Philippines. All these trends, he lamented, brought great harm to the environment.[14]

Over time Lindbergh developed a keen interest in so-called primitive tribes, visiting the Philippines and Africa to study how the inroads of modern civilization were transforming these pre-modern societies. Living in the suburbs and working in urban centers, Lindbergh believed his own lifestyle had stressed "life's accomplishments" as opposed to life itself. He spent time in East Africa with the semi-nomadic Masai tribe. He slept in their huts, ate their food, and joined them on their hunting forays. For Lindbergh, the Masai seemed to enjoy a real freedom that didn't exist in modern society.

Collectively, these experiences compelled him to rethink his own civilized values in light of a society that appeared to him as more natural and authentic.

There was a certain nostalgia over the past that overcame Lindbergh in his mature years. "Within a fraction of my lifetime," he observed, "I saw New York parking space disappear, the waters of Long Island Sound become polluted, and the coasts of Maine and Florida packed to the shoreline with houses and motels. The distant howl of a superhighway and the thunder of jet aircraft in the sky broke into the tranquility of my New England home. Rampant pressures of improved technology and increasing population were rapidly destroying what my Masai friend and I considered freedom."[15]

As Lindbergh approached old age he became nostalgic for the rural past he had once known, a world he uniquely had observed from the air. Science and

▲ Charles Lindbergh meets with Wernher von Braun in the 1960s. A lifelong rocket enthusiast, Lindbergh took a keen interest in the American space program, in particular the Apollo missions to the moon.

A multicolored beaded knife belt given to Lindbergh by native Americans in Alaska, circa 1932

technology—once considered by Lindbergh as unalloyed benefits for humankind—now seemed threatening, at odds with some of the values he had defended throughout his life. He yearned for some redemptive path that would dampen the destructive power of science and allow for the preservation of the "wisdom of wildness" he had observed in Africa.[16]

Even with his growing commitment to the preservation of the environment, Lindbergh retained confidence in rocketry as a positive expression of modern technology. Going back to his early support of Robert Goddard, he had viewed the development of rockets as an important priority, an avenue toward full expression of his futuristic temperament. In the Cold War context, for Lindbergh, the need to build missiles was a key element in any program of national security. But his more fundamental interest was in the civilian side of rocketry, in particular the NASA Apollo program to make a lunar landing. He met many of the astronauts and attended launches at Cape Kennedy in the heyday of the Apollo program in the 1960s. For the astronauts, Lindbergh's flight across the Atlantic in 1927 represented an epic moment in human flight, an inspiration for all those engaged in air and space travel. Lindbergh linked his own world of long-distance flying to the new world of space travel by writing the introduction to Apollo 11 astronaut Michael Collin's book *Carrying the Fire* (1974): "Of course, there is a future for us in space, just as there was in air. We can put manned stations on the moon if we want to. We probably can set foot on Mars.

east africa

Charles Lindbergh made a remarkable journey to Africa in late 1962, visiting the Kenya-Tanzania borderlands and taking up residence with the Masai people. His trip took him to the remote Rift valley, where the Masai lived as a seminomadic tribe. While civilization had made many inroads, the Masai still managed to maintain the essence of their traditional society, as evident in their animist religion and the ritual of young men killing a lion with a spear as part of the passage to manhood.

The invitation to visit Africa came from a Masai tribal leader, John Konchellah, who had met Lindbergh at a conference in Switzerland. Konchellah was a tall and striking figure who spoke impeccable English and wore a business suit. The only hint of his Masai heritage was his enlarged ear lobes. Konchellah was a member of the Kenyan parliament and moved easily among Europeans,

but he retained strong ties with his tribe. Interestingly, Konchellah knew little of Lindbergh's flying exploits, but welcomed him warmly to his homeland. Lindbergh quickly accepted the invitation.

Anne Morrow Lindbergh wrote of African wildlife

When Lindbergh visited Kenya for the first time, he rejected the option of an organized safari in favor of a solitary trek into the interior in a rented car. The projected sojourn in Kenya, in Lindbergh's mind, offered an avenue to explore how the traditional society of the Masai had maintained their tribal identity in the face of modern civilization. At the

time of his appearance in Kenya, the Masai still lived in a vast territory filled with wild animals—elephants, lions, giraffes, zebras, wildebeests, rhinos, wild dogs, and hyenas, among others. Being a seminomadic people, they occupied this extraordinary region as their ancestral home, a beautiful domain in the shadow of Mount Kilimanjaro.

While among the Masai people, Lindbergh lived in a thatched hut, took meals with his hosts, and despite the language barriers engaged in a series of conversations with the Masai on their life. At one point he joined a Masai cowherd, where men and boys, dressed in their distinctive red blankets and armed with spears, moved their herds of oxen. When Lindbergh reluctantly departed the Masai, Konchellah gave him a special shield that had been made for him.

The trip had been organized with the cooperation of the chief game warden of Kenya, who allowed Lindbergh access to other parts of the region. Lindbergh told his government hosts that he did not like staying

Lindbergh with Ian Grimwood, park administrator, in Kenya, 1964

in first-class hotels or using cities like Nairobi as the base for his study of Africa. He preferred the primitive conditions in the interior, a chance to live in rugged terrain, to sleep on the ground, and to eat the food of the Masai. On later trips, in 1964 and 1965, his itinerary expanded, including a meeting with the celebrated archeologist Dr. Louis S. B. Leakey. The work of Louis and Mary Leakey expanded Lindbergh's appreciation for the role of Africa in human development.

Anne Lindbergh joined her husband on a separate trek into the primitive interior, including the domain of the Masai people, where they experienced life at a considerable distance from civilization. Driving in a Land Rover into the interior, they pitched their tents near a water hole in a remote stretch of territory. Here, outside the city lights of Nairobi or any settlement, Charles and Anne witnessed the movement of elephants, giraffes, and other animals. The next morning, Masai herdsmen with their cattle joined them at the water hole. Such experiences in the untouched interior prompted in Lindbergh a sense of nostalgia for the primitive past and a deep appreciation for the ability of the Masai to manage and

On one trip to Africa, Charles Lindbergh met celebrated scientists Louis and Mary Leakey, shown here with a skull fragment 600,000 years old.

preserve their traditional lifestyle. For Lindbergh, who had once championed science and the march of modern civilization, there was now a belated appreciation of indigenous peoples and their values.

The African trips made a profound impact on Lindbergh and his evolving ideas about the interaction of civilization with the natural environment. He increasingly used his global celebrity to lobby government leaders for environmental issues. Lindbergh's diverse agenda included advocacy of a ban on whale hunting, an effort to save the huge land turtles on the island of Aldabra in the Indian Ocean threatened by the construction of an American air base, and work to preserve the Arctic

wolves from extermination, among other issues. He joined the World Wildlife Fund and worked diligently to promote a vast array of conservation initiatives.

Lindbergh's article "Is Civilization Progress?," a declaration of his new concerns for the environment, appeared in *Reader's Digest* in July 1964. In it, he reflected, "When I am in Africa, I feel this miracle of life, for one is constantly surrounded by it." This sense of life led him to conclude that the progress of civilization would not be made "by our amassment of knowledge, or by the discoveries of our science, or by the speed of our aircraft, but by the effect of our civilized activities as a whole upon the quality of our planet's life—the life of plants and animals as well as that of men."[17]

Lindbergh's trips to Africa set the stage for similar visits to Indian tribes in Brazil and the indigenous tribes in the Philippines. His dedication to conservation now emerged as a major commitment, one that would dominate the remaining years of his life.

Such adventures continue to be tantalizing. But whether we travel in a jet transport or in a space-craft, we still look down, or back on life on the crowded surface of the earth as both our source and our destination."[18]

While Lindbergh's interests had broadened beyond aviation, he took time to enter the great debate in the 1960s on the building of the Supersonic Transport (SST). Both the Russians with their Tu-144 and the Anglo-French consortium with their Concorde had entered the competition to develop a modern airliner capable of supersonic speeds. The Concorde, in many respects, was the ultimate refinement of transatlantic flight Lindbergh himself had pioneered, flying in three hours the distance the *Spirit of St. Louis* covered in over thirty-three and a half hours in 1927. Lindbergh still served on the board of directors for Pan American Airways and remained a staunch advocate of commercial airline development, but the proposed SST ran counter to other priorities in his life. In his testimony before Congress, he argued against governmental subsidies for the SST, arguing along two lines, one economic and the other environmental. Lindbergh believed the SST, in terms of passenger-carrying capacity, was small and not at all economically profitable for the equation

▲ *Charles Lindbergh in a primitive hut. When he visited the Philippines in 1970, he stayed in a similar structure.*

▼ *Charles and Anne Lindbergh spent considerable time in the Florida Everglades, a natural area they wished to conserve for future generations.*

of "seat-mile" costs projected for the aircraft. More fundamental to Lindbergh were the untold costs to the environment. He strongly believed the SST could pollute the upper atmosphere and that the excessive noise of sonic booms made by the plane would make it an unnecessary nuisance. Lindbergh's authoritative voice, to the surprise of many, helped to defeat the American version of the SST.[19]

In the late 1960s Lindbergh visited Hawaii, staying overnight at a friend's home on the eastern tip of Maui. The beauty of the island, still largely untouched by suburban housing developments, immediately captivated him. "In the early morning," he wrote, "you can stand on one of Maui's beaches and watch day break in either east or west, judging by the pinkness of cloud—the double sunrise of Pacific islands. The constant roar of a white cascade behind you is answered by periodic roars of white-foam waves in front. Depending on which way you turn, you wade into fresh water pools or dive through a breaking sea."[20]

In time, Charles and Anne Lindbergh obtained land and built a modest A-frame cottage on Maui as their own hideaway. They came to Maui several weeks each year to live in this beautiful, if austere, home, a tropical version of their seaside home on Illiec in the 1930s.

the wisdom **of wildness**

In the last ten years of his life, Lindbergh wrote several articles and delivered public addresses about primitive cultures, conservation, and the environment. The following are excerpts:

In the jungles of Africa, I became more aware of the basic miracle of life. . . . Lying under the acacia tree with the sounds of dawn around me, I realized more clearly facts that man should never overlook: that the construction of an airplane, for instance, is simple when compared to the evolutionary achievement of a bird; that airplanes depend upon an advanced civilization; and that where civilization is most advanced, few birds exist. I realized that if I had to choose, I would rather have birds than airplanes.

—"Is Civilization Progress?," *Reader's Digest,* July 1964

There is in wildness a natural wisdom that shapes all earth's experiments with life. Can we tap this wisdom without experiencing the agony of reverting to wildness? Can we combine it with intellectual developments of which we feel so proud, use it to redirect our modern trends before they lead to a worse breakdown than past civilizations have experienced? I believe we can, and that to do so we must learn from the primitive. . . . The human future depends on our ability to combine the knowledge of science with the wisdom of wildness.

—"The Wisdom of Wildness," *Life,* December 22, 1967

Alaska is one of the key areas of the world, as regards conservation, so what you do here is going to be watched closely by the entire world. . . . It is absolutely necessary that we take steps now to protect what to us at this time seems commonplace. . . . There is nothing we can do anywhere in the world that is more important than to protect our natural environment. . . . I would like to emphasize that cooperation between hunters and conservationists is extremely important. Both want to preserve the species of animals and both want to preserve the habitat of our wildlife.

—address to the Alaska legislature, March 19, 1968

Man must feel the earth to know himself and recognize his values. I believe that, like the mythical Antaeus, man is invincible only so long as he keeps close and sensate contact with the earth.

—"Feel the Earth," *Reader's Digest,* July 1972

Nature's essential wisdom is shown in the selection through which life evolved to the splendor, variety and balance that existed before the advent of the human mind. I believe our civilization's survival depends on our ability to discern this wisdom and to combine it with our scientific knowledge in directing the technological forces we have turned loose in this 20th century.

—"Lessons from the Primitive," *Reader's Digest,* November 1972

Acacia tree and sunset in Africa

◀ *Lindbergh meets with Laurance S. Rockefeller on the Tonga Coast in May 1972. Rockefeller, a noted conservationist, had helped fund the Grand Teton National Park and shared with Lindbergh an enthusiasm for the development of national parks in the United States.*

Here, too, Charles Lindbergh enjoyed the privacy and an unhurried lifestyle. The locals respected his desire for insularity and rarely disturbed him. In time the Lindberghs became acquainted with many of the islanders, shopped at the local general store, hiked, and swam in the ocean. In many ways, Maui was an idyllic setting in which to spend their last years. But even with his residence on Maui, the inveterate traveler Lindbergh continued to make trips to distant parts of the globe. Maui always offered a special serenity, a place of refuge for Lindbergh each year.

Life took a dramatic turn in October 1972, when Charles Lindbergh learned in the course of a routine physical examination that he had cancer of the lymph nodes. In the months that followed Lindbergh underwent a variety of therapies, but his condition gradually worsened, though it was punctuated by interludes of renewed vitality. Slowly, he retreated from public life, resigning from the board of Pan American World Airways and cutting back his involvement with environmental advocacy groups. He spent time with his family, wrote to friends, and attended to the details of his will. One poignant episode in his leave-taking came when he visited his hometown of Little Falls, Minnesota, to dedicate a new reception center for his childhood home. On the steps of his home, Lindbergh made an appeal for environmental awareness and action. He also asked publisher William Jovanovich to take custody of his voluminous memoir, *Autobiography of Values*, and guide it to publication.

island home

Charles Lindbergh first visited the small Hawaiian island of Maui in 1968 as a guest of former Pan American World Airways executive Sam F. Pryor Jr. A close friend, Pryor had built a lovely home on Maui at Kipahulu, on the eastern tip of the island.

Lindbergh's stopover in Maui, on his way home from a trip to the Philippines, came at a decisive moment in his life. He stayed overnight in Pryor's beach house, where in isolation and quiet he experienced firsthand the striking beauty of the island.

Lindbergh was so taken with Pryor's retirement hideaway, he asked whether there might be some land available to build his own home on Maui. To his surprise, his old colleague offered him five choice acres. When Lindbergh asked Pryor what the cost would be for the land, Pryor told him there was no cost. Knowing that the Pryors prized their collection of over ten thousand antiques dolls, the Lindberghs arranged to buy them a valuable

A rainbow appears over a Hawaiian landscape

collection of nineteenth-century mechanical dolls, the cost for which was roughly equivalent to the price of the land.

The Lindbergh-Pryor friendship had been forged at Pan Am, where both men assisted Juan Trippe in transforming the airline into a major international air carrier. Lindbergh's name alone gave Pan Am great legitimacy and influence. Pryor's role as executive vice president had been less visible but essential: He had overseen Pan Am's public affairs office, the operation that advanced the airline's interests in congress and among myriad political leaders across the globe. Pryor was highly regarded for his skills at lobbying and his pivotal role in setting up Pan Am's vast network of international routes. There was also a curious footnote to their friendship: Sam's uncle, St. Louis banker Edward B. Pryor, approved the loan of $15,000 that had paved the way for the building of the *Spirit of St. Louis*.

On Maui the Lindberghs built an A-frame home, which was situated near the beach. The Maui getaway was a simple and

Lindbergh's A-frame home on Maui

austere structure with no electricity. Charles and Anne Lindbergh typically visited their beach house twice a year, spending about six weeks on each trip. Lindbergh delighted in watching the sunrises and sunsets from the beach, taking walks into the forests, traversing streams, visiting waterfalls, and studying the rich flora and fauna of the volcanic island. In time the island became part of Charles's personal identity, his own special context from which to advocate the preservation of the environment. As his death approached in the summer of 1974, Lindbergh chose Maui as his last resting place.

Anne Morrow Lindbergh found Maui to be a beautiful locale, a sort of tropical version of their former island home at Illiec off the coast of Brittany in the 1930s. But now in advanced age she was less willing to accept uncritically the privations that came with their Maui home, especially when she would be isolated on the island during her husband's frequent trips. Shortly after the Lindberghs took possession of their new home on Maui, they discovered that the builders had not done a competent job in fitting the A-frame structure to resist the ravages of the weather

on Maui. On one memorable occasion, a violent rain storm exposed a leaky roof and defective drainage, setting the stage for the structure to be inundated with water and mud. No less a problem were the many insects, lizards, and rats that besieged the Lindbergh household. While Charles and Anne never lost their affection for the beauty of Maui, there were moments when their home's severe lack of creature comforts posed a challenge.[21]

While a resident of Maui, Lindbergh took the initiative to promote conservation policies. "Primitive ways," he wrote, "have almost disappeared. The impact of twentieth-century transportation, economics, and politics will produce results as far beyond our present vision as statehood and hotel-ridden Waikiki were beyond a Hawaiian's vision a hundred years ago."[22] Consequently, he joined the clamor to expand designated wilderness areas on Hawaii and to proclaim Diamond Head as a national monument. He spoke with local and national politicians to advance the cause of conservation. He and Anne contributed generous funds for local Hawaiian conservation efforts, taking a keen interest in the campaign

Sunset on Maui

to extend the boundaries of the Haleakala National Park in Maui.

At the end of his life, Lindbergh wrote about the island he had chosen as his final home: "Men and women about [Maui] show how the islands blend the races of the world. In this blending, you see Hawaii's past entering its future and recognizing the value of establishing great parks."[23] In many ways, Maui had became a metaphor for Lindbergh's mature consciousness on the eve of his death in 1974.

As his health visibly declined, Lindbergh went to considerable effort to plan his death and funeral, working out a checklist with precise instructions on how and where he would be buried. He spent more and more time on Maui to rest and recover between radiation treatments and decided, for this climactic chapter in his life, that it would be his final resting place. His funeral plans called for a highly scripted memorial service with a distinctly Hawaiian flavor and no eulogies. The funeral ceremony called for the local Christian minister to preside, but only Hawaiian hymns were to be sung. He choose an eclectic group of readings that included excerpts from the Bible and the Hindu Munkaka Upanishad, the writings of Gandhi and St. Augustine, and a Navajo prayer, among other works.[24] Keeping with the simplicity of his Maui lifestyle, Lindbergh decided to be buried in a rustic wooden casket, dressed in simple garb consisting of gray cotton pants and a khaki shirt, and without shoes.

By the summer of 1974, Lindbergh knew that it was time to make his last trip from Connecticut. Arrangements for his

▲ Charles Lindbergh chose for his burial site the graveyard of the Kipahulu Congregational Church on Maui. He requested a simple burial in a rustic wooden casket.

▶ The last known photograph taken of Charles Lindbergh.

▼ The Lindberghs' Maui home.

final flight to Maui were not easy because of the advanced state of his cancer, but a cooperative doctor was secured to sign the necessary papers certifying that Lindbergh was fit to fly. He took a regularly scheduled United Airlines flight from New York to Honolulu, resting on a stretcher in the first-class cabin and accompanied by Anne. The Lone Eagle arrived in Maui on August 18, and his death followed eight days later on the morning of Monday, August 26, 1974.

As he had planned, Lindbergh was buried in the graveyard of the local Kipahulu Congregational Church. His grave is adorned with a simple headstone of granite from Barre, Vermont, that carries a partial inscription from Psalm 139: "If I take the wings of the morning, and dwell in the uttermost parts of the sea."

◆ During the 1960s and 1970s Lindbergh had regained his status as an American hero, respected by politicians and the public. He met with NASA astronauts and the nation's leaders and used his political influence to promote his new passion, conservation of the environment. He traveled to visit conservation sites around the world. Lindbergh's last visit home was in 1973, for the dedication of his homestead in Minnesota.

◆ ◆

Charles Lindbergh persists in historical memory as a transcendent figure. His milestone flight from New York to Paris in 1927, flown nonstop and alone, triggered a frenzy of hero worship, arguably the first incarnation of media-driven celebrity in the twentieth century.

Such global stardom came suddenly, and throughout his storied life, Lindbergh struggled in vain to control the momentum of this unparalleled fame. He lost any comfortable measure of privacy, a condition of life that proved to be irreversible and fraught with tragedy. With fame, however, Lindbergh discovered a lifelong platform to promote his ideas and causes, often outside the narrow confines of the aviation world.

A vast crowd greets Lindbergh in a ticker-tape parade in New York City during his triumphal return home from his transatlantic flight in 1927.

When Lindbergh conquered the Atlantic Ocean in 1927, people began to call him "Lucky Lindy," a nickname he disdained for its gross distortion of fact. He correctly understood, as we do today, that his triumph in the competition for the Orteig prize had not been the product of chance but the consequence of careful planning, the calculated performance of a superbly designed airplane, and no small measure of personal discipline on the part of the pilot. Calling the young Minnesotan "Lucky Lindy" became a form of popular shorthand, a way for Lindbergh's stunned contemporaries to explain the passage of the *Spirit of St. Louis* across what appeared at the time to be an insurmountable ocean barrier separating North America from Europe.

Over time Lindbergh's personality became more manifest, and he revealed himself to be a complex and enigmatic figure in American life. His initial appeal stemmed from his youthful good looks, modesty, and self-effacing charm. For an adoring public, Lindbergh's extraordinary courage in making a solo crossing of the Atlantic mixed harmoniously with his understated personal style. The public was slow to realize his high seriousness, his probing intellect, and his belief in the power of technology to remake the world. Lindbergh emerged as a man with life goals quite at odds with the garden-variety stunt pilot of his era.

Lindbergh's decision to take his fabled *Spirit of St. Louis* on a national tour, just weeks after the historic

▲ *Charles Lindbergh with helmet and goggles became a familiar image to Americans after 1927. The public viewed the Lone Eagle as the symbol of aviation itself.*

▼ *A commemorative box depicting Lindbergh and the* Spirit of St. Louis.

transatlantic flight, mirrored this reality. On one level, the tour represented an effective way to respond to an intense public yearning to see their new hero. But, on a more fundamental level, it offered a meaningful way for Lindbergh to showcase aviation at a time when the airplane had not gained full acceptance as a safe and reliable mode of transportation.

Later, with his wife, Anne Morrow Lindbergh, he made a series of dramatic survey flights across vast regions of the globe, over continents and oceans, to herald a future world linked together by commercial airlines. In the post-1927 period, Lindbergh became the appealing and ubiquitous face of aviation, and he actively promoted the development of pioneering airlines such as TAT (later TWA) and, later, Pan American World Airways. For Lindbergh, the airplane was at the cutting edge of modernity, and he used his celebrity to promote this air-mindedness.

There was also a certain irony to Lindbergh's life: he yearned for privacy, but his promotion of certain causes—aviation, scientific inventions, rocketry, nonintervention in World War II, defense of the environment and wildlife—meant he could never escape public scrutiny and controversy. Even when subject to attack for his views and ostracized for a period in American political life, Lindbergh never really fell from grace. The trajectory of his life went in many directions, and for some, his advocacy of conservation offered redemption. No one could or would forget the flight of the

Spirit of St. Louis, which had become a defining moment in the twentieth century.

For those seeking to understand Lindbergh's life and legacy, his identity as a pilot provides the logical point of departure. Lindbergh became interested in aviation at a tender age, a time of youthful dreams of flying in the boundless blue sky of Minnesota. With awe, the young Lindbergh read of the exploits of Eddie Rickenbacker and other aces in World War I. Once he gained flight training and purchased his own airplane, he demonstrated a natural bent for flying, always at ease in the air, cool and competent at the controls in any emergency. Wherever he flew—as a barnstormer executing death-defying aerial maneuvers, winning his wings in the army air corps, or flying the storm-tossed routes of the airmail—Lindbergh displayed what the writer Tom Wolfe would later popularize as the "right stuff."

Lindbergh's flight log as a pilot included "stick time" at the controls of a great variety of aircraft, from World War I–era biplanes to the B-29 Superfortress, from *Luftwaffe* warplanes to modern jet aircraft. Front-line military pilots in the Pacific war lauded him for his quick mastery of the F-4U Corsair and P-38 Lightning fighters, an aptitude for flying that set the stage for Lindbergh—then in his forties—to participate in combat operations. While in the

▲ Charles Lindbergh adorns a special section of the New York Times on May 29, 1927, after his historic flight. The paper devoted sixteen pages to his accomplishment.

▼ Lindbergh at the controls of his Miles M-12 Mohawk aircraft in 1936.

Pacific, he demonstrated his technical knowledge of aircraft by offering Fifth Air Force pilots a technique to expand the range of their aircraft.

Lindbergh was a keeper of checklists. This impulse for control became a thread that ran throughout his life: He kept elaborate checklists for his transatlantic flight in 1927, even devised his own elaborate criteria seeking out an ideal mate, and when facing terminal cancer made detailed plans for his funeral and burial. His father had taught him self-reliance, and this character trait served Lindbergh well throughout his life. At the Ryan factory in San Diego, when the *Spirit of St. Louis* was being designed and built, Lindbergh oversaw every detail, even as he studied reference books on meteorology and navigation of the North Atlantic in anticipation of his historic flight. His associates—often with some frustration, as in the case of the Ryan workers—viewed him as a perfectionist. For Lindbergh the assertion of personal mastery over machines and circumstances was a way to dampen fear in any emergency and to reduce the role of chance in all his flying endeavors.

He was always the pilot, never the passenger, in life's journey. Mixed with his disciplined approach to life was a personal willingness to risk danger, to seize the proper moment to achieve a worthy end.

▼ *Charles Lindbergh at the controls of a P-38 Lightning fighter, date unknown.*

"If I have been lucky, it was because I got fitted out with a perfect ship, equipped by men who took every care and precaution. Nothing was overlooked, and from the first we never had any trouble or setback." —Charles A. Lindbergh

If Lindbergh lacked a solid formal education, he read widely, invariably focusing on themes that captured his restless imagination. His mechanical bent and engineering skills only complemented his intellectual pursuits. A belief in science had been ingrained into the young Lindbergh by his mother and her family. This dedication to science led to a remarkable collaboration with Nobel laureate Dr. Alexis Carrel in the development of the perfusion pump. Following his own intellectual interests, Lindbergh explored pathways that led to controversy, in particular his views on race, civilization, and war. His sure hand as a pilot often eluded him in the public arena, where his principled approach to issues prompted fierce opposition in some quarters.

In the face of adversity, Lindbergh embraced the same stoicism his father had shown when ostracized because of his opposition to World War I. The younger Lindbergh possessed his father's maverick dis-

position, always stubborn in the defense of his ideas and unwilling to answer his critics, even in cases where the hyperbole of his detractors did great damage to his reputation. Following World War II, however, he altered his approach to many issues, but remained slow to acknowledge past errors, preferring to stress what he believed to be the threads of continuity in his thinking. Lindbergh's moral rectitude would always anger his critics and puzzle his friends.

Anne Morrow Lindbergh was at the epicenter of Charles Lindbergh's life for nearly a half century, from their marriage in 1929 until her husband's death in 1974. From the beginning Anne participated fully in Charles Lindbergh's world of aviation, learning to fly, serving as a navigator and radio

> ▶ Home to Harold Nicolson and Vita Sackville-West for over twenty years, Long Barn, pictured here in October 1933, was leased by the Lindberghs for two and a half years until the threat of war grew near.

operator on long-distance survey flights, and even qualifying as the first woman to be licensed as a glider pilot. Their marriage proved to be a complex and enduring union, punctuated with shared triumphs and incomprehensible tragedy. During its formative years, Anne lived in the shadow of her husband, playing a supportive role in the scheme of things. In popular parlance, Charles and Anne were often called the "First Couple of the Skies" or the "Eagle and His Mate." Even as Anne found her place in the sphere of aviation, she endeavored to carve out a meaningful life for herself as a wife, a mother, and a professional writer. She yearned as well for privacy and solitude. If deeply committed to her husband's values, she was less combative and stubborn in any crisis. Over time she became more independent in her outlook and found more her own voice than an echo of her husband's.

In their separate ways, they weathered the pain of the kidnapping and murder of their firstborn child, Charles A. Lindbergh Jr. The prolonged firestorm of press and radio coverage, which engulfed the police and the courts, caught them unawares. No less alarming, popular interest in every aspect of their lives brought new and plausible dangers for their second son, Jon. For them, America had become untenable. The Lindberghs chose exile in England, an abrupt

▲ The celebrated couple of the air, Charles and Anne Lindbergh, were active in the 1930s, making survey flights for future airline routes and representing flying as a safe mode of transportation.

move that shocked many Americans. The Lindbergh kidnapping became a benchmark in American culture and a cautionary tale of the pitfalls of celebrity.

A new home in England offered a temporary sanctuary from the media and celebrity seekers, but Lindbergh's new life as an émigré brought in its wake fresh challenges and career pitfalls. His inspection tours of the German air force, made at the behest of the American government, catapulted the air hero into political controversy. Lindbergh fulfilled his intelligence tasks well, but his independent ways soon led him down pathways quite separate from the narrow agenda of gathering intelligence on a potential enemy. His highly publicized, if selective, praise of Nazi Germany and his subsequent quixotic campaign to keep America out of war eroded Lindbergh's exalted public image in ways that he could neither control nor reverse.

Lindbergh revealed a certain moral blindness in his initial assessment of Nazi Germany. Anne Morrow Lindbergh later described this prewar orientation to Nazi Germany as naive. Lindbergh himself perceived the outward reality of the "New Germany" as something historic—the early economic strides of the Nazi regime, the new sense of political unity and order, the apparent vitality of the people, and the growing prowess of the German military. By contrast, he viewed Britain and France as weak, in a state of economic decline, and extremely vulnerable to the German military in any future war. Lindbergh opted not to speak out clearly on the darker side of Nazi

Germany, although privately he found the regime's repressive policies and anti-Semitism abhorrent. In retrospect, Lindbergh's inexplicable silence, his failure to have spoken forcefully on these matters, tarnished his legacy, leading to a long period of ostracism in American life.

Hovering at the edge of Europe—and, for Lindbergh, a greater challenge to civilization—was Soviet Russia. He ardently believed that communism was a geopolitical threat. With the advent of World War II in Europe, Lindbergh argued for strict American neutrality and a negotiated peace. He appeared on radio, made speeches, and wrote magazine articles to express his deeply felt concerns over America's involvement in war. For the United States he advocated the alternative of a strong defensive military posture, not an active intervention in the war on the side of Great Britain and France. His critics, then and now, have argued that Lindbergh failed to see clearly in the 1930s the emerging struggle between totalitarianism and democracy, one of the larger themes that defined the twentieth century. Lindbergh's detractors asked: How could he, as a defender of civilization, have ignored the overt threat that Naziism represented to Western humanistic values?

Whatever Lindbergh did or said in those turbulent decades reflected his own best judgment. He always acted alone. His actions mirrored an elusive and often paradoxical personality, a private man with precise views, who only rarely associated himself with groups sharing his outlook. While it is difficult to

▲ Charles Lindbergh never met Adolf Hitler on any of his five visits to Nazi Germany, although he was often accused of being a devotee of Hitler by his enemies.

▶ Just days after his transatlantic flight, Lindbergh inspects his Spirit of St. Louis at a hangar at Le Bourget Airport.

fathom all the factors at play or reach clear conclusions as to his motives, it is apparent that he fell victim, as did many of his contemporaries, to what one might call the totalitarian temptation. Lindbergh was impressed with the outward dynamism of Nazi Germany, in the same manner that others on the political left were awestruck with the claims of the Soviet Union to be on the cutting edge of the future. Both totalitarian regimes seemed to represent revolutionary answers to the economic woes and political chaos of the times. Also, both regimes ostentatiously engaged in huge public-works projects, even as they constructed concentration camps and built vast military machines. There was a bright and dark side to each regime, and sympathetic visitors, more often than not, chose to view them in terms of pros and cons, stressing the former and ignoring the

latter. Lindbergh fell into this intellectual trap, making his own list of pros and cons for Nazi Germany and failing to gauge properly the intrinsic evil of Nazism already evident in the prewar years. A corollary of this thinking was to exaggerate the decline of the democracies or to see clearly in the prewar context the imperative to defend them against the threat of totalitarianism. Only the passing of time revealed the military weaknesses of Nazi Germany or the internal contradictions that ultimately brought about the fall of communism in Russia.

Lindbergh's silence on the evils of Nazi Germany had not meant approval, for in private he was disturbed by the Nazi policies. His reluctance or ingrained reflex not to clarify his views in public only deepened the public's misperception of him. Lindbergh personally rejected anti-Semitism, one of

HE SAID THAT HE WOULD DO IT AND HE DID!

▲ Lindbergh's contemporaries were stunned by his extraordinary flight over the Atlantic, then considered a vast ocean barrier separating North America and Europe. His aerial feat represented a genuine act of heroism, given the times and the nature of aeronautical technology.

the more serious charges made by his critics, but in the absence of an active and clear statement of his views, his reputation suffered dramatically in the 1930s and 1940s.

In spite of the controversies that dogged him later in life, Charles Lindbergh will be remembered as one of the great figures of the Air Age, perhaps second only to the Wright brothers. Other aviators of his time have slipped into the fog of history because their flying exploits lacked the historical impact of Lindbergh's solitary crossing of the Atlantic in 1927. His book *The Spirit of St. Louis* will continue to garner well-deserved attention as a literary masterpiece, not just as a chronicle of one of the most remarkable flights in history. His spirited crusade against America's entry into World War II, whatever his personal motivations, placed Lindbergh at odds with the drift of history and, for many, the strategic interests of American foreign policy. Lindbergh's advocacy of the environment and wildlife in his mature years suggested his evolving personal outlook and personal priorities.

For over seventy-five years, Charles Lindbergh has both dazzled and perplex us. Now, as aviation enters its second century, many continue to ponder Lindbergh's life and legacy. His epic flight in 1927 demonstrated the power of the airplane to alter our sense of time and space. We remember and admire Lindbergh's personal heroism. And many are inspired by his fervent campaign to preserve the natural environment. Lindbergh lived a rich, if controversial, life—one that will persist in our historical memory.

▶ *Charles Lindbergh and the Spirit of St. Louis. Lindbergh spoke to the role of "luck" in his fabled career,* *pointing to the fact that with the Spirit of St. Louis he possessed a "perfect" airplane. For Lindbergh,* *careful planning, not what others incorrectly labeled as luck, shaped his fate.*

notes

Abbreviations have been used for two frequently cited works in the notes:

AV: Charles A. Lindbergh, *Autobiography of Values* (New York: Harcourt, 1978).

SSL: Charles A. Lindbergh, *The Spirit of St. Louis* (New York: Scribner's, 1953).

Introduction

1. Brendan Gill, *Lindbergh Alone* (New York: Harcourt Brace Jovanovich, 1977), 1.
2. Igor I. Sikorsky, *Story of the Winged-S* (New York: Dodd, Mead & Company, 1941), 171.
3. Ibid., 181.
4. Ibid., 227.
5. *SSL,* 12.
6. Ibid.
7. *SSL,* 13.
8. Ibid.
9. *SSL,* 14–15.
10. Ibid., 15.

Chapter 1

Handwritten quotation: *AV,* 310.

1. *Aircraft Yearbook* (New York: Aeronautical Chamber of Commerce of America, Inc., 1928), 3.
2. *AV,* 7–8.
3. *SSL,* 244.
4. Charles A. Lindbergh, *"We"* (New York: Grosset & Dunlap, 1927), 145.
5. Ibid., 145–46.
6. Ibid., 161.
7. *AV,* 70º71.
8. Charles A. Lindbergh, *"We"* (New York: Grosset & Dunlap, 1927), 212.

Chapter 2

Handwritten quotation: Quoted in T. Williard Hunter, *The Spirit of Charles Lindbergh: Another Dimension* (Lanham, MD: Madison Books, 1993), 31.

1. *SSL,* 166.
2. Richard Byrd, *Skyward* (New York: Blue Ribbon Books, 1928), 240.
3. *SSL,* 177.
4. *SSL,* 186.
5. *SSL,* 187.
6. Ibid.
7. *SSL,* 191–92.
8. *AV,* 299–300.
9. *SSL,* 197.
10. Ibid.
11. *SSL,* 204.
12. *SSL,* 227.
13. Ibid.
14. *SSL,* 227–28.
15. *SSL,* 295–96.
16. *SSL,* 297.
17. *SSL,* 322–23.
18. *SSL,* 331.
19. *AV,* 11.
20. *SSL,* 362.
21. Ibid.
22. *SSL,* 388; *AV,* 12–13.
23. *AV,* 12.
24. Ibid.
25. *SSL,* 393.
26. *SSL,* 399.
27. *SSL,* 465.
28. *SSL,* 486.
29. *AV,* 310.
30. *SSL,* 492.
31. Edwin L. James, "When Lindbergh Reached Paris," *New York Times,* May 26, 1927; reprinted in A. C. Spectorsky, ed., *The Book of the Sky* (New York: Appleton-Century-Crofts, 1956), 51–57.
32. Ibid., 54. It should be noted that Lindbergh was a captain at the time of his flight, not a colonel.
33. Ibid.
34. Charles A. Lindbergh, *"We"* (New York: Grosset & Dunlap, 1927), 225.
35. Carlyle MacDonald, "Lindbergh Does It!" *New York Times,* May 22, 1927.
36. *AV,* 311.
37. F. Scott Fitzgerald, quoted in Paul Sann, *The Lawless Decade* (New York: Crown, 1962), 162.

Chapter 3

Handwritten quotation: *AV,* 310.

1. Brendan Gill, *Lindbergh Alone* (New York: Harcourt Brace Jovanovich, 1977), 157.
2. *AV,* 78.
3. *AV,* 310.
4. Frederick Lewis Allen, *Only Yesterday: An Informal History of the 1920s* (New York: John Wiley & Sons, 1931; reprint 1977), 165.
5. Nick Komons, *Bonfires to Beacons, Federal Civil Aviation Policy Under the Air Commerce Act, 1926–1938* (Washington, D.C.: Smithsonian Institution Press, 1989), 112.
6. Brendan Gill, *Lindbergh Alone* (New York: Harcourt Brace Jovanovich, 1977), 161.
7. Eric Hodgins and F. Alexander Maguon, *Sky High* (Boston: Little, Brown, and Company, 1929), 316.
8. Harry F. Guggenheim, *The Seven Skies* (New York: G. P. Putnam's Sons, 1930), 215.
9. Ibid.
10. Brendan Gill, *Lindbergh Alone* (New York: Harcourt Brace Jovanovich, 1977), 184–85.
11. Ibid., 193.
12. James D. Newton, *Uncommon Friends: Life with Thomas Edison, Henry Ford, Harvey Firestone, Alexis Carrel, & Charles Lindbergh* (New York: Harcourt, 1987), 256–57. Italics are from the original.
13. Ibid., 257.
14. Ibid.
15. Ibid., 258.
16. Anne Morrow Lindbergh, *North to the Orient* (New York: Harcourt, 1935), 138.
17. Ibid., 50–51.
18. Anne Morrow Lindbergh, *The Flower and the Nettle: Diaries and Letters of Anne Morrow Lindbergh, 1936–1939* (New York: Harcourt Brace and Company, 1976), 25.

Chapter 4

Handwritten quotation: Charles A. Lindbergh, "Aviation, Geography, and Race," *Reader's Digest,* November 1939, 65.

1. Letter to Lindbergh is contained in a special report, "Air Intelligence Activities, Office of the Military Attaché American Embassy, Berlin, Germany, August 1935–April 1939," prepared by Truman Smith between September 1954 and September 1956 (Yale University Library, 1970), 23.
2. Truman Smith, "Air Intelligence Activities," June 1953, 26.
3. Robert Hessen, *Berlin Alert* (Stanford, California: Hoover Institution, 1984), xv–xvi.
4. Robert Graves, *The Long Week-End: A Social History of Great Britain, 1918–1939* (New York: W. W. Norton, 1963), 409–10.
5. Truman Smith, "Air Intelligence Activities," June 1953, 20–27.
6. Ibid., 30.
7. Anne Morrow Lindbergh, *The Flower and the Nettle, Diaries and Letters of Anne Morrow Lindbergh, 1936–1939* (New York: Harcourt Brace and Company, 1976), 100.
8. R. J. Overy, *The Air War, 1939–1945* (New York: Stein and Day Publishers, 1981), 22–23.
9. Robert Graves, *The Long Week-End: A Social History of Great Britain 1918–1939* (New York: W. W. Norton, 1963), 442.
10. Truman Smith, "Air Intelligence Activities," June 1953, 157.
11. Katharine Smith, "My Life," unpublished manuscript, 103–104. This work was made available to the author by Fred Beck of Falls Church, Virginia.
12. Ibid.
13. Ibid.
14. Ibid., 105.
15. Ibid., 105–106.
16. Ibid, 106.
17. Ibid.

18. *Vital Speeches of the Day* (New York: City News Publishing, 1940, 751.

19. William Mitchell, *Skyways: A Book on Modern Aeronautics* (Philadelphia: J. B. Lippincott, 1930), 71.

20. Albert Fried, *FDR and His Enemies* (New York: St. Martin's Press, 1999), 214.

21. Anne Morrow Lindbergh, *War Within and Without: Diaries and Letters of Anne Morrow Lindbergh, 1939–1944* (New York: Harcourt Brace and Company, 1980), xxii.

Chapter 5

Handwritten quotation: Charles A. Lindbergh, *Of Flight and Life* (New York: Charles Scribner's Sons, 1948), 50

1. *AV*, 23.

2. *AV*, 23.

3. Brendan Gill, *Lindbergh Alone* (New York: Harcourt Brace Jovanovich, 1977), 203.

4. A. Scott Berg, *Lindbergh* (New York: Putnam, 1998), 434.

5. Ibid., 435.

6. Ibid., 437.

7. *AV*, 23.

8. *AV*, 24.

9. A. Scott Berg, *Lindbergh* (New York: Putnam, 1998), 448.

10. Richard Kirkland, *Tales of a War Pilot* (Washington, D.C.: Smithsonian Institution Press, 1999), 26.

11. Ibid., 28.

12. A. Scott Berg, *Lindbergh* (New York: Putnam, 1998), 457–58.

Chapter 6

Handwritten quotation: Charles A. Lindbergh, *Of Flight and Life* (New York: Charles Scribner's Sons, 1948), 47.

1. *AV*, 345.

2. A. Scott Berg, *Lindbergh* (New York: Putnam, 1998), 465.

3. *AV*, 350.

4. *AV*, 344.

5. *AV*, 348.

6. *AV*, 348.

7. *AV*, 349.

8. Letter of Charles Lindbergh to Elizabeth Sikorsky, October 1972, courtesy of Sergei Sikorsky.

9. *AV*, 28–29.

10. *AV*, 29.

11. A. Scott Berg, *Lindbergh* (New York: Putnam, 1998), 488–90.

12. Quoted by T. Williard Hunter, *The Spirit of Charles Lindbergh: Another Dimension* (Lanham, MD: Madison Books, 1993), 116.

13. *AV*, 32.

14. *AV*, 33–34.

15. *AV*, 40.

16. *AV*, 42–43.

17. Charles A. Lindbergh, "Is Civilization Progress?," *Reader's Digest*, July 1964, 73.

18. Michael Collins, *Carrying the Fire: An Astronaut's Journey* (New York: Farrar, Straus and Giroux, 1974), xii.

19. T. Williard Hunter, *The Spirit of Charles Lindbergh: Another Dimension* (Lanham, MD: Madison Books, 1993), 107; A. Scott Berg, *Lindbergh* (New York: Putnam, 1998), 538.

20. Charles A. Lindbergh, introduction to *Maui: The Last Hawaiian Place*, by Robert Wenkam (San Francisco: Friends of the Earth, 1970), 25.

21. T. Williard Hunter, *The Spirit of Charles Lindbergh: Another Dimension* (Lanham, MD: Madison Books, 1993), 131–35.

22. Charles A. Lindbergh, introduction to *Maui: The Last Hawaiian Place*, by Robert Wenkam (San Francisco: Friends of the Earth, 1970), 25.

23. Ibid.

24. A. Scott Berg, *Lindbergh* (New York: Putnam, 1998), 557–58.

Epilogue

Handwritten quotation: Quoted in James E. West, *The Lone Scout of the Sky* (Philadelphia: John C. Winston Publishing Co., 1927), 83.

acknowledgments

No book, particularly one about the life and legacy of Charles Lindbergh, can be fashioned in isolation. A host of people helped to shape the concept and ultimate design of *Lindbergh: Flight's Enigmatic Hero*. Early on, I made the decision to write the narrative in close proximity to Lindbergh's own writings. This attentiveness to primary materials led to the study of other contemporary accounts of Lindbergh, some known, others largely ignored. In the quest to read extant primary materials, I found some insightful contemporary accounts, hitherto ignored. For example, Dr. Fred Beck, a historian of modern German history, provided me with his personal copy of the unpublished memoir of Kay Smith, the wife of Truman Smith, who served as American military attaché to Berlin from 1935 to 1939. The Kay Smith recollections of Charles and Anne Lindbergh became an invaluable source, one revealing the perspective of a person close to the scene in Germany in the 1930s. Dr. Beck also served as a key resource on Lindbergh's friendship with Truman Smith. I turned as well to Dr. Robert S. Kreider, who was my major history professor as an undergraduate in college. Kreider grew up in the 1930s, and he made trips to Germany just before and after World War II. His perspective on those years was insightful in all respects.

Others offered timely inspiration and concrete assistance. Gene Eisman, a skilled editor and an informed reader on aviation history, weighed in on more than one occasion, asking probing questions and offering alternative viewpoints. Stephen Hardesty also read and commented on selected chapters. My own long-standing personal interest in Charles Lindbergh, in large measure, can be traced to Judy Hardesty, who also served as a reader of the manuscript and offered historical materials for the book project. Glen Sweeting, my former colleague at the Smithsonian National Air and Space Museum, also provided expert historical consultation on a host of topics related Lindbergh's visits to Nazi Germany. Nova Hall provided expert reference on the life of his grandfather, Donald Hall, and the plane he designed, the *Spirit of St. Louis*. Rick Leyes, another former colleague and historian of aircraft propulsion, provided expert assistance on the technology and historical impact of the Wright Whirlwind engine. Lawrence DiRicco, a talented researcher and expert on aviation history, helped to fill in some missing data on a number of photographs related to Charles Lindbergh. Sergei Sikorsky and Igor Sikorsky Jr., two sons of aviation pioneer Igor I. Sikorsky, provided firsthand accounts of the friendship of their father with Lindbergh. They also regaled me with their memories of the visits by Charles and Anne Lindbergh to their parents' home. Most of all, I wish to thank Patricia Hardesty for her patience and support. She often took time from her own busy schedule to read and comment on the emerging manuscript.

I have enjoyed working with the team at Tehabi Books, in particular editor Garrett Brown and art director Vicky Vaughn. Garrett displayed exemplary skills as an editor, always patient and expert in his work with me. I remain appreciative of his many timely shipments of books, articles, and selected historical materials during the research phase. Vicky worked diligently to seek out illustrations on the saga of Charles Lindbergh from diverse sources across the country. I enjoyed working with her on the demanding chores of photo research. Working with the Tehabi team sustained my enthusiasm for the book project, especially on those occasions when unforeseen problems threatened our established deadlines. Charles Lindbergh was a complex person, and during this project we all discovered that the fashioning of an illustrated book on the Lindbergh phenomenon proved to be equally complex.

Tehabi would like to acknowledge the following individuals: Amanda Claunch at the Missouri Historical Society, for her diligence in helping us locate photographs; John Bolthouse at the San Diego Aerospace Museum, for his generous assistance and support; and Reeve Lindbergh, for her thorough critique of the proofs and for kindly granting us permission to use images from the Missouri Historical Society collection. We would also like to thank our editorial intern, Kati Franco, for her assistance in crafting the gatefold flight timeline.

image credits

Front cover: Library of Congress (LC-USZ62-93443). **Back-cover:** a, Minnesota Historical Society; b, San Diego Aerospace Museum; c–e, Lindbergh Picture Collection, Manuscripts and Archives, Yale University Library; f–g, San Diego Aerospace Museum; background, ©Tom Nebbia/CORBIS. **Front flap:** a, Lindbergh Picture Collection, Manuscripts and Archives, Yale University Library; b, San Diego Aerospace Museum. **End sheets:** San Diego Aerospace Museum. **Page 1:** Allen Airways Flying Museum, 619-596-2020, allenairwy@aol.com/Rick Starkman Photography, **2–3:** Library of Congress, Prints and Photographs Division (LC-USZ62-115128), **4–5:** San Diego Aerospace Museum, **6–7:** San Diego Aerospace Museum, **8–9:** ©Bettmann/CORBIS, **10:** San Diego Aerospace Museum, **12:** Jeff Christensen/Reuters/TimePix, **13:** Illustration by Peter Horjus, **14a:** Carving by Erik Lindbergh, **14b:** The X Prize Foundation, **15a:** The X Prize Foundation, **15b:** Lindbergh Picture Collection, Manuscripts and Archives, Yale University Library, **16a–17:** San Diego Aerospace Museum, **16b:** NASM (78-14972), **16c:** San Diego Aerospace Museum, **17a, b:** ©Bettmann/CORBIS, **18:** Illustration by Peter Horjus, **19:** ©Bettmann/CORBIS, **20a, b:** ©Bettmann/CORBIS, **21:** Underwood & Underwood/CORBIS, **22a:** ©Bettmann/CORBIS, **22b:** Allen Airways Flying Museum, 619-596-2020, allenairwy@aol.com/Rick Starkman Photography, **23a:** Igor Sikorsky photos made available to Von Hardesty, **23b, c:** Allen Airways Flying Museum, 619-596-2020, allenairwy@aol.com/Rick Starkman Photography, **24:** NASM (90-8831), **25:** CORBIS, **26a:** Lindbergh Picture Collection, Manuscripts and Archives, Yale University Library, **26b:** Allen Airways Flying Museum, 619-596-2020, allenairwy@aol.com/Rick Starkman Photography, **27:** NASM (77-8848), **28a–29:** San Diego Aerospace Museum, **28b:** ©Bettmann/CORBIS, **28c:** San Diego Aerospace Museum, **29a:** Minnesota Historical Society, **29b:** ©Bettmann/CORBIS, **29c:** Missouri Historical Society, St. Louis, **30:** NASM (A42065), **31:** Illustration by Peter Horjus, **32a:** Photo by Nelson, Minnesota Historical Society, **32b:** Library of Congress, Prints and Photographs Division (LC-USW3-16610-C), **33a:** Hand-lettering by Peter Horjus, **33b:** Lindbergh Picture Collection, Manuscripts and Archives, Yale University Library, **34:** Minnesota Historical Society, **35a:** San Diego Aerospace Museum, **35b:** Allen Airways Flying Museum, 619-596-2020, allenairwy@aol.com/Rick Starkman Photography, **36a, b:** Minnesota Historical Society, **37a, b:** Lindbergh Picture Collection, Manuscripts and Archives, Yale University Library, **37c:** Allen Airways Flying Museum, 619-596-2020, allenairwy@aol.com/Rick Starkman Photography, **38a:** Photo by John M. Noble, Minnesota Historical Society, **38b:** Lindbergh Picture Collection, Manuscripts and Archives, Yale University Library, **39a:** San Diego Aerospace Museum, **39b:** Lindbergh Picture Collection, Manuscripts and Archives, Yale University Library, **40a:** San Diego Aerospace Museum, **40b:** Library of Congress, Prints and Photographs Division (LC-USZ62-99814), **40c:** Lindbergh Picture Collection, Manuscripts and Archives, Yale University Library, **41a:** Allen Airways Flying Museum, 619-596-2020, allenairwy@aol.com/Rick Starkman Photography, **41b:** San Diego Aerospace Museum, **42a–43:** Missouri Historical Society, St. Louis, **42b:** Missouri Historical Society, St. Louis, **42c–e:** San Diego Aerospace Museum, **43a–c:** San Diego Aerospace Museum, **44a, b:** San Diego Aerospace Museum, **44c:** San Diego Aerospace Museum, **44d:** NASM (78-12207), **46a, b:** Allen Airways Flying Museum, 619-596-2020, allenairwy@aol.com/Rick Starkman Photography, **47a–h:** ©Bettmann/CORBIS, **48:** San Diego Aerospace Museum, **49a:** Missouri Historical Society, St. Louis, **49b:** San Diego Aerospace Museum, **49c:** San Diego Aerospace Museum, **50–51:** San Diego Aerospace Museum, **51a:** San Diego Aerospace Museum/Photographer Donald Hall, **51b:** Missouri Historical Society, St. Louis, **52a–53:** San Diego Aerospace Museum, **52b–53:** San Diego Aerospace Museum/Photographer Donald Hall, **52c, d:** San Diego Aerospace Museum, **53a, b:** San Diego Aerospace Museum, **54a:** San Diego Aerospace Museum, **54b–55:** San Diego Aerospace Museum, **54c:** San Diego Aerospace Museum, **55:** San Diego Aerospace Museum, **56–57:** San Diego Aerospace Museum, **58a–59:** San Diego Aerospace Museum, **58b:** NASM (NAS-53691), **58c:** San Diego Aerospace Museum, **59a–62:** Missouri Historical Society, St. Louis, **59b:** San Diego Aerospace Museum, **60:** George Silk/TimePix, **61:** Missouri Historical Society, St. Louis, **62:** AP/Wide World Photos, **63:** San Diego Aerospace Museum, **64:** Illustration by Peter Horjus, **65:** San Diego Aerospace Museum, **66a:** NASM (A-627), **66b:** NASM (A-627A), **66c:** Photo by Monroe P. Killy, Minnesota Historical Society, **67a:** ©Bettmann/CORBIS, **67b:** Underwood & Underwood/CORBIS, **68a, b:** San Diego Aerospace Museum, **69:** San Diego Aerospace Museum, **70a:** San Diego Aerospace Museum, **70b–71:** San Diego Aerospace Museum, **71:** Hand-lettering by Peter Horjus, **72–73:** Lindbergh Picture Collection, Manuscripts and Archives, Yale University Library, **74:** NASM (A49499A), **75a:** Library of Congress, Prints and Photographs Division (LC-USZ62-103897), **75b:** Library of Congress, Prints and Photographs Division (LC-USZ62-106868), **76a:** San Diego Aerospace Museum, **76b:** San Diego Aerospace Museum/Photographer Donald Hall, **78a, b:** San Diego Aerospace Museum/Photographer Donald Hall, **78c:** San Diego Aerospace Museum, **79a:** NASM (94-8820), **79b:** Missouri Historical Society, St. Louis, **79c:** San Diego Aerospace Museum, **80a:** Paul A. Souders/CORBIS, **80b:** Missouri Historical Society, St. Louis, **81a, b:** Missouri Historical Society, St. Louis, **82a–83:** San Diego Aerospace Museum, **82b:** Missouri Historical Society, St. Louis, **82c:** Missouri Historical Society, St. Louis, **84a–85:** ©Jim Zuckerman/CORBIS, **84b:** Allen Airways Flying Museum, 619-596-2020, allenairwy@aol.com/Rick Starkman Photography, **85:** Missouri Historical Society, St. Louis, **86a:** Allen Airways Flying Museum, 619-596-2020, allenairwy@aol.com, **86b, c:** Missouri Historical Society, St. Louis, **86d:** San Diego Aerospace Museum, **87a:** NASM (A41359), **87b, c:** San Diego Aerospace Museum, **88:** Yann Arthus-Bertrand/CORBIS, **89:** Michael Nicholson/CORBIS, **90a–91:** ©Bettmann/CORBIS, **90b:** Mansell/TimePix, **92a:** Allen Airways Flying Museum, 619-596-2020, allenairwy@aol.com/Rick Starkman Photography, **92b–93:** Lindbergh Picture Collection, Manuscripts and Archives, Yale University Library, **93:** Lindbergh Picture Collection, Manuscripts and Archives, Yale University Library, **94a–95:** San Diego Aerospace Museum, **94b:** Lindbergh Picture Collection, Manuscripts and Archives, Yale University Library, **94c:** Hulton-Deutsch Collection/CORBIS, **94d:** San Diego Aerospace Museum, **95a:** Time Magazine, Copyright Time Inc./TimePix, **95b:** Pictures Inc./TimePix, **96:** San Diego Aerospace Museum, **97:** Illustration by Peter Horjus, **98a:** Missouri Historical Society, St. Louis, **98b–e:** Lindbergh Picture Collection, Manuscripts and Archives, Yale University Library, **99a, b:** Allen Airways Flying Museum, 619-596-2020, allenairwy@aol.com/Rick Starkman Photography, **99c:** Lindbergh Picture Collection, Manuscripts and Archives, Yale University Library, **99d:** Lindbergh Picture Collection, Manuscripts and Archives, Yale University Library, **100–101:** Lindbergh Picture Collection, Manuscripts and Archives, Yale University Library, **102a:** NASM (78-17771), **102b:** NASM (A3865), **103:** NASM (A4587C), **104a–d:** Allen Airways Flying Museum, 619-596-2020, allenairwy@aol.com/Rick Starkman Photography, **105a:** Missouri Historical Society, St. Louis, **105b:** Allen Airways Flying Museum, 619-596-2020, allenairwy@aol.com/Rick Starkman Photography, **106a:** Hand-lettering by Peter Horjus, **106b:** Allen Airways Flying Museum, 619-596-2020, allenairwy@aol.com/Rick Starkman Photography, **107a:** Allen Airways Flying Museum, 619-596-2020, allenairwy@aol.com, **107b:** Lindbergh Picture Collection, Manuscripts and Archives, Yale University Library, **108–109:** Lindbergh Picture Collection, Manuscripts and Archives, Yale University Library, **111a–c:** Allen Airways Flying Museum, 619-596-2020, allenairwy@aol.com, **112a:** Underwood/CORBIS, **112b:** Lindbergh Picture Collection, Manuscripts and Archives, Yale University Library, **113a:** Lindbergh Picture Collection, Manuscripts and Archives, Yale University Library, **113b:** ©Bettmann/CORBIS, **114–15:** Lindbergh Picture Collection, Manuscripts and Archives, Yale University Library, **115a, b:** Lindbergh Picture Collection, Manuscripts and Archives, Yale University Library, **116a–17:** Lindbergh Picture Collection, Manuscripts and Archives, Yale University Library, **116b–f:** Lindbergh Picture Collection, Manuscripts and Archives, Yale University Library, **117a–c:** Lindbergh Picture Collection, Manuscripts and Archives, Yale University Library, **118–19:** Lindbergh Picture Collection, Manuscripts and Archives, Yale University Library, **119a, b:** Lindbergh Picture Collection, Manuscripts and Archives,

further reading

The literature devoted to Charles Lindbergh is immense, beginning with his transatlantic flight in 1927 and continuing into the twenty-first century. This select bibliography is, at best, a mirror on some of the more compelling titles. The Centennial of Flight in 2003 has been a stimulus for additional histories and interpretative pieces on Lindbergh, both in full-length books and articles. Any serious student of the Lindbergh saga will be challenged to keep pace with this ever-growing body of historical literature.

The narrative for *Lindbergh: Flight's Enigmatic Hero* has been based largely on Charles Lindbergh's own writings and, to a lesser extent, those of Anne Morrow Lindbergh, a set of core materials essential for any analysis of the complex life and career of Charles Lindbergh:

"We": The Famous Flier's Own Story of His Life and Transatlantic Flight (1927). This short book, written in a straightforward, even restrained, manner, echoes Charles Lindbergh's desire to avoid the hyperbole and distortions evident in many contemporary news accounts of his 1927 transatlantic flight.

Of Flight and Life (1948). This short book keynotes Charles Lindbergh's post–World War II worldview. The book signaled his evolving sensibility about science and moral values.

The Spirit of St. Louis (1953). This celebrated memoir by Lindbergh won a Pulitzer Prize, garnering a huge readership and serving as the basis for the 1957 feature film of the same name, starring Jimmy Stewart. The narrative is in the present tense, telling the story of his solitary passage across the Atlantic in a vivid fashion. The text is punctuated with numerous flashbacks to dramatic episodes from Lindbergh's life. This book became a literary event in the 1950s and remains an aviation classic.

Autobiography of Values (1978). This abridgment of Lindbergh's huge rambling memoir, which at the time of his death was in manuscript form, provides the most systematic presentation of Lindbergh's mature outlook, with asides into pivotal episodes in his life.

There are certain minor writings of Charles Lindbergh that are worthy of study: Lindbergh's own chronicle of his formative years, *Boyhood on the Upper Mississippi* (1972); his diaries, in particular the *Wartime Journals* (1970); and his numerous magazine articles and speeches, some dating back to the 1930s, which are too voluminous to describe in detail here.

The literary legacy of Anne Morrow Lindbergh, in particular her diaries and letters, provides another avenue to comprehend the life of Charles Lindbergh. Her first book, *North to the Orient* (1935), is a beautifully written account of the survey flight she and Charles took across the Great Circle route over Canada to the North Pacific in 1931. In the same genre, she published *Listen! The Wind* (1938), which provides an account of flying from Africa to America. Her most controversial book was *The Wave of the Future: A Confession of Faith* (1941), which appeared to many to be an apologia for Nazi Germany. Anne Morrow Lindbergh's most remembered title is *The Gift from the Sea* (1955), an essay on the changing role of women in society. Her diaries and letters constitute a valuable historical record: *Bring Me a Unicorn* (1972); *Hour of Gold, Hour of Lead* (1973); *Locked Rooms and Open Doors* (1974); *The Flower and the Nettle* (1976); and *War Within and Without* (1980). The introductory essays folded into these anthologies provide Anne's perspective on the many controversies that surrounded her husband.

Secondary sources on the life and career of Charles Lindbergh are numerous, with the first histories appearing as early as 1927. Harry F. Guggenheim's *The Seven Skies* (1930) represents an early and serious effort to place the Lindbergh achievement in the broader context of aviation progress. Placing Lindbergh's achievements in proper perspective would be a continuing challenge for writers, biographers, and historians in the decades that followed. A. Scott Berg's biography *Lindbergh* (1998) stands out as the most authoritative and insightful assessment of Lindbergh's life. A recent book by Reeve Lindbergh, daughter of Charles and Anne Lindbergh, entitled *Under a Wing: A Memoir* (1999), offers a unique perspective from a family member.

A number of writers and historians have attempted to give meaning to the Lindbergh phenomenon over the years, with varying degrees of success. Frederick Lewis Allen's *Only Yesterday: An Informal History of the 1920s* (1931), written in the depths of the Great Depression, remains a baseline document, although marred by a certain superficiality. Brendan Gill's *Lindbergh Alone* (1977), if subject to both praise and criticism, is a provocative character study. Lesser known but equally insightful is T. Williard Hunter's *The Spirit of Lindbergh: Another Dimension* (1993).

Friends of Charles Lindbergh also have left interesting retrospective accounts: John Grierson, *I Remember Lindbergh* (1977), and James D. Newton, *Uncommon Friends, Life with Thomas Edison, Henry Ford, Harvey Firestone, Alexis Carrel, & Charles Lindbergh* (1987). One excellent source of information on Charles Lindbergh and Truman Smith is Robert Hessen, editor, *Berlin Alert: The Memoirs and Reports of Truman Smith* (1984). The unpublished memoirs of Kay Smith, the wife of Truman Smith, are insightful,

especially for the visits of the Lindberghs to Nazi Germany. For a more recent and harsh assessment of the officer class in the American army, including Truman Smith, there is Joseph W. Bendersky, *The "Jewish Threat": Anti-Semitic Politics of the U.S. Army* (2000).

A multitude of articles have appeared on the life and legacy of Charles Lindbergh, too many to mention in this small place. One recent historical essay by A. K. S. Rayl in *Lindbergh* (2002), published by the Lindbergh Foundation, offers an honest and insightful overview of the life of the famed aviator.

Over the years, the staff of the Smithsonian National Air and Space Museum has produced a number of interesting books on Charles Lindbergh and his airplanes, many richly illustrated. David A. Romanowski has compiled a general reference volume, the *Official Guide to the Smithsonian National Air and Space Museum* (2002), with sections related to Lindbergh aircraft. For a recent commentary on Lindbergh and an excellent technical profile of the *Spirit of St. Louis* airplane, see Dominick A. Pisano and Robert van der Linden, *Charles Lindbergh and the Spirit of St. Louis* (2002). R. E. G. Davies also has published an illustrated volume touching on the Lindbergh saga, *Charles Lindbergh: An Airman, His Aircraft, and His Great Flights* (1997). An older but still insightful anthology on the historical significance of Charles Lindbergh is *Charles A. Lindbergh: An American Life* (1977), edited by Tom D. Crouch and published on the occasion of the fiftieth anniversary of Lindbergh's transatlantic flight.